What Would You Do If You Had No Fear?

What Would You Do If You Had No Fear?

Living Your Dreams While Quakin' in Your Boots

DIANE CONWAY

Inner Ocean Publishing, Inc.
Maui, Hawai'i
San Francisco, California

Inner Ocean Publishing, Inc.
P.O. Box 1239
Makawao, HI 96768-1239
www.innerocean.com

Printed on recycled paper.

Cover and book design by Suzanne Albertson

Publisher Cataloging-in-Publication Data
Conway, Diane.
    What would you do if you had no fear? : living your dreams while
quakin' in your boots / Diane Conway. — Makawao, HI : Inner Ocean, 2004.
      p. ; cm.
    ISBN: 1-930722-42-7 (pbk.)
    1. Self-actualization (Psychology) 2. Success. 3. Fear of failure.
4. Quality of life. I. Title.
    BF637.S4 C66 2004
    158.1—dc22 0412

DISTRIBUTED BY PUBLISHERS GROUP WEST

*For information on promotions, bulk purchases, premiums, or educational use, please contact Special Markets:
866.731.2216 or sales@innerocean.com.*

To my friend, my buddy,
my sweetie,
Brian Conway

CONTENTS

PART 1

What Would You Do?

PART 3

Living the Fearless Life

FOREWORD

I love this book, and I love the question it asks: What would you do if you had no fear? Diane Conway's question changed my life when I heard it: it gave me a kind of awakening, and it continues to ring through the chambers of my mind. When I am faced with bureaucracies or menopause, a scary world, a sagging butt, a teenage child, I ask myself the question again, and more times than not, I act on what I answer.

I am doing things now I would never have thought possible. I have taped the question to the wall in my office. It emboldens me when I am working, or being a parent, a daughter, an activist, a more-and-more alive human being. It's a question that gently nudges me in the direction of bravery, of being true to myself—of saying "no" to people when I mean no, of saying "yes" when I really and truly want to do something. It's helped me with relatively small things, like wearing shorts when it is hot, even though I am shy about the condition of my thighs, or like calling back advice nurses and demanding that I be seen that day. It's helped me get out of bad relationships, and summon the courage to slog through rough patches in good ones.

Both the question and the book have helped so many people find support within themselves to live braver and more authentic lives—to quit jobs or seek more challenging ones, to get on planes and fly to wild places, or to call forth the courage to stay and face hardship. These are stories of women and men who have moved beyond their fears in order to change, to soar, even to fail, whose adventures and humanity can't help but inspire the rest of us: A man who rescued the family dog during the Oakland Hills fire, while every house in the neighborhood burned around him. A woman with Stage Four cancer who thought her life was over, until she met a man with whom she could dance to life—a partner who also has Stage Four cancer. An ex-convict who, after thirty years in San Quentin, now walks across the United States seeing the world for the first time, and who has been taken in by a highway patrol officer, not to jail—but to the officer's home.

The men and women interviewed for this book relate their long-hidden dreams and fears and surprise themselves with their answers to the question, and the new directions their lives have taken as a result. As Conway writes, "Going for our heart's desires is possible while quaking all the way."

Courage is usually fear that has said its prayers, and fears shared are gifts we give each other. To speak them out loud opens our hearts, so that the fresh air and sunshine of identification can flood in, the miracles that spring forth when we are heard. Humor is restored, and with it come breath, and hope, and the possibility of breaking free from the isolation that binds us, our worries, and our doubts.

This is a deeply spiritual book, as humans pursue the truth of their spiritual identities—that they are free, gorgeous, fabulous, and capable of amazing themselves (and us). It is filled with hints and tips and gentle nudges on how the reader, too, can get over the fears of being rejected, failing, facing the future, and looking foolish, and instead shoot for the moon, for more joy, deeper exploration, harder laughter, and—do I even dare to use this word? —actualization.

That's exactly the word I would use if I had no fear of looking like a born-again, New Age–type Californian, even though I am. Actualization.

This book may very well change your life, giving you the faith to give up a job you hate or a person who is no longer any fun at all. These people and their stories will move you, charm you, inspire and entertain you. They'll make you cry, and they'll make you try to help your dreams come true, whatever your age, whatever your circumstance and challenges. Diane Conway is going to feel like your new best friend. She has such a gift of communication, a unique way of listening to ordinary people, to their hopes and fears, to the hilarious and poignant details of their journey. She's a cross between Studs Terkel and Fanny Flagg—intelligent, spiritual, wise, and hilarious. Trust me—you're in for a wonderful ride.

Anne Lamott

INTRODUCTION

Take the Dare!

"Life is either a daring adventure or nothing.
To keep our faces toward change and behave like free spirits
in the presence of fate is strength undefeatable."
HELEN KELLER

In some mysterious and profound ways, asking and answering the question "what would you do if you had no fear?" produces a divine flash that sets in motion assistance from out of the blue.

I first began asking this question to participants in my workshops and retreats. Many found themselves naming their dreams and desires for the first time—and the results stunned them. No sooner had they spoken their heart's desire out loud than serendipitous meetings and incidents began to spring up in their life. Some people applied to medical school, others quit soul-numbing jobs, and still others took trips they'd dreamed of for years. A fireman called with the jubilant news that he was taking flying-trapeze lessons. An interior designer fulfilled her life long dream and moved to Rome.

The feedback to this simple question stuns and surprises people. A circuit court judge, aboard a ferry on San Francisco Bay, began to laugh when he heard the question. After half an hour of trying to answer, he'd run the gamut from grim to joyful and decided: "You know, I'd resign my appointment and explore a tribal justice system like the Maoris in New Zealand."

Those who read and ponder this question seem to gain a temporary reprieve from the limits they ordinarily place on their lives. They begin to explore the life not lived and that alternative set of choices that linger in the recesses of the mind. Why do our desires and dreams linger? They beckon us, call our name, because they are waiting for us to inhabit the life we were meant to live. They are waiting for us to listen to our highest calling.

The stories in this book relate that life-changing flash when you stop wishing, get off the sofa, take a shower, and mail the manuscript, or when you're honest with a lover while crying and laughing with giddy abandon. As you read, you'll learn more about the courage it takes to be human and fully alive. You'll witness everyday miracles. And with any luck, you'll make some of your own. Following the stories, you'll find some suggestions called "Life Challenges," ideas designed to engage your mind and move you toward greater fulfillment as you ask yourself, "What would I do if I had no fear?"

I wrote this book and I grapple with this question because I have been crippled by fears and doubts all my life. It's been said that we teach best what we need to learn. Interviewing people and hearing the stories of ordinary heroes have profoundly changed me—their experiences have spurred me on, even though there were many times when I would cry out in despair, thinking that I didn't have what it takes to see my own dreams through.

The miracle of this book is that it exists at all—after a number of rejections I'd abandoned the project to a bottom drawer. Still, I knew that it had merit and I'd send energy to it and pray about it. Then my friend Karen, the woman whom I do retreats with, asked if she could show it to a friend who worked for a publisher. I said, "Yes, but don't tell me what they say. I can't stand another rejection." A week later I met with the publisher, and here it is.

To have my dream manifest in such a magical way has been amazing. It is sweeter because it came about in a way I could never have predicted. The saying "you can't get there from here" comes to mind. The message I wanted to convey to readers from the start was that when we have a dream it is a real, living thing with a life of its own. We don't always have to be super achievers, or even know how it will come into being. I am a woman with lots of dreams but frequently shaky faith and truckloads of self-doubt, and my dream came true. If mine can, I know yours will also. Don't quit before your miracle.

Take this journey with me, your slightly neurotic guide. Let me believe for you as others have believed for me.

PART 1

What Would You Do?

"What would you do if you had no fear?"

"I don't think I'm creative, but I want to be. I'd take painting and writing classes, preferably in Tuscany." —WORKSHOP PARTICIPANT

"Buy a piece of land and build my own home." —THERAPIST

"Stop obsessing about what others think of me." —GRAPHIC DESIGNER

"Take my dog and go to the lake a friend told me about." —OVERWORKED COUNTER PERSON

"Act as if my life is going to work out." —CEO AT AIRPORT

"Start selling the jewelry I design." —EMPLOYEE AT A BEAD STORE

"Give a $100 bill to someone who has said or done something to inspire me, like the waitress who was kind when I needed it." —MEMBER OF A SUPPORT GROUP

"The need to find meaning in the universe is as real as the need for trust and for love, for relations with other human beings."
MARGARET MEAD

The hard questions in life send most of us to the freezer for Ben and Jerry's. It takes courage to ask ourselves questions like: What should I do with the rest of my life? Am I making a contribution to my world? Am I following my heart or only my head? Am I on the right path?

We get so caught up in the daily grind, the million and one things that are on our To Do lists, that we don't stop to listen to the whisperings of our heart. Life gets away from us. Occasionally, we need to stop, ask, listen, and shake things up. Then we can move toward making our lives more livable, more joyful, and more real. The chapters that follow contain stories of people who have taken the time to ask the big questions. May they inspire you.

But first, go get your Chunky Monkey ice cream.

CHAPTER 1

Who Would You Be?

"All my life I've always wanted to be somebody.
But I see now I should have been more specific."

JANE WAGNER, *THE SEARCH FOR INTELLIGENT*
LIFE IN THE UNIVERSE

Freedom to Choose

"To choose is also to begin."
STARHAWK

We think of our lives as being determined by the grand choices we make, the earth-shaking decisions such as: who should I marry, what house should I buy, what the devil am I gonna have for dinner? But a lot of life is in the details, the small moment-to-moment decisions and choices we come to all the time.

I've always had a hard time making up my mind. It actually seems as if there are several minds in my head and none of them can agree. There's infighting, relentless lobbying, and squabbling galore. Some people call this state of mind "the committee."

When we want to make a big life change, the fear of the unknown often lurks around the corner. The task seems daunting, and at moments like that, I like to think of the construction of the Pyramids; even such magnificent structures could only go up one brick at a time. You don't have to carry the entire pile of bricks at once—when choosing to do things differently, you only have to make one choice at a time, and one choice is frequently magic. We decide to take a different route to work. We choose to say "no" to an activity or commitment that brings no joy. We pick out a fabulous pink top. We take a day trip somewhere new. The freedom from fear happens one action, one thought, one choice at a time.

Ever try on a sexy pair of shoes and just know you'll walk away a different woman, more confident, full of "Yeah, Baby, I'm cute" sass? I've seen a man put on a sharp suit that totally changes his demeanor. When we make a decision, it's good to grab an object that will symbolize the choice and anchor it. You could carry a little metal angel in your pocket, wear khaki shorts that scream "Safari!," or sport a fabulous new haircut. Symbols, lucky charms, and talismans are a great way to remind us how far we've come and where we wish to go.

"I got my ears pierced and drank a Fuzzy Navel," says Deanna of her declaration of independence at age twenty-six. These served as her lucky charms.

Deanna's face looks like the very illustration of a luscious, wild woman: her mop of go-to-hell red hair and green eyes make you wonder why God created any other color combinations for humans; her green rhinestone sunglasses match her eyes; her vitality and love of life hit you like a bright, fluffy pillow.

Hard to imagine this vibrant woman was ever anything but independent, but Deanna was not always this way. For nearly half of her forty-two years, she felt paralyzed. The fear of making mistakes was what kept her locked in a life she hated. She was terrified of even the smallest choices. "I would get a panic attack anytime I had to choose, even off a menu. I would just close my eyes and point like a child."

Her parents belonged to a fundamentalist sect that did not allow much of anything, and certainly not freedom of choice.

She says that for years she did not even know what kind of clothes she liked. She and her sisters wore whatever her mother brought home from the Goodwill that fit. It cracks her up that the people she knows now always say, "What a great sense of style you have." And "Oh, that is so Deanna!" Just as Gertrude Stein once infamously quipped, "There is no there," Deanna says that for years of her life there was no "her" there.

When she left her first marriage at age twenty-six, it was the first time she'd ever been on her own. Her parents and then her husband had controlled every single aspect of her life. Until then, like a fish in a fishbowl, she didn't realize how small her life was. Her husband made all the decisions just as her parents had, and there was no room for dissent.

When she told her mother about the abuse in her marriage, her mother said, "Oh, Deanna, what is forty years of misery for all eternity?" Her mother's meaning was clear: Deanna should stay in that marriage forever, no matter what. That comment finally pushed her over the edge and out of the marriage. Her first act of independence was getting her ears pierced; when lightning didn't strike, she was amazed. Next, she drank a Fuzzy Navel, flavored with Peach schnapps, and again she wasn't struck down. Her ticket out of fear-based living began with small choices.

Once out of her cage, she pursued freedom with a vengeance, taking consciousness-expanding classes and reading books on personal growth. Only after several years did she fully realize how bad her marriage had been and what a diminished life she'd been living. It takes time away from a situation to see it clearly.

Today she says, "It takes a lot of life to figure out who you are. Now I know who I am, I'm me."

Deanna's core need is freedom—but it took half a life of emotional incarceration for her to discover and pursue her deepest desire. Ever since Deanna woke up to her wild woman inside, she's become a creative dynamo. Her graphic design office features purple walls, gold drapes, and fairy artwork everywhere—it's magical. Her mind dances with so many sugar-plum-fairy ideas that she made up a sign that reads, "I forbid any new ideas to enter."

In addition to her graphic design work, she's written several books, designed accessories, and displayed her art work in galleries. She produced a mural in her town that depicts a Mission Blue butterfly. This is the only place in the world where Mission Blues live and the only place where this one-of-a-kind woman lives.

She's found her outrageous self and has a husband and two boys who love her for being who she is.

Not long ago, Deanna was telling a friend about some wild thing she was planning, and the friend said, of Deanna's husband, "He lets you do it?" She laughed. "Lets me? Ha, no one has permission to let me anymore. I let me!"

"Freedom breeds freedom. Nothing else does."
ANN ROE

✬ LIFE CHALLENGES ✬

Ask yourself, "Am I waiting for someone or something to let me be me?" Think about what you'd do if you weren't waiting.

Write your declaration of independence.

Get a symbol of your dream and keep it with you.

While Alive, Live!

"You're alive. Do something. The directive in life is so uncomplicated. It can be expressed in single words. Look, Listen, Choose, Act."
BARBARA HALL

Fred made a lot of noise after he found his voice. He was an accountant who sounded as if he'd just jumped off the back of a boxcar on a freezing morning after smoking three packs of Camels and drinking a fifth of Jim Beam.

Fred drank at least that much for years. He'd sit on a barstool in some longshoreman's bar on San Francisco Bay and curse the lucky suckers who were doing something with their lives. The sailors whipping by on the Bay looked like freedom personified, while Fred felt as if life were literally passing him by. He was a barstool dreamer, too lost in an alcoholic fog to do anything. In his forties, he hit bottom and sobered up.

With the liquor gone and his head clearing, like many people who have been let out of the addiction prison, he didn't want to waste a minute more wishing and hoping—he decided to be a doer. He dove into sailing lessons and crewed on sailboats every weekend, becoming one of the lucky suckers he had envied. He took improvisation acting classes, and his boxcar voice was all of a sudden on radio ads that featured New Jersey tough guys and ex-cons. In a funny paradox, he was playing the type of man he used to be. Kids at the library loved story time when Fred was Mr. Grumpy.

He started renting an apartment in Paris for two months every year, and then the trips got longer and more frequent. He became a beloved favorite of the expats. He relished the art, language, culture, and food in France. Fred was a man amazed: an actor, sailor, and part-time Parisian. Fred recently passed away but while alive, he lived.

✩ LIFE CHALLENGES ✩

Make a list of all the things you want to do before you die.

Think of someone you know who has lived fully. Take them out for coffee and discover their secret.

What lucky suckers do you envy? Become one.

I Wish . . .

"Yesterday they told you you would not go far.
That night you open and there you are.
Next day on your dressing room they've hung a star.
Let's go on with the show."
IRVING BERLIN, "THERE'S NO BUSINESS LIKE SHOW BUSINESS"

Sometimes we don't know what we want; we only know that our present life doesn't quite fit anymore. Todd says, "I didn't like where I was but I didn't know where else I wanted to be." One step toward a lifelong love affair with music changed everything.

In musical theater, there are people with pitch-perfect tone and the technical skills to hit all the right notes. And then there are the rare talents who embody the spirit of the song—who can "sell" the song, in musical parlance. These people make you believe. When you sit in a dark theater and hear these virtuosos perform, you get chills. Like the best of them, Todd seems born to play the lead in any musical theater production.

As a little boy, Todd was fearful of things other kids took for granted. But he had the gift of music; he could play the piano by ear from age five. Alone in his room he entered another world, separate from the stunts and rough life of the Southern boys in the neighborhood. He would listen to his idol, Elton John, for hours. Todd even memorized all the liner notes in the albums. His favorite was *Goodbye Yellow Brick Road.*

Still, Todd, now thirty-nine, relates, "I never had the grand plan like some driven performers who plot out a career A to Z." He's amazed at his good fortune, like a kid in a candy store: "I didn't set out to do this, and I never dreamed I'd have this success and personal fulfillment from loving what I do."

Not so long ago, Todd was stuck in an administrative job that did little more than pay his bills; he was good at it, but he definitely had no passion for his job. Something was missing. Six years ago, when Todd moved to Atlanta, he started voice lessons with a coach. This led to an audition for a regional musical theater. One day he watched the TV program *Inside the Actors Studio*, which was featuring an interview with Barbra Streisand, who said something like (in Todd's recollection): "When you make a move or a decision, things happen to back you up." Taking that advice to heart, Todd let go of his day job as soon as he heard he'd been cast for the production. He's been working in theater every since and wonders at this amazing turn of events. What had seemed like a pipe dream, so far out of reach, was now a reality.

It was as if this life in the theater were just waiting for him to move into it, to own it. Todd gets philosophical when he tries to make sense of his abrupt life change and good fortune: "I wonder about this whole predestination thing.... Am I a character that's already written and I'm living out the play? Do I really have control of any of this? Or does a higher hand plan it even when I think I'm choosing from free will?"

Despite his initial success, though, Todd soon endured a string of flops, and for a time he stopped performing. He went into a dark questioning period, asking himself, "What am I doing? Maybe I don't enjoy this anymore, maybe the pressure is too great."

He even began to diminish his talent and, he says, "I started almost to hate doing what I love." He'd run into the same obstacle many performers eventually face: the fickleness of the business, and the lack of security that goes along with it. But these doubts often don't last, as performers again get the itch to put on the greasepaint and hear the roar of the crowd. Abandoning talent leads to pain, which luckily brings us back to using our talents. Todd realized he was throwing his gift back in the face of the creator who gave it to him, and he got back on stage. He came out of this experience with a good offer to work with really talented people.

Todd now makes a great living doing what he loves. He's had some peak experiences, including singing the national anthem for the Atlanta Braves and being in the chorus at the opening of the Olympics.

But his biggest thrill was the opportunity to sing back-up for an Elton John recording session. Todd says, "It was surreal, never, ever, did I think I'd be at that level." He told Elton's guitarist, "I've known you guys all my life, I just never met you. Thank you for what you have done for my life."

The little boy, who battled fear, had met his idol. Today Todd gets to do Elton John numbers in shows—with his wild costumes and his ability to sell a song, he brings the essence of Elton to life.

Today, Todd says, "I look at the way my life turns out in a good way. I look back at all the fears I had and I don't have them anymore. I was the kid who was afraid of so many things, wouldn't even get a driver's license when all my friends couldn't wait to get theirs."

In answer to the question "what would you do if you had no fear?," Todd says he'd write a musical. "Deadlines motivate me. It's almost like the less time I have, the more I get done," he says. I gave Todd a deadline and told him I'd be encouraging him to fulfill this dream. So far his life has proven that talent can triumph and that, even though we don't always know the path we're on, miracles can happen to put us in the divine spotlight.

In the beginning of the musical *Into the Woods*, Cinderella sings, "I wish...." In two notes, Todd says, the song brilliantly depicts the longing and hope with which every dream begins. At the end of the show, Cinderella again sings, "I wish...," symbolizing a new beginning. There is always something new to wish for. We are not aging if we keep wishing. Remember that the sweet dream you hold is holding you.

"... and then the day came when the risk to remain tight in a bud was more painful than the risk it took to blossom."
ANAÏS NIN

☆ LIFE CHALLENGES ☆

Start with "I wish..." and write fifty things you wish for.

Find a class or a coach, and begin studying something you have an itch for.

Make a list of your childhood pleasures. Rediscover some today.

CHAPTER 2

Where Would You Go?

"The impulse to travel is one of the hopeful symptoms of life."

ADELINE AINSWORTH

Say "Yes"

*"I would not creep along the coast, but steer out in mid-sea,
by the guidance of the stars."*
GEORGE ELIOT

Saying "yes" to life opportunities is like opening a secret door or finding buried treasure; it is like loving yourself enough to take a risk. Have you known people whose first response to any suggestion or invitation was "no"? In improvisational comedy classes, the very first lesson is that you always say, "Yes, and...." If your improv partner says, "We are little green people and we only eat figs," you say, "Yes, and I love figs. What an aphrodisiac." You always play along. When we say a knee-jerk "no" in improv or in life it stops the action.

Practice saying "yes" to life. Your results may not be as far-reaching as those in the following story, but who knows. Why not try?

Janet first learned to sail small boats at Girl Scout camp but didn't really keep up with it after that. In her early thirties Janet worked in Boston, for a financial institution. A friend from her women's group issued an open invitation, to the group, to come sailing in Florida. The friend, Carol, and her husband, Don, owned a boat down in the Keys.

Janet was the only one who took Carol up on the offer, the only one who said yes. This "yes" started an odyssey that would last years. Janet flew down to Key Largo and boarded the *Domicile*, a top-of-the-line, forty-nine-foot Liberty sailing sloop, for a three-day cruise to the Bahamas. The minute they hoisted the sail Janet threw up. But she was hooked by the silence, the salt air, and the dolphins. She got along well with Carol and Don. They made several stops along the way, and at the end of the trip Janet flew home from Nassau and went back to work as a financial analyst.

Next time, the trip lasted two weeks, Turks and Caicos to Puerto Rico. Janet discovered that she only would get seasick for the first three days, and after that she would be fine.

Then she got the call to go out for three months from Boston to Saint Lucia in the Caribbean. As fate would have it, the international corporation she worked for was offering layoffs, so she volunteered and got three months' severance pay. As she says, "I got paid to sail. And anyway, my friends all said I looked funny in a business suit."

The Gulf Stream can be nasty, and she experienced her first storm on the way to Bermuda. Icy water flooded the cabin, and the sixty-foot main sail got jammed and wouldn't come down. In the middle of the storm Janet volunteered to be hoisted about forty feet up the mast in a bos'n chair. This is a feat so daring that when they sailed into Bermuda, people who'd heard about it on the radio lined up in the marina to meet her. When you're at sea, Janet says, no matter what comes up you have to deal with it and you have to do it right now. There's no repair ship coming; it's you and the boat. After this trip, Janet really had her sea legs.

The next call came from Carol and Don: "Wanna go across the Pacific?" Janet flew to Panama and met up with them. They went through the canal and over to the Galapagos Islands. Janet says, "I got to swim with penguins, tortoises, and sea lions. There were even marine iguanas that swim." She marveled at the blue-footed boobies and the birds' intricate mating dance.

After twenty-one days at sea, they arrived in the Marquesas, where Paul Gauguin, lived, painted, and is buried. His love for the tropics is reflected in the warm colors and glowing people in his painting. Janet could be speaking for Gauguin or anyone who's ever caught Polynesian paralysis—the dreamy, lush feeling that only a tropical island can produce—when she says, "These beautiful children would follow me around like I was Petunia Pan. Here I was on the most gorgeous beach, with kids tagging along bringing me shells and teaching me the name of each. They pulled an old beach chair under a palm tree and made me sit, like I was a queen. One child climbed the tree, threw down coconuts while others opened them, and we all drank coconut milk." Long way from Boston and a business suit.

Sailing is a multinational world, and Janet loved meeting people from everywhere, who all became friends when they encountered each other on tiny specks of land in the middle of vast oceans. Because sailors have to make sure they get through certain ocean passages before the stormy season begins, they often meet up on the same islands, repeatedly reuniting during their journeys as they all race to beat the weather.

Janet and Carol and Don sailed to the Tuamotu Islands, in French Polynesia, following the footsteps of Thor Heyerdahl, who sailed the handmade balsa wood raft *Kon-Tiki* from Peru to Tuamotu in 1947 to prove that the Polynesian people could have migrated from South America. Later Thor sailed from Morocco to Barbados with a crew of seven on the papyrus reed boat *RA-2* to prove that the Egyptians could have sailed to the New World. Like Heyerdahl, Janet was part of that rare world of explorers who set off and lose sight of land, trading the known world for the exotic.

Eight months after starting out in Panama, Janet, Carol, and Don landed in New Zealand. The couple whom Janet had lived with all these months, through all these adventures, decided that they'd done all the sailing they wanted to do for the moment. They sold the boat and flew home. Because she wasn't ready to go home, Janet says, she "found a couple of options." In the sailing community people are always looking for crews. Janet decided to sign on with a man who owned a thirty-eight-foot sailboat.

Janet kept in touch with her parents via email; her dad was very excited that she was headed for the island of Espiratu Santo where he'd been posted during WWII. He helped liberate the islanders from Japanese occupation. When Janet mentioned this to a man she met on the island, he told his friends, and then everyone wanted to meet the daughter of a man who had helped free them. Janet says, "I felt like a celebrity."

Her experiences rewarded her with a strong sense of reverence and respect for other cultures. "I'm a visitor in someone else's home," she says. "These countries and islands are their home."

She had been gone two years when her parents, who were in their seventies, got their first passports and flew to meet her in Pohnapei, Micronesia. Janet says, "I was living my dad's dream. He'd always talked about trips like this. But I had to tell my mother, 'Don't get your hopes up about my relationship with this skipper because it's not going to last.'"

The adventures at sea strengthened her faith. "When I was on deck at night and saw the stars stretching from horizon to horizon, I knew something made all this—it is not an accident. And the power that created the earth, sea, and sky gives you strength when you need it. Wherever I turned, I could see the hand of a higher power. There's just too much evidence; it can't be coincidence."

Janet arrived in San Francisco two and a half years after she'd started from Panama.

The lessons Janet took from her life at sea—about coping with whatever comes your way, and not balking at the most frightening events—continue to inspire her every day.

✫ LIFE CHALLENGES ✫

Say "YES!" Think YES. Be YES.

Take a ride away from the city lights, look at the stars, and ask them for inspiration.

Ask yourself, "Do I have a suit that doesn't fit my soul?"

Purple Bandanna

"Nothing's far when one wants to get there."
QUEEN MARIE OF ROMANIA

The main thing that was stopping Kathleen from pursuing her dream of traveling to foreign countries was that she didn't have anyone to travel with. "When I travel I feel so alone," she says. "I feel safer with another person." She also wanted a buddy to share the memories after the trip.

The second thing stopping her was her lack of paid vacation time. For a self-employed bookkeeper, taking time off could mean a loss of income or clients.

Most of her previous travels were of the armchair variety, reading travel logs and seeing films set in exotic locations. She originally wanted to travel with a boyfriend. After relationships with two men who had no interest in going to the Far East, she gave up that idea.

"For several years, I was stuck in my living room paralyzed by fear. Those who knew me never had any inkling that I was unable to realize my dreams. I was outgoing, had created my own business, and had an exciting social life. I saw friends travel, and I was excited for them but green with envy.

Kathleen attended one of my retreats and when we did the "what would you do if you had no fear?" process, she says, "Immediately, I knew what I'd do. I was the first to make my declaration. 'I would go to Vietnam' popped out of my mouth before I had a moment to think about it."

Kathleen says that this simple exercise empowered her. The act of speaking her dream out loud enabled her to feel it might be possible. At the end of the retreat Kathleen was given a gift that symbolized adventure to her, a purple bandanna. For the first time she surrendered to the fact that she might have to do her trip alone or not at all—but this time she was willing to go for it.

As fortune would have it, on the ride home, her retreat buddy told her that she'd be interested in going. Neither had known that the other was interested in a trip to Vietnam and Cambodia. But the act of speaking the dream set it in motion. It is as if the universe were just waiting for us to have the nerve to say what we want, and as soon as we do, all sorts of help, material and spiritual, comes our way.

Kathleen's planning began in earnest. Many times during the process, she asked herself, "Can I really do this? But the energy from the retreat stayed with me and I kept plodding through all the arrangements."

First, she had to educate herself about tours. She surfed the Web and found a tour agency based in Hanoi.

Second, she tackled the financial part, doing extra projects for clients and breaking the news that she was leaving for three weeks during the busiest the time of the year.

She boldly boarded the plane, saying, "I left with faith in my ability and God at my side." Through the entire trip, her mantra was "Try everything and have no fear." She did.

Arriving in Hanoi, Kathleen and her companion were met by a wonderful guide, Truong Nguyen Manh. "He made the city sing," she says. They spent a night on a Chinese junk on Ha Long Bay and sampled all that Hanoi has to offer.

The next stop was Ho Chi Minh City (Saigon) in South Vietnam. One of the reasons Kathleen wanted to see Vietnam was because she grew up with war news on the TV in her living room every night. While there, she saw many reminders of the war and talked to many men who had served with U.S. soldiers.

They toured the incredible Caodai Buddhist temples, where an enormous globe with the "divine eye" hangs above the altar, along with a sign reading *Van Giao Nhat Ly* ("All religions have the same reason"). Behind the gilded letters is a picture of the founders of the world's great religions: Mohammed, Laotse, Jesus, Buddha, and Confucius.

Kathleen says, "We toured the Cui Chi tunnels and took a river-boat up the Mekong River, stopping along the way for incredible food and shopping. In a rural town, we were approached by waiters in the restaurant. They put on their favorite song and we all sang 'Hotel California.'"

Next in the women's Far East odyssey was Cambodia. A speed-boat took them to one of the wonders of the world, Angkor Wat. These temples, built between the ninth and fourteenth centuries, are adorned by statues of heavenly nymphs.

In Cambodia they dined on spiders fried in hot oil, rode ele-phants, and became heavenly nymphs in a hot air balloon.

"This is one of the greatest experiences of my life. We met some of the nicest people, and I am still in touch through email with Truong, who turned out to also be a reporter for the *Vietnam Economic News*. He sent me a recent issue; he'd quoted me about bird flu. Bless his heart for giving me my fifteen minutes of fame in Vietnam."

Kathleen now has pictures to prove she lived her dream. Around her neck she wears the purple bandanna. One year later, Kathleen attended the retreat and gave the bandanna to a woman who wanted to go to Eygpt.

"It is the soul's duty to be loyal to its own desires.
It must abandon itself to its master passion."
REBECCA WEST

✦ LIFE CHALLENGES ✦

Declare a desire today.

Make a list of all your unfulfilled desires.

Go buy a purple bandanna.

Far-Away Places with Strange-Sounding Names

*"Through travel I first became aware of the outside world;
it was through travel that I found my own introspective
way into becoming a part of it."*
EUDORA WELTY

Sylvia married when she was twenty-two and had not experienced much of the world. After five years of a happy marriage she wanted to stretch her wings—not to leave the marriage but to travel alone.

She planned to go to Africa for three weeks. In her backpack were a Lonely Planet guide to East Africa, travel documents, and a camera. She had a general plan of what she wanted to do and see but absolutely no idea of what lay ahead. Those three weeks turned into a life-changing three-month trip.

The first thing Sylvia did was join a short organized safari to Northern Kenya; this gave her the grounding to go out on her own.

She kept her options open, letting the land and people guide her. She traveled by trains, in the back of crowded pickups, and in buses stuffed with thirty people plus noisy goats and chickens.

Although she started out alone, she didn't stay that way long; she continually hooked up with fellow travelers

The journey took her north through Uganda to Zaire to see the gorillas of the Verunga Mountains. There was war in Rwanda. "We could see shellfire across the range," Sylvia reports. "We didn't have visas, but after a small bribe, we were allowed to stay twenty-four hours and make the trek up and back to see the gorillas."

Next she traveled to Tanzania, the Serengeti, the Mount Kilimanjaro base camp, and Zanzibar.

Sylvia says, "I can't begin to describe all the wonder and magic I experienced . . . red Columbus monkeys jumping from behind a tree to play peek-a-boo and then stealing our cookies when we weren't looking, hyenas rubbing their backs on my tent."

Sylvia's words are like thirty-second videos. She describes "the cinnamon, sweet aroma as the ferry pulled into Zanzibar." In Uganda, she rounded a river bend to see "two bull elephants bathing in the sunset as hippos swam around our boat and brightly colored Kingfishers dove for their supper."

Now, a few years after her trip, she says that people think she was incredibly brave to go, but ironically the idea of staying put in her comfortable life scared her much more than going to Africa. "It is a greater fear that forced me to go seize this opportunity," she says. "The fear of not going, the dread of living my life without seeing these breathtaking places and experiencing the awe-inspiring cultures. Ultimately it is the fear of being alive and not living that is most fearful."

✬ LIFE CHALLENGES ✬

Listen to your heart and soul—what are they nagging you to explore?

Spread your wings. Close your eyes and imagine yourself taking flight.

Tell a loved one how important it is to live your heart's desire.

Foreign Affair

"Life, that is Paris! Paris, that is life!"
MARIE BASHKIRTSEFF

"I don't know whether to kill myself or go bowling," Jan quoted Woody Allen. Our support group was meeting on a chilly October night in Jan's Sausalito houseboat. Week after week we had been holding her dream of finding a mate. There are times when we cannot believe for ourselves that our dreams can come true. At these times it's good to have a friend who believes for us. She claimed not to have had a date since Watergate. Throughout the years, Jan had watched friend after friend get married while she collected magenta and slime-green bridesmaid dresses. This night she cried, "I'm turning forty on November 5, and if I don't do something bold, I'll go crazy!" Jan had some money saved and wanted to do something big and bold. She put out two possible birthday ideas: either get liposuction on her thighs, or go to Europe for the first time. I asked her, "Jan, what would you do if you had no fear?" She said, "Europe!" The group cheered. She'd always dreamed of going to Europe with a soul mate; she'd always envisioned herself in romantic, postcard-style shots. This night she realized she might never get there if she kept waiting for him to arrive.

She booked a two-week trip to London and Paris. She didn't go with the intention of meeting a man, but that didn't stop me from praying daily that she would at least have safe sex with a dangerous European. Jan was way out of her comfort zone when she had a cupcake in her room on the fortieth anniversary of her birth. Things in London were lonely.

Jan took the Eurostar to Paris. She attended an event at the American Church, a gathering place for people who speak English. Roy, an Englishman who'd been working in Paris for seven years, chatted her up. The next day Roy called. He had packed a very French picnic. Thus started Jan's love affair with Roy and with Paris.

My prayers had been answered. Jan came back from the trip with a glow like the sun breaking over the Eiffel Tower and a smile like the *Mona Lisa*. She told our group, "I met my soul mate." We were nervous that this would be a flash-in-the-pan foreign affair. We were all wrong!

She and Roy visited back and forth. In June, Jan called me in a panic and I rushed over to the houseboat. She'd been downsized and had lost her job. We looked at each other and yelled, "Paris!"

My prince, Brian, the best packer ever, helped Jan organize and put things in storage. At the San Francisco airport, he hugged her goodbye, and Jan cried at the enormity of starting a new life in a new country with a new man. She was really going out on a limb. Brian reminded her, "Planes fly both ways."

A couple of years earlier, Brian and I had helped Jan move into a houseboat, and we'd fallen in love with it. We had been living in a boring beige condo that was so not us. We talked to her landlady and moved in as Jan moved out.

Jan and Roy were married on February 17, 1998. The candlelit wedding at a European-style hotel on a cliff above San Francisco Bay was a magical fairytale. Jan glowed: she looked like a forty-one-year-old vision. Brian was the best man. I had helped her shop for the dress at pretty much every bridal shop in London and Paris. Today, Jan and Roy have a five-year-old son named Branton and they live happily a block away from the Champs-Élysées.

✿ LIFE CHALLENGES ✿

Ask yourself, "What would I do for love if I had no fear?"

Identify a dream you can accomplish before your next birthday.

Imagine your ideal city. Do research on the Internet, find pictures, and put them on your refrigerator.

The World Awaits You

"Survival is important, but thriving is elegant."
MAYA ANGELOU

Some people travel the world. Some travel only a few hundred miles in their lifetime.

There are people who never venture out of their village. The conditioning that says, "Stay here, danger is over there," is strong in some cultures and countries. Fear-provoking messages are passed down for generations. I heard a story about a woman who was preparing a roast for the oven; her daughter asked her, "Why do you always cut off a piece on both ends?" Her mother replied, "I never thought about it, I guess I do it because my mother did." She got curious and called her mother, asked the same question and got this response: "I had to cut the ends off because the pan was too small."

Hours are spent on therapists' sofas trying to get out of a small pan and into a larger world. There's a great Billie Holiday song that goes, "Mama may have, Papa may have, but God bless the child that's got his own." In life, if we want to be happy and productive and discover new worlds, we have to "get our own."

"Beauty was blond hair and blue eyes," says Nicky, a beautiful woman of color from Cape Town, South Africa. In her mid-twenties, she looks like a model, with long, dusty black hair and luminous, large eyes. Nicky wishes she had grown up with the idea of being able to do anything in life. When she was a child, the thought that she could live an open life free of political, societal, and family restrictions was foreign. Most of the restrictions she encountered, no matter the source, were based on fear.

South Africa during apartheid was a world of haves and have-nots, with many signs that read, "Reserved for Whites Only." Like indigenous peoples everywhere who find themselves displaced by foreign colonists, Nicky's family had been relocated from Upper Cape on lovely Table Mountain to dusty, flat Lower Cape.

The day Nicky was born, a protest was in full swing, and the acrid smell of tires burning filled the air, making it hard to breathe. The police had closed off the exits from Nicky's family's neighborhood, fighting back the crowds with rubber bullets and tear gas. Even if her parents had had a car they couldn't have gone to the hospital, so Nicky was born in her parents' bed. She literally started life in the midst of fear and fighting. She slept in that same bed with her parents and two other siblings until she was nine years old.

Nicky was taught by her mother to accept things as they were and not to make waves. You get used to bad treatment, Nicky says, but at times she thought, "How can you just sit there and take it?" For instance, there was a Whites Only beach only half an hour away.

The beach that allowed blacks was hours away so if her family wanted to go to the beach they had to get up at four o'clock in the morning, pack food and blankets, and change trains twice. The beach was a strip of sand directly adjacent to the railroad tracks and not very restful when the train roared past. The kids had a special name for the beach because of the sewage pipes that drained into the water.

Of course, it was fear of the consequences of stepping out of line that kept people in line. And Nicky's family saw those consequences firsthand when Ashley Kriel, a young local activist hero, was killed in front of his family in his mother's house. The community who loved him carried his coffin through the streets. As a nine-year-old, Nicky sat on a stool by the window when her father commented, "There wasn't room for a red ant," because the street was so crowded with mourners.

The whole social order was based on fear and prejudice; everyone feared the Other. The whites in power feared losing control; the blacks feared the iron hand of the whites.

It's no wonder that all her life Nicky felt like a second-class citizen, inferior and not good enough. She sums it up: "I feared myself." When apartheid ended, she was fearful of entering the blond, blue-eyed world: "If I go out in the world, what will people think of me? Maybe I don't know how to act or what to talk about? I'm not good enough and I will surely fail."

As she looks back on how she chose a larger life, Nicky points to a series of serendipitous happenings and chance encounters. There may be fear in the world and hatred in the world, but there is also a power working that endeavors to lift individuals up. In Nicky's life, there were women who saw good, strong things in her that she did not see for herself.

Nicky had not heard Marianne Williamson's words ("We ask ourselves, Who am I to be brilliant, gorgeous, talented, and fabulous? Actually, who are you not to be?"), but she was beginning to feel tiny stirrings of personal power nonetheless.

She saw peers who did not risk anything in their lives and ended up in a cycle of poverty that repeated the past. Her friends had lots of children and lived in cramped houses like their mothers before them. Nicky was fearful of making waves, but more afraid of never seeing waves at all.

Nicky was working in an upscale department store in Cape Town when a young woman came in to buy shoes and said she was leaving on a cruise ship. "There's an agency right here in Cape Town that books people to work on ships called Blue Ensign. Check it out," the woman told Nicky.

Nicky didn't think much about it until six months later, when she was bored and looked to see if the company was in the phone book; it was, and she sent a resume. Two weeks later she had an interview, and two days after that she received a letter welcoming her to Princess Cruises. Nicky thought it was a form letter and tore it up. Four weeks later the company called and asked, "Can you leave on a ship in one month?" She was afraid to tell anyone in her family except her older sister. Like adventurous children everywhere since time immemorial, she elected to wait until the last minute, until all the arrangements had been made, to tell her parents and siblings. This was the point of no return for her new life. She gathered everyone together and dropped the bomb, and they laughed, thinking it was a joke.

In an effort to keep children safe at home, countless numbers of mothers have reported the horrors that wait around the corner, over the mountain, and across the sea. Following in that rich tradition, Nicky's mother was horrified. "This can't be real," she said. "They'll get you away and use you for bad movies. It's dangerous. How will you get home? You'll get stranded and they'll take advantage of you and put you in a little cell somewhere." Nicky thought, "I trust my instincts, and I'm not a helpless child."

While quaking in her new shoes, she boarded a plane to join the ship. It was her first time ever out of South Africa, and she'd never been on a vacation in her life.

She went on a luxury ship to work in the gift shop, one of the best jobs on a ship. Every port was new; every person she met had taken a risk to leave their homeland to work on the ship. The ship's crew included thirty-four different nationalities, and though the cabins were small, for many of the workers it was a luxury to have a bunk of one's own.

Nicky's job has taken her all over the Caribbean, through the Panama Canal, to Alaska and the Baltic. The risk she took has shot her out into the wide world, where she's met more people from more countries in a couple of years than most people meet in a lifetime. She works with people she was once afraid would judge her.

I read Nicky her story and we both hugged and cried—a white woman who grew up in the South during the end of segregation and a black woman from South Africa, apart no more.

Nicky still has fears, but she doesn't let them cripple her. She's seeing places her friends and family in Cape Flats haven't even head of. Once a little girl who thought she'd never be good enough without blond hair and blue eyes, Nicky has learned the truth of what Oprah says: "Love and trust yourself."

✬ LIFE CHALLENGES ✬

Pay attention to chance meetings and serendipitous happenings.

Call the number that will lead to an adventure.

Walk over the hill, around the bend, or sail away even for a half a day.

CHAPTER 3

How Would You Live?

"There are homes you run from and homes you run to."

LAURA CUNNINGHAM

Mistress of the Rancho Esperanza

"The very least you can do in your life is to figure out what you hope for. And the most you can do is to live inside that hope."

BARBARA KINGSOLVER

During one of my retreats, Nellie stated that she did not know what the next step was in her life. She only knew she had a desire "to be alone and find out who I am. I want to have the time to do the creative projects boiling up inside."

When she did her treasure map, the collage of scenes she wanted in her life, Nellie let go of preconceived ideas and just let her heart and intuition choose the pieces. Her treasure map had pictures of houses in the country, gardens, and arbors—altogether, nothing like the urban life she was living. Later she started journaling to keep discovering what was in her heart.

Today, a couple of years after that retreat, Nellie says, "Many times in my life I've longed for something, then achieved it and been disappointed. But this place is better than I could have planned. This was a dream I didn't know I wanted." Nellie tells me this as I sit in her vineyard under a huge walnut tree. She is the mistress of a two-acre ranch in the Valley of the Moon. It's a magical place in the California wine country. Her house was built in the 1930s and features hardwood floors, spacious rooms, and a beautiful garden. The arms of an ancient oak form a canopy over the house. Two three-foot-high stone pillars stand on either side of the dirt drive.

Nellie, a vivacious woman in her early sixties, says she has always been afraid. No one would know it to look at her, especially after they consider her accomplishments: going to Russia and China on humanitarian missions, acting on stage, doing commercials, and performing in films.

Nellie's childhood looked like a fairytale from the outside. She grew up in a mansion in the Pacific Heights neighborhood of San Francisco that enjoyed views of the Golden Gate Bridge and the Bay. But inside the house, her violent father would fly into a rage and terrorize the family by firing guns into the fireplace. Nellie, then a child with a child's perspective, became convinced that good moments actually caused bad times. So she suffered from thoughts of impending doom when things were going well. As a result, Nellie says, all the problems in her life have come from fear. It paralyzed her to the extent that she stayed in both bad relationships and situations, even as an adult.

When she married, she and her husband moved across the street from her parents' palatial home to another Georgian four-story mansion. Thirty-five years of her life were spent in a marriage that did not nourish her. Nellie raised five children, all the while battling fear and using alcohol to cope.

Her unhappiness led her to a therapist, and that led her into recovery. Without alcohol clouding her perspective, her life began to crack open, and light shone in. The day came when she was ready to end the marriage. It was liberating. Nellie remained in San Francisco to keep acting. She hired an agent and won parts in lots of commercials and long-running plays. She never considered living anywhere else.

Nellie came down with coronary artery disease a year ago after returning from two weeks in China. It was a shock because she's very fit, regularly exercises, and eats a healthy diet. There was no real treatment for her disease, but the doctors advised her to slow down radically. Then a small idea emerged, and she thought, "I can't act anymore and do the nerve-racking rounds of auditions. Being in a room with fifty women who all look the same, competing for the one spot on a television show is not going the help me relax. Nor is the drudgery of going to the theater seven days a week." All of a sudden she could see an escape hatch, like Alice's hole; she could stop doing something she thought she had to do.

Nellie's body demanded that she stop acting. Next, she thought, "I don't have to stay in San Francisco. I can scout new places." She'd been attracted to the Sonoma area, and she found herself a realtor and looked at the compulsory three awful properties. One day her realtor called and said, "Get here now! Something just came on the market. In this tight housing market you've got to see it now!"

Nellie was chattering away as they drove into a driveway through two ivy-covered stone pillars. She was still talking a blue streak as they walked up the stairs and opened the front door. Then she shut up, awe-struck—she knew without a doubt that this was the place of her heart. This house was what she'd been waiting for all these years. But after buying it, she could not move in for several months. Meanwhile her beloved dog got sick and died. Nellie felt as if she also experienced a small death inside herself. Her fears began to attack her, and she worried that she wouldn't live to move into her dream home.

Through years of dealing with fear, Nellie had developed a system for fighting it. First, she prayed for faith. She practiced going around the fear by doing an action, any action, and taking the next logical step that was in front of her. In making arrangements for the move, sometimes she'd pick up the phone and the old paralysis would strike and she'd have to put it down. But Nellie would give herself credit for the effort. At least she'd picked the phone up, and next time she could make the call. This is the way she walked through the fear.

She had concerns about moving to a community where she really had no friends, as well as fear of making a mistake and fear of living alone. But she said to herself, "All I have to do is what I've been guided to do. I just have to get there, and then I'll find out my next step. I can't sit here and get the benefit of the risk without taking the risk. The worst that can happen is it's a mistake and I can always sell and move again. But I must know what is waiting for me in what feels like my dream existence."

Today, Nellie imparts her love of theater to teens by volunteering at a local drama department. She's working on a children's book about fairy spirits that live in theaters.

After moving in, Nellie was inspired to remove the ivy that had encircled the pillars for so many years. The previous owners had never touched it. Underneath the ivy, in the peeling lettering, she beheld the words "Rancho" on the left and "Esperanza" on the right. "Esperanza" means "hope" in Spanish. Nellie had found her "home of hope" and received a divine confirmation. Nellie's life now looks pretty much like her treasure map of several years ago. It was the divine destiny waiting for her even before she knew she wanted it.

"Ah! There is nothing like staying at home, for real comfort."
JANE AUSTEN

☆ LIFE CHALLENGES ☆

Imagine a life that feels like a blessed sigh.

Ask yourself, "What place in the world feels like my spiritual home?"

Create a treasure map.

A Safe Haven

"Surviving meant being born over and over."
ERICA JONG

ometimes our worst fears do manifest. It's horrible, excruci-
atingly painful, and unfair. We want to break things and
scream. We want the sun to go out. We wonder how we'll ever
get the will to go on. I'm humbled and grateful to the people who
have told me about their losses. The fact that they lived though fears
and pain gives me courage.

There are no quick fixes or pat answers in dealing with fear, loss,
and pain. However, sharing them with someone else takes some of
the sting away. I feel privileged when people confide these feelings to
me. They are giving me a gift—the gift of knowing that if they faced
the worst and lived, I can also. In talking with Maitreya, I got this
sense strongly.

"All my life I've feared losing people, especially my parents. I was
afraid of being emotionally alone and having to take care of myself,"
Maitreya says.

She has reason to feel insecure and afraid—raised by her junkie
mom, Maitreya spent her childhood moving from one undesirable
place to another, fourteen times in ten years. Home was a series of

abandoned buildings, cold-water flats, and vans. Life was full of midnight moves, drug deals in doorways, characters on the fringe, and the need to look over your shoulder all the time. Childhood for this girl was a shadowy, scary place.

Maitreya's saving grace was her intelligence. After test results showed her to be "gifted" in the second grade, she was able to stay in one school (for gifted students) throughout her schooling, instead of being shuttled from school to school every time she and her mother moved. At the gifted school, she found kind teachers who offered much-needed emotional support. She excelled in learning, and education became an anchor in the turbulent seas of her young life.

When she was eleven, life at home deteriorated even further, and Maitreya struggled between the desire to save her mother and the need to save herself. Despite her strong feelings of guilt and responsibility for her mother, she called her father for help.

When he arrived in San Francisco, the conditions his daughter were living in appalled him. He said the apartment "smelled like death." He took Maitreya back to the East Coast with him.

Even as she began to live a more secure life, Maitreya carried in her the memory of how shaky life could be, how thin the line between having a home or being homeless, having food or being hungry. The illusion of security that many people experience was not a luxury Maitreya could depend upon. When she visited her mom once or twice a year, she had to contend with the horrible feelings that she was abandoning her mother every time she left. She also experienced the pain of seeing her half sister follow in their mother's footsteps and experiment with drugs.

One day, while she walked with her father in New York City, Maitreya saw a person sleeping on a hot-air grate and instinctively thought, "I'm going to help people like that."

She grew up and continued to excel academically, earning a college degree on full scholarship. Next she received her law degree at the University of California, Berkeley. Maitreya says, "All my life I've been told I was brash and argumentative so I decided to become a criminal defense attorney."

Today, Maitreya speaks for people who reside in the shadow world she was once a part of. "I've run into my mother, with a different face, several times," she says. Her clients are drug addicts and people accused of violent crimes, the "reviled members of society." Maitreya feels lucky to be their defender: "It's a privileged role to be a person who can't pass judgment on others."

Despite her career success, though, life had more pain in store for this woman: she saw her sister die as a result of being addicted and not taking care of herself. Shortly after that loss, Maitreya's dear father died.

Several years ago, Maitreya met a woman and they fell in love.

When she and her partner decided to have a baby, Maitreya carried the child and her partner's brother provided the sperm. During Maitreya's pregnancy, her mother came to visit for Christmas, and while there she was diagnosed with ovarian cancer. Maitreya and her best friend drove her mother home—which turned out to be a crack house with people passed out on the floor in the middle of the day. Shortly before Maitreya gave birth to her daughter, Maitreya's mother died.

The girl who'd been so afraid of loss had now lost everyone in her immediate family. After you lose people tragically and in a short period of time, Maitreya says, it feels like you just can't stand it. It seems as though the grief will swallow you whole. A terror rises up when you realize you're alone.

Maitreya has come to know that the only real security comes from within. That the real home is what is in your heart. She's learned to be less dependent on things and people outside of herself.

Although Maitreya's greatest fear came to pass, it did not kill her. She sums up her life lessons: "I don't have to give up on myself and my life no matter what happens. I don't need much to have a great life."

Today, Maitreya is raising her daughter, Eve. The demons that plagued her mother have been healed in Maitreya. Eve can grow up in a safe garden.

"I have a lot of things to prove to myself.
One is that I can live my life fearlessly."
OPRAH WINFREY

✧ LIFE CHALLENGES ✧

Write all the positive things you wish you had been told as a child and say them to yourself every day for a week.

Help a child. Become a mentor, a Big Brother or Big Sister, or a tutor.

Pray for healing for all the wounds of childhood.

Airstream Dream

*"Stand firm in your refusal to remain conscious during algebra.
In real life, I assure you, there is no such thing as algebra."*
Fran Lebowitz

One hundred well-meaning people can tell you why your dream is silly, impractical, stupid, and unworkable. Don't listen to them. In my own case, I never made better than a grade C in twelve years of school. I had severe learning disabilities, Attention Deficit Disorder, and dyslexia. Teachers put me at the back of the class and never called on me, and I was humiliated when I failed the seventh grade. By freshman year in high school, the guidance counselor told me I'd be going into "distributive education." Wow, that sounded good, a real plan and program for me. Then I discovered that "the plan" called for me to get out of school at noon and go to work as a clerk in Woolworth's. Get it? I'd "distribute" cheap costume jewelry, dust mops, and goldfish in little plastic bags to the buying public. Whee, I'm set for life now!

I grew up thinking I was stupid and could not learn. It wasn't until years later that I got encouragement from friends who told me I was bright and had a way with words. I took a night class and earned my first A ever.

Back when I was in school I would have never dreamed I'd be able to write. I still can't do the grammar, but I love stringing words together and telling stories. And I discovered you can hire people to handle grammar!

If I had accepted what I was told about myself, I would have sold myself short.

Ann's another true original. She knew what she wanted all along, but it took her years to stop listening to others.

"I let someone or other talk me out of living my dream for forty years," Ann says in her Southern, butter-dripping-off-a-biscuit voice.

Ann's first glimpse of her dream life came at the tender age of seven, in her home state of North Carolina, when a relative on the "trashier" side of the family rolled into the driveway in a putrid yellow camper trailer.

This "one-room wonder" had a bed and minuscule kitchen with a cool table that folded up against the wall. The bathroom was called an "S. S. S." because you could sit, shave, and shower all at once. To Ann's eyes it was heaven. "My daydreams centered on having a camper of my very own from that day forward."

When she was twenty-one, Ann says, "my spouse-equivalent and I got jobs in the glamorous entertainment industry (i.e., we became carnies working at fairs)." Ann considered herself a "fake carnie" because they stayed in cookie-cutter motels. She begged the boss for a trailer, like the real carnies, but he protested that motel accommodations were much classier.

The same plot replayed every few years, with one person after another telling her why she couldn't do what she wanted.

Ann just wanted to live like a gypsy in a "one-room wonder."

But she settled down and bought a fixer-upper house, which she shared with her mother.

Finally, Ann took some metaphysical classes and "began to listen more to the voices telling me what I could do and less to the ones telling me what I couldn't." She couldn't wait any longer on her dreams.

Even after repair work, her house only yielded a measly $16,000 when she sold it. Many a helpful man told her that she couldn't find a new home with that amount of money. She didn't listen to them. She listened to herself.

She spent $9,000 for a used trailer, $6,000 for a truck, and $1,000 to stock up. Ann hit the road with her seventy-eight-year-old mother and a sixteen-year-old cat. "I haven't been sorry one day since," she says. They've been on the road for four years now, stopping here and there to work and socialize.

Ann describes life on the road like so: "Sometimes I have all the time in the world and no money, and sometimes it's money and no time. Sometimes I have lots of friends close by (all new), and sometimes all my friends are hundreds of miles away. But I know that there are more new friends just up the road. I know there is either work for me to do ahead or a fabulous place to rest. I know there'll be sunsets to take my breath away and a rock to sit on until I catch it again. I know that the daydreams I escaped to in the bad times were pointing me towards the reality I love today. And if folks call me trailer trash—why, I know they're just jealous of me and my interesting, exciting, illuminating, entertaining, and fabulous trailer-trashy life."

✬ LIFE CHALLENGES ✬

Think of something you've been told you aren't good at. Do it.

What have you dreamed of since the first day you saw it? Go get it.

Be a gypsy for a day, week, or month.

CHAPTER 4

What Can You Survive?

*"Success or failure of a life, seems to lie in more or less
the luck of seizing the right moment of escape."*

ALICE JAMES

Escape to Freedom

"I wanted you to see what real courage is,
instead of getting the idea that courage is a man
with a gun in his hand. It's when you know you're licked
before you begin but you begin anyway and
you see it through no matter what."
HARPER LEE, *To Kill a Mockingbird*

Sometimes life deals us something we are completely powerless to control or escape. However, men and women do survive unimaginable events and unbelievable cruelty. The power of the human spirit to survive is incredible, and in the most horrible situations people will find ways to help one another. Every time an individual hangs onto a shred of hope and takes one more breath, a tyrant looses. In extreme conditions, the smallest act of kindness—a shared scrap of bread, a hand on the shoulder, the gift of a smile—can make all the difference. And in the worst of worlds people do defeat fear and survive.

Those who have faced the worst possible, most dangerous situations report that there comes a time when there is a tiny window of escape and you must squeeze through it right then or it'll be gone.

Eleanor lives in a snug house with a lovely, lush backyard. As we sit down at her kitchen table, the first thing she does is show me the tattoo on her left forearm: 75030. Then, with complete clarity, she begins to recall the events that happened more than sixty years ago.

In 1938 Berlin, Eleanor's Jewish father began to see what was happening to the Jews. He desperately wanted to save his son and daughter, so he took them to board a ship bound for the United States. Nazi doctors stood on the dock accepting or rejecting each child. Eleven-year-old Bernie was accepted. Fourteen-year-old Eleanor was rejected because she was nearsighted. Bernie, one of the lucky Jewish children who escaped, was raised by Jewish foster parents in Santa Barbara, California.

By a cruel turn of fate, one child was taken to a safe, gorgeous seaside town on the California coast while another was thrown back into the ghetto in Berlin.

Three days after putting Bernie on the ship, Eleanor's father died of a heart attack. After his death, Eleanor began to see Jews confined to the ghettos, with their freedoms taken away one by one. She watched while a synagogue was set on fire. The firemen did nothing to quench the flames, but stood by to make sure the neighboring buildings did not catch fire. Then one day she went to school and found that all the teachers had been taken to the camps.

When she was nineteen, her mother, who was Christian, wanted to visit her own brother. Eleanor reminded her that she (Eleanor) was not allowed on public transportation because she was half-Jewish, but her mother insisted and they went.

They left a note, to a friend who was coming to visit, on the kitchen table. The Gestapo went to their house looking for that friend and found the note.

At five o'clock the next morning, the Gestapo pounded on the door of her uncles' house and arrested Eleanor, charging her with riding on the train. After being interrogated by the Gestapo, she was put on a train under guard.

In the odd way that memory works, she recalls the name of the guard on one leg of the journey; he gave her a little of his sandwich. She asked him where she was being taken. He surely knew but wouldn't answer.

Eleanor arrived at the camp in Buchenwald on a freezing February night. All the prisoners were immediately sent to the wash house, where everything they had was taken away. There were hundreds of other women, who were all forced to strip naked, shower, and have their heads roughly shaven to the scalp.

Eleanor recalls that even though many of the others were strangers to her, they had been distinguishable as individuals while they had hair. After their hair was shaved, she says, "we didn't know each other anymore."

Each woman was then tattooed with a number and given a

garment that had been taken from someone who had already been killed. Eleanor received a wool dress, which she wore for the next two years.

The unheated barracks had wooden bunks built into the wall. The five women in each bunk shared one horse blanket. Each night, they huddled together to keep warm. The guards were brutal, forcing twenty women at a time to stand outside in the freezing air to use one bucket to relieve themselves.

Next to Eleanor, a twelve-year-old Dutch girl died of typhus.

Then one day Eleanor was transported to Auschwitz, where she made a friend named Rita. During her imprisonment at Auschwitz, Eleanor survived three "selections." The guards would line up the prisoners and divide them into two groups, based on how strong they were: one group would be sent directly to the gas chambers, and the other group would continue to do forced labor.

Six weeks before the end of the war, the Nazis wanted to remove the evidence of their atrocities. They took the prisoners who were able to walk on what was to become known as the death march. At this point, Eleanor weighed only eighty pounds. Malnutrition had devastating effects on her: not only were all her teeth loose, but there were holes on the inside of her mouth and black spots on her skin. And yet her hair had grown back.

Her friend Rita was not allowed on the march, because she was too weak to walk. She gave Eleanor her wool coat. This coat helped to save Eleanor's life.

The prisoners were forced to march in bitter cold. They had no warm clothes, they were starving, and their shoes were the unforgiving wooden clogs they'd been issued in the wash house. No one had socks, but some wrapped rags around their feet and legs. Besides the physical misery, these people were emotionally bankrupt from witnessing the horrors they had seen and grief-stricken from watching family members die. The only thing that had kept Eleanor going was the hope that one day she would see her brother, Bernie, and her mother again.

During the march, when someone stumbled or fell, he or she was shot in the back of the head. On one leg of the march, Eleanor noticed three girls escape without being seen. Eleanor had a moment of knowing that she had to be fearless and escape or she would surely die. She decided to risk the fear of being shot in order to gain her freedom and her life. When she saw her chance, she rolled into a ditch and lay there for hours until the line passed. She fled into the woods and removed the Star of David from Rita's coat. In the cold, with no shelter, Rita's warm coat helped Eleanor stay alive.

After her escape she was still not safe, as she could easily be shot as an escapee at any time. She had escaped in Poland, and her home was in Berlin. There were weeks of traveling ahead of her, all of it dangerous. But small miracles started to happen almost immediately after she escaped. Eleanor vividly remembers the kindness of so many strangers and even soldiers.

Over and over she recounts instances of people sharing food with her. Over and over she says it was a miracle. Once, a young boy came by on his bike, stopped, and said, "You look hungry." He gave Eleanor a little piece of cake. It was her twenty-first birthday.

When some German soldiers came upon her, she made up a story about being from a nearby town that had been bombed. One of the soldiers was from that town. He asked her what street she lived on. She felt a minute of intense fear because she'd never been to the town she'd named. If he realized she was lying, she could easily be sent back to the camps or shot. But luckily a friend in the camp had come from this town. They'd memorized each others' addresses so they could find each other after the war if they survived. Eleanor gave the girl's address, and the soldiers believed her. They even gave her some of their food. Another miracle.

After the war, Eleanor and her mother returned to the family home. Their house was the only one on the street that had escaped bombing, as the Nazis had used it as their headquarters.

One day, Eleanor opened the door to a young man in a U.S. Army uniform—it was her brother, Bernie, all grown up. He later arranged for his mother and sister to come to Santa Barbara. There,

Eleanor met and married a Jewish man who had been interned in a camp in India. They had a son and daughter. She named her daughter Rita, after her friend and savior from Auschwitz, the infamous camp that had put one million people to death.

Altogether, during the Holocaust, nearly six million Jews were killed, as well as two and a half million Christian Poles, and half a million gays, gypsies, and disabled people.

In June of 1981, Eleanor, her husband, and her daughter, Rita, all went to the world gathering of Jewish Holocaust survivors in Jerusalem. During that same trip, the mayor of Berlin invited all the survivors from that city to come for a visit, all expenses paid.

Miraculously, Eleanor was reunited with her old friend Rita, whom she named her daughter after. Eleanor still keeps a picture of the two of them taken on that Berlin trip.

If this woman had not survived, Eleanor's daughter, Rita, would not be here. And since Eleanor's daughter was the therapist who helped me out of a dark period, I would not be writing her mother's amazing story.

Eleanor, Rita, and I make a full circle: one woman who has had the courage to fight fear and escape terror, one woman who helps people walk out of the dark, and one who now tells a story of the synchronicity and miracle of it all.

*"In spite of everything
I still believe that people are really good at heart."*
ANNE FRANK

✨ LIFE CHALLENGES ✨

Help someone escape from a painful experience.

Consider your freedoms, and cherish them.

Look back on your life to discover the miracles you may
have experienced.

Facing the Fire

"It's not that I'm afraid to die, but I'm terribly, terribly afraid not to live."
FRANCES NOYES HART

O nce at Lake Tahoe, David and his family had watched their family dog, Baxter, power up hills and over boulders. The black, fuzzy cockapoo was then and there dubbed a "four-wheel-drive dust mop."

On Sunday, October 20, 1991, David decided to go to his law office to get some work done while it was quiet. After working for awhile, he went across the street to get some coffee, where he ran into his old friend Elihu Harris, the mayor of Oakland, California. They sat down to chat, and the mayor's cell phone rang. He told David, "There's a big fire up in your neighborhood." They went outside, looked up in the direction of David's house, and saw a huge plume of smoke. The both yelled and ran for their cars.

They would not know it until later, but this was to be the worst Bay Area fire since the 1906 San Francisco earthquake and fire. The location of David's house, in the Oakland hills, had been ripe for a fire. It was a steep, wooded area with heavy underbrush, and the roads in the hills were narrow and winding. This type of terrain was known as a firefighter's nightmare.

David got to the bottom of the hill, about a mile from his house. The police had already cordoned off the road and were not letting anyone up the hill. There were about a hundred frantic people at the barricade. David frantically scanned the crowd for his wife and daughter. He heard, "Daddy, Daddy, Baxter! Baxter's at home." He saw terror in his nine-year-old's eyes.

David was determined to try to get through the barricade in order to reach his house and Baxter. He noticed a newspaper reporter whom he knew who was riding a motorcycle. They both slipped past the officers, and David hopped on the back of the bike. They went roaring up the hill. "We go halfway up the hill and we're confronted with a 300-foot tower of flames, about forty feet wide, sucking so much wind that gravel is biting into our faces. This tower of flame is literally a firestorm, which creates a tornado effect. The tower is red and hot, very hot," David reports. "Later I would see 200-year-old oak trees turned to powder, houses disintegrated, nothing left."

With a sense of relief, he noticed that his friend's lovely home, which had always looked like a storybook vision, was untouched. But all around it homes were burned or burning. Then, he says, "suddenly, wham! Fire blows out all the windows at once and the house is fully engulfed."

David's reporter friend took the picture that appeared in the paper the next day. The full-page photo showed David grimacing, with his hands pressed hard against both sides of his head.

He begged the reporter to give him a ride to his house, but the reporter said, "No way." When the reporter friend relented, though, David climbed on again and they flew through the fire and smoke, every house burning as they went by, until they reached David's home. He was scared, to say the least. The reporter said he wasn't waiting. David yelled, "I'm not going in—just getting the dog."

Fear makes people do funny things, and David wonders why he broke down the garden gate instead of just unlatching it. But he crashed through at a dead run. "Baxter leaps into my arms—he'd never done that before—and we run back down the side of the house just as the motorcycle is leaving. He sees me and stops and I climb on with Baxter in my arms. We race down the hill—I don't think we were breathing at all—and we don't stop until we reach the barricade."

As David continues his story, he says that nothing was the same after that event: "My ex-wife said the whites of my eyes were completely black. But I will never forget the look of gratitude on my daughter's face. Thirteen years later it seems like yesterday. It's not often we get to be a hero in our kids' eyes."

This fire destroyed 2,843 homes and took twenty-five lives. About 150 people were injured, and the estimated dollar loss was over $1.5 billion.

David's home survived in the odd way that some homes do during fires, although all the homes around it were gone. Baxter lived to a ripe old age of seventeen years, grateful to the end.

"The real trick is to stay alive as long as you live."
Ann Landers

✿ Life Challenges ✿

Save a life.

Go adopt a dog.

Put out the fire of your fearful thoughts.

Dancing with Death

"Fear cripples the soul, so you just have to fight it."
DIANE KEATON

"As I stare at the video camera, I ask myself what I will say to my children. Do I speak to them about truths of divine order and the innate goodness of God—two things I don't believe in anymore? Do I smile bravely into the camera and tell them that it's my time to go?" Cheryl wondered during the lowest point in her fight with cancer, after she was told she had only six months to live. She was making a video for her children while struggling with her own grief: "Sadness falls around me like a suffocating cloak as once again I repeat the steps in an agonizing waltz with my mortality— one, two, three; one, two, three; fear, anger, sadness; fear, anger, sadness."

For almost ten years, Cheryl has been on a physical and emotional roller coaster. It started with finding a lump in her breast while swimming in Hawaii. A tall, voluptuous woman, Cheryl thought, "I love my breasts, and I'll be damned if I'll lose one." But to save her life, she had a mastectomy. Cheryl had always believed in a higher power, but during the chemotherapy and more surgery, she hung onto her belief in God "by a thread."

Cheryl finished the treatment. Her hope resurfaced, and her mantra became "Fear into faith, fear into faith." Feeling more in control, she began rebuilding her life again—work, friends, yoga. She even had a couple of dates while wondering if there was a dating manual that covers the subject of telling a man, "Oh, by the way, I had a mastectomy."

She went to the Center for Attitudinal Healing in Sausalito, which was started by Gerald Jampolsky, who wrote *Love Is Letting Go of Fear*. Talking with others who also had life-threatening illnesses was a relief to Cheryl. They buoyed her spirits around dating and told her, "You won't have to deal with losers because any man who will truly accept you will be a winner."

Then, two years later, on Mother's Day, Cheryl was in San Diego with her children. Again, just like what happened in Hawaii, she felt as if she couldn't breathe while she was swimming, as if her lung had collapsed.

Her doctor confirmed her worst fears: Stage Four terminal cancer. It had metastasized into her ribcage and lungs and produced a total of twelve tumors. Cheryl's doctor had always been a source of strength over these difficult years, but when she heard this news she fell into his arms and sobbed, "This isn't fair!" In her hopelessness she cursed God. She now believes, "In that moment, in my pure hatred of God, I was the closest I have ever been to my Creator."

This upbeat woman—whose presence in a room had always signaled fun and laugher—was devastated. She tried a new experimental drug. She lost her beloved hair, thirty pounds, and her will to live. As Cheryl sank lower and lower, she made the video for her children because it felt as if all hope were lost.

At her lowest point, a friend insisted that Cheryl go to a healing circle, where she was finally able to pour out all her feelings of despair. Slowly, with the help of others, she's been able to tearfully release much of the pain. The horrible fear that has gripped her like a vice since the terrible diagnosis has receded.

Cheryl has become a healer herself and gives the gift that has been given to her, helping others to recover their hope and faith. Her journey to study healing and faith has taken her around the world to India. From a frightening diagnosis came a journey through worlds both spiritual and physical that she would have never known existed.

Today, although the cancer has returned and is in her bones, she has recovered her own faith. She walked into a party two years ago, and a man across the room was thunderstruck by her energy and beauty. They married a year ago. Her higher power put a powerful, fun-loving man in her life. A man who completely understands her path because he has Stage Four prostate cancer. They joke, "Together, we're Stage Eight!" Eight, coincidentally, is the symbol of eternity.

Cancer is a horrible thief, but today Cheryl dances with death instead of fighting it, and now she has a divine dance partner.

"Without faith, nothing is possible. With it, nothing is impossible."
MARY MCLEOD BETHUNE

✩ LIFE CHALLENGES ✩

Ask yourself, "What situation can I stop fighting and dance with?"

Consider the possibility that a bad situation may be taking you to your highest good.

Fight fear and turn your attention to what you would do or be.

PART 2

Living Your Dreams (Quaking or Not)

"What would you do if you had no fear?"

"Wear boas!" —WOMAN IN SWEATS

"I'd ask some people out. That's scary, but the fear of being alone forever is bigger." —GYM MEMBER

"I'd fall in love again."
—DIVORCED COUNTER PERSON AT STARBUCKS

"I'd say hello to every person I see."
—CUSTOMER AT THE CAR WASH

"Tell people what I think. Be like a New Yorker."
—SURFER/COMPUTER PROGRAMMER

"I love my life and it is full, but I wonder if I'm doing things that make a difference. I would probably use my skills to raise money for charities full time."
—EVENT PLANNER

"Dreams are...illustrations from the book
your soul is writing about you."
MARSHA NORMAN

P eople in my workshops frequently comment, "Oh, my
mother, friend or co-worker could really use this! Why don't
more people reach out to expand their horizons?" I tell them
it takes bravery to look inside, to summon the courage to change,
and many people aren't willing. We can't pull others along but we can
celebrate the fact that we are on the journey of discovery.

This section of the book offers stories of people who have found
the courage to make positive changes (while still being afraid), taken
chances, and started over when their lives took a wrong turn. The stories remind us that taking one small step in the direction of our
heart's desire will reap rewards. And sometimes just the act of being
willing is the reward.

Goethe has described the magic that occurs when one is willing, even for a moment, to break the bonds imposed by fear: "Until
one is committed, there is hesitancy, the chance to draw back, always
ineffectiveness. Concerning all acts of initiative or creation, there is
one elementary truth that the ignorance of which kills countless
ideas and splendid plans: that the moment one definitely commits
oneself, then Providence moves too. All sorts of things occur to help

one that would otherwise never have occurred. A whole stream of events issues from the decision, raising in one's favor all manner of unforseen incidents and meetings and material assistance which no person could have believed would have come their way."

CHAPTER 5

Breaking Through the Fear

"I have not ceased being fearful, but I have ceased to let fear control me. I have accepted fear as a part of life, specifically the fear of change, the fear of the unknown, and I have gone ahead despite the pounding in the heart that says: turn back, turn back, you'll die if you venture too far."

ERICA JONG

One City Block

"Courage is being scared to death and saddling up anyway."
JOHN WAYNE

The first thing we need to know to break through our fears and begin living our dreams is that we all have fears. We aren't bad, weird, or unique for having fears. The paradox is that the last thing we want to admit is the first thing that will set us free. When I ask people to tell me about their fears, it opens up a whole new world. Admitting our fears acts as a magic spell to dissipate them. Plus, when we talk to others about our fears, we experience the exhilaration of discovering we're not alone.

Many people spend lots of energy and money trying to look like they aren't afraid—and many times they fool us. We think, "How could that dude in the brand new Jag be insecure?" or "She has the perfect body and the hair I always wanted—she's got it made."

Our fears faced are our gifts. The greatest gift someone can give me is to tell me her fears and insecurities, because then I can say, "Me, too! I'm not perfect either." I can learn more from people who are perfectly flawed and perfectly human than from the seemingly perfect ones.

Two people I met by chance, on one block, gave me the gift of their vulnerability. Talulah caught my eye right away. Her outfit made her look as if she'd stepped out of an animated Disney feature. She was accessorized! Her dark hair was streaked with Nuclear Red. Flowers added splashes of color to her 1940s dress, and she wore tights with huge pink and green flowers. To complete this Technicolor dream was a thrift-store coat in lime green with matching fake-fur collar and cuffs; the tiny moth holes were hardly noticeable. I love a woman who has the nerve to kick it, fashion-wise.

I asked her what her fears were, and she said, "Definitely, number one is relationships. So much can go wrong. There's dating and the awkwardness of first dates. There's online dating and finding the person has nasty surprises, like a wife. Then there's getting close and getting hurt and the mother of all relationship fears: ending up alone." Talulah said that if she had no fear she'd love to jump off a mountain. Did she mean hang-gliding, I asked her, but she said, "No, just sail off like a bird." I could see how she might be able to do just that with her fantastic plumage. I could also see her finding a mate who would appreciate a true original.

Next I ran into a friend, Peter, who has a sort of Indiana Jones air. After a childhood filled with abuse, he suffers from posttraumatic stress. He has said, "You know you're in trouble when the therapist just shakes their head after hearing your story." He's never told me the details of his past, out of respect for me, and I'm glad. Some things you hear, paint a picture that haunts you forever.

Peter said he can't even imagine asking himself what he would do without fear because he lives with fear daily. The effects of his trauma and abuse make it seem as if life has to be lived on red alert, and he is hyper-vigilant. Meeting him, you would never know that fear is the undercurrent of his life, because he's charming, chivalrous, and ready to laugh. He learned to hide all of his feelings, especially fear, from his fighter-pilot father, who gave Peter the message: "Fear is not an option. Don't talk about it; don't show it." Peter grew up hardening himself, living by the mantra, "I don't need anything from anyone, ever."

For years and years in therapy he's worked on being vulnerable and more willing to trust. Peter has done a lot of things that would make other men afraid—outward, physical things—but it is the internal world that he wants to heal.

He said, "If I could be in a relationship where the whole story was known and there was still trust and intimacy...if I could have that and be comfortable and relaxed with someone..." His voice trailed off. This is a man brave enough to face his demons and to work on healing past scars.

I know that the very act of speaking our dreams and being honest creates a window for them to manifest; therefore, the breakthrough has began for Talulah and Peter.

When I think of all the people I pass by in one city block, I realize that all of them have unique fears, hopes, and stories of the ordeals they have survived. I only talked to two people, but they gave me the gift of being real.

> *"If you banish fear, nothing terribly bad can happen to you."*
> MARGARET BOURKE-WHITE

✧ LIFE CHALLENGES ✧

Pick a block, any block, and talk to three people.

Practice loving the unfinished parts of yourself.

Tell someone your fears.

Seminary Stephen

"When your heart speaks, take good notes."
ANDY MELLON

S tephen explains, "I always had an interest in mystical and spiritual matters, but it was not until joining the Episcopal Church when I was in my mid-twenties that I started to feel the pull towards the ministry."

Stephen had been laying the foundation for a solid career in graphic design, working for a small studio on a new magazine. He was paid well, enjoyed the work, and found he was quite good at it. At the same time he started getting active in his church, teaching Sunday school to three- to five-year-olds, and serving on the parish council.

He was invited to come to work as the parish administrator, and because he spent a lot of time at his graphic design job thinking of spiritual matters, he decided to go for it. He accepted the job and gave notice. Stephen says, "In a sort of biblical moment cementing the wisdom of my decision, the magazine went belly-up on my last day at the office. I was packing up my desk while all my coworkers were in a general staff meeting being told that the company was folding the next day." He worked in the church office for two years and decided to apply to the diocese to enter the seminary.

In thinking about becoming a priest, Stephen faced fears, a fear of failure and a fear of not being good enough. "Those are probably the two main fears behind everything I do," Stephen says. "Dealing with them has largely been a process of coming to accept that my qualifications have nothing to do with why I am doing what I am doing. When I told one of the priests at my church that I doubt I'm good enough, he jokingly replied, 'Well, you'll never get any better.' His point was that I am the way I am because that's how God made me, and I haven't really got any choice in the matter." Stephen realized that being called to the priesthood had nothing to do with being qualified, for most prophets weren't qualified. "I am made in the image of God," he says. "Self-improvement is an oxymoron."

Stephen's take on fear is: "I think that the matter of fear is central to the experience of being a Christian. Fear, not hate, is the opposite of love. The reconciling work of religion is to try to move ourselves from lives lived in fear to lives lived in love. This happens through forgiveness and service to others. These actions break down the barriers that divide people from one another and from God." Stephen believes that "Fear can reasonably be identified as the source of the world's ills. Fear of scarcity motivates acts of aggression." This happens on a small scale when a hungry person steals bread and on a larger scale when one country takes over another. "Fear is a cutting off from the recognition of our common humanity," Stephen adds. Of course, he says, some fears are reasonable—the fear of walking alone down a dark alley at night; most people have a healthy desire not to be harmed.

The message he would give to help people combat fear is to be honest with ourselves by admitting that we have fear, "In a weird way, our fear is the very thing that can help us move away from fear—but only once we acknowledge that we actually have it. Christianity teaches forgiveness of others and ourselves. By admitting our fear we are seeking forgiveness. Or, put another way; don't be afraid of being afraid."

✿ LIFE CHALLENGES ✿

Forgive your fears and love yourself, warts and all.

Ask yourself in what do you put your faith.

When in trouble, consider the possibility of a loving higher power.

Driving Force

"Fear is a question. What are you afraid of and why?
Our fears are a treasure house of self-knowledge if we explore them."
MARILYN FRENCH

It's important to respect our fears as well as our strengths. We're all unique. Sometimes all it takes to overcome some fears is to learn a new way or a new skill.

Karen is a woman who feared something many of us take for granted. She says, "I always had this 'thing' about driving. I was convinced that if I got behind the wheel it would mean certain death for me and countless others." Because she lived in big cities with good public transit, her fear of driving really wasn't an issue she had to confront. However, people would look at her as if she had two heads when she admitted she was vehicle-challenged. They were openly critical, making comments like, "Everyone can drive. How do you survive? Is it even possible to go anywhere without a car?" In the land of the free and the home of the Buick, not knowing how to drive is a dirty little secret. It's so shameful that even Oprah hasn't done a show about it.

When Karen met her sweetheart and they moved out of the city, she knew that the gig and her bus pass were up. She was trapped in suburbia without a license.

On one of my retreats, Karen told the group of women her secret and said that if she had no fear she'd learn to drive. She knew that asking relatives or friends—or worse, her significant other—to teach her was a recipe for dysfunction.

Karen found Judy, a driving instructor whose specialty was teaching phobic people to get in the driver's seat and stay there. Karen says, "Judy's approach was brilliant in its simplicity. She was calmness personified. She only gave positive feedback. No matter how many rules of the road I broke, she was encouraging: 'You're doing great! Good job, I can see you've been practicing.'"

During the months that Karen was learning to navigate the highways and byways, a newspaper reporter was also taking driving lessons. The reporter interviewed some of Judy's students and wrote a wonderful story that highlighted Judy's remarkable teaching abilities. Karen passed her driving test after only two trips to the Department of Motor Vehicles.

Shortly after Karen got the coveted piece of paper, her license, the article about Judy's driving school ran on the front page of the Sunday *San Francisco Chronicle*. Karen's picture was right there next to the story. Karen says, "There I was, looking smug, sitting behind the wheel of my Mercury Sable. How many others get to be on the front page for leaning to drive? Overcoming my life-long fear was headline-making news."

✩ LIFE CHALLENGES ✩

Ask yourself what learnable skill would expand your horizons, and make a plan to learn it.

Decide what you could teach a friend or a child to enrich their life, and do it.

Pick the fear you want to overcome and forget the ones you don't—you don't have to do everything.

Baby Steps

"Only when we are no longer afraid do we begin to live."
DOROTHY PARKER

Sometimes we have a goal or dream that seems so out of reach that we get frozen in the fear and don't make any progress. We may think we want to climb Mount Everest. If you're like me, your mind will immediately come up with all the reasons why you won't be able to do it. My mind magnifies the possible problems and forgets to tell me the wonderful things that can come from pursuing my goal. The scary speech I deliver in my mind goes like this: "So you want to climb a mountain? Ha! Sister, let me give you a reality check. You don't have a clue how to go about it. You can't go a morning without a latte. You have a tendency to whine and that's not attractive to fellow climbers. Girl, you better forget it and just stay home."

Within five minutes of contemplating the goal, I've successfully talked myself completely out of it. This is where the value of taking baby steps comes in.

Don't abandon or jettison your dreams because you don't know how to do the whole thing or you think you aren't capable of doing it. Get in the habit of breaking down goals into the tiny, manageable steps. Also, don't fall into the trap of thinking you can only feel fulfilled if you climb the highest mountain. You may take a day climb that turns out to be a life-changing experience. It could be the happiest, most exhilarating day of your life; you could meet your soul mate on a rocky outcropping. Take a step toward your dream, and do it soon.

One day I talked to an interesting man in the Laundromat; he looked to be in his sixties, with close-cropped gray hair. I asked him what he'd do if he had no fear. He was thoughtful, and then replied, "Well, I have a thirty-six-foot sailboat, which I take out two to three times a week. If I had no fear I'd probably sail around the world alone." After a few moments, he amended his answer to: "Well, I'd sail around the Farallones alone." The Farallones, about thirty miles off the coast of San Francisco, are a group of islands inhabited only by birds. Sailors say that once you are "out of the Gate," meaning the points of land between the Marin Headlands and San Francisco, you are in dangerous seas.

The man in the Laundromat related that he's always remembered the movie *What about Bob?*, in which Bill Murray plays a neurotic man paralyzed by fears. In one of the funniest scenes, Bob, tied to the mast of a sailboat, screams in fear and exhilaration. The little boy in the film tells Bob, "You know, you're going to die one day, so what is there to fear?"

My sailor said he's always remembered those lines: "We all know the end of the story. We will die one day. So I don't know why we all hold back because of fear."

He asked me what I'd do if I had no fear, and I told him I'd finish this project and have the nerve to send it out in the world. We looked each other in the eye.

"I hope you complete one of the sails."

"I hope you finish the book."

It was like falling in love for ten minutes.

✬ LIFE CHALLENGES ✬

How to "baby-step" your dream: write the goal or dream on a piece of paper.

Start breaking the steps to the goal down into the smallest, most doable increments. If you are more visually inclined, make a dream diagram. Put the goal in a center circle and draw spokes off the main circle. At the end of each spoke will be a smaller circle with the steps you need to do. Keep making spokes and circles until you get to small actions (baby steps) you can start working on now.

For instance, to plan climbing a mountain, the baby steps might be: (a) check out adventure travel companies, (b) join the Sierra Club and start weekend hikes, and (c) register for a climbing class. The smallest baby step will be simply picking up the phone and calling for information. Remember to enjoy the process because at least half the pleasure is in the planning.

Dream Up a New Life

"Imagination is more important than knowledge."
ALBERT EINSTEIN

We can actually dream up a new life. Think of a filmmaker deciding on a project, say *The Lord of the Rings*: he or she finds a location that looks right, casts the people who fit the characters, and dresses them in period clothes. Nothing happens until someone "sees" how the story will look and sound. Nothing happens until someone makes a decision to create his or her dream of the particular story. Nothing happens until someone dreams it up. Imagination is always the first step.

Every material thing we see was once just a tiny sprig of a thought in the mind of a person or in the divine mind. We can easily access this creative power and make our own world patterned from our heart's desire. People who have never worked with visualization may think it's too simple to work. However, we all visualize, all the time. It's just that the mind usually comes up with a picture of what will happen if things go wrong.

The fact is, every worry and fearful thought is really an act of visualizing something bad, something we don't want. Some wise person once said, "Either pray and don't worry or worry and don't pray." It does take work to redirect the mind toward the creation of love and adventure stories and away from scary movies. Like a film reviewer, impose a ratings system on your thoughts, a "thumbs up" for good visions and "thumbs down" for the bad ones.

Dreaming up, or visualizing, exactly how your ideal life would look can be a tool that produces unfailing results. There are a couple of ways to do this.

Visualizing is slightly different from meditation, but both begin with closing our eyes, getting calm, and dropping a line into our peaceful core. Then you create your own story of how you want your life to be. Since you're the creator, make it good!

Visualizing is like opening the door to the universe's warehouse; you can go into the room labeled "home" and pick and choose the elements that you want. For instance, visualize what's heavenly to you. "See" the style of your ideal home, the colors you'll paint the walls, the kind of furnishings you like, what your special chair will look like, and the view from the kitchen. And remember that even if your ideal doesn't turn into something real immediately, or for years even, the time you spend visualizing and creating can be such a pleasant experience nonetheless. While I was visualizing my dream home, I realized I'd like to have bright colors, so I painted my gate and my front door purple. This change makes me so happy; it's a way of achieving some of my dream until the rest manifests. One day soon,

I know that the house behind my purple door will be bigger and have more closet space!

We make "movies" every night when we create imaginary worlds in our dreams. Use the power of your imagination to make a movie of your heart's desires. Just in case you think, "I'm not creative, I can't do this," remember the "monster movies" we let our minds make. But your brain can also create romantic comedies and tales of triumphing over the odds. In this film, you are the star.

The second way to use your imagination is to create a visual map of your ideal world. To do this, get a stack of old magazines and start clipping pictures of things you want. Also, clip powerful phrases that reflect what you want to experience and feel. Glue them on a piece of poster board or in your journal. This "treasure map" becomes a visual record of your future good, and the process of making it engages the right (i.e., creative) side of the brain.

A former student showed me the treasure map that she had made in one of my workshops three years ago. At that time she was living in a boring apartment, feeling stuck, and longing for a mate. The treasure map featured lots of pictures of her ideal life. Two of the images were of a rustic cabin in the woods, and one showed a man and woman sitting by a stream, with ducks floating by. She said she had to show it to me because she was so amazed at the power it had. Since then, she has met a man who is building a house in the redwoods, and he proposed to her by a river! This stuff works.

People have told me that in working with the "what would you do if you had no fear?" question, ideas and images start to bubble up from their subconscious. You may notice a nudge to explore new life options; you may see that your subconscious mind knows things that your conscious mind did not. History offers many stories of composers, writers, and inventors "going to sleep" on a problem and discovering the answer in a dream, or seeing the solution clearly when they pick up the project again with fresh eyes. Einstein said, "You cannot solve a problem with the mind that created it." People who have a spiritual practice or a belief in a higher power know that tapping into the divine mind and asking for direction or an intuitive thought or decision frequently produces miracles.

> *"I have found that you have only to take that one step toward*
> *the gods, and they will then take ten steps toward you.*
> *That step, the heroic first step of the journey,*
> *is out of, or over the edge of, your boundaries*
> *and it often must be taken before you know*
> *that you will be supported."*
> JOSEPH CAMPBELL

☆ LIFE CHALLENGES ☆

Imagine yourself doing, being, and having your wildest heart's desire.

Make a visual representation of your dream.

Picture your ideal home, relationship, vacation, and job.

CHAPTER 6

Be Bold

"Normal is a cycle on a washing machine."

EMMYLOU HARRIS

Be Real

"When you are content to be simply yourself
and don't compare or compete, everyone will respect you."
Lao-Tzu

"If people really got to know me, I'm afraid they would see I'm a fraud." This thought was expressed by many of the people I spoke to. At the deepest level of being many of us harbor the fear of being our unique selves and letting the world see who we really are. This fear expresses itself in various ways, but mainly in a misguided belief that who we are is not enough and that we are not worthy.

We all compare our insides to others' outsides. And it is not a fair comparison.

I am frequently a mass of insecurities and contradictions. I look at those around me and perceive them to be together and confident. A duck glides gracefully across the water, but underneath the little feet are pumping like mad. Like the duck, I feel the waters raging underneath my surface, but I only see the accomplished gliding of others.

This core insecurity also drives us to try to tailor our desires to please others and to seek approval. Fritz Perls, who developed Gestalt therapy, has wisely advised, "I'm not in the world to live up to your expectations and you're not in the world to live up to mine." And, no matter how hard we try, most times we can only make guesses about what others want.

In response to the "fear" question, one women declared that, without fear, "I'd speak what's in my heart. I'd take up more space it the world. I'd make more noise. I'd sing in my apartment without worrying about bothering the neighbors. Bottom line, I'd be more me."

A man related, "I'd disappoint more people. I stayed in a relationship too long. I was unhappy but didn't want to disappoint the woman I was involved with. Her enthusiasm overrode my indifference."

There are many ways to access and accept our authentic selves. Two tools that may seem quite different but in reality work the same psychic muscles are meditation and martial arts.

Meditation drops a line into our core and taps into universal spirit and divine energy. Not only do we connect with something larger than our finite minds when we meditate, but we also can listen to the "still small voice" and come to know who we are, what we want, and what pleases us. Meditation can give us the feeling that the world is open and waiting.

Martial arts, or self-defense training, teach us how to honor and protect our being. All the martial arts start not with a physical exercise but with an attitude—the attitude is that there is something worth protecting and fighting for. In most self-defense disciplines, the first lesson we must learn is how to make noise, how to verbally defend our life and space. Martial arts also teach us how to avoid conflict while still standing our ground.

In my classes I encourage people to speak aloud their long-buried dreams and desires. Meditation and martial arts help in the excavation of the authentic self. The act of being able to verbalize desires shakes things up in the psyche and rearranges the DNA of desire. In workshops people learn that speaking one's truth brings into being the miraculous.

After classes in which people have spoken their desires and learned tools to make them a reality, I give each student a beaded bracelet spelling out the word "fearless." This reminds participants who they are and offers a way for them to hold, or make real, their dreams.

Six weeks after one class, I received a note from a woman who, although young, had pretty much given up hope. A series of losses had just about knocked the life force out of her. But there is always a divine spark in people, no matter how small and tentative, and speaking our truth helps to rekindle it. She emailed me, "The class was a wonderful experience for me. I ended up taking that radical self-defense class. I'm already signed up for the next level, where you learn to kick some serious butt if you are in danger. I feel empowered for the first time in years. I didn't realize how my life had gotten away from me. Also, I've been dating for the first time in months and months. Whenever I'm afraid to do something, I look at the 'fearless' bracelet and I decide to go ahead and do it anyway, or at least part of it."

In my own life, a stranger broke into my apartment in the middle of the night and raped me when I was one week away from my thirty-fifth birthday. My illusion of safety was shattered, and I knew that I was not prepared mentally or physically to protect myself. People offered me lots of advice, but the one offer that meant the most to me came from a male friend who said he'd guard me all night so I could sleep. The offer was an affirmation that I did not have to be alone in this terrible experience.

I did two things after the attack. First, I demanded that the university I was attending start a group for survivors of rape. Women who came related every imaginable story, sometimes saying that they'd been raped years ago and never told anyone. Healing took place among the tears. We felt we were finally with people who understood and who heard us.

Second, I started to learn to defend myself. This put me in touch with my fierceness.

In both meditation and martial arts, we can learn that the ability to say a strong, nonnegotiable "no" is the beginning of being able to say "yes." We all have thousands of "no's" we've never said. When our nay means nay and our yea means yea, then we are on the road to being the bold, daring, original humans we are meant to be.

"If I be you, who'll be me?"
ANONYMOUS

✡ LIFE CHALLENGES ✡

Take a self-defense class.

Ask yourself who or what you need to say "no" to.
Say it.

Take a meditation class or listen to a guided
meditation CD.

Movie Star Moxie

"People in the land of LaLa look like expensive wax fruit."
ERICA JONG

A ll it takes is a half hour of channel-flipping to prove the point that the entertainment industry's "ideal" is narrowly defined. In a world where size zero is standard and every feature and flaw must be fixed, it's great to see someone unique, a person who doesn't fit the mold. It's a victory when the "non–wax fruiters" get a shot.

Jan is a generous-sized woman who loves to wear hats, so when she went for an interview to be a film reviewer, the station manager said, "You could be conceived of as a freak and laughed off the air." (This is one industry where the people in power actually say things like that to your face.) A walking encyclopedia of film, Jan only got the interview because her friend was the manager's secretary. But the station manager admired her guts and style and told her she could do six spots.

That was years ago, and today she's still appearing on television and radio and writing columns. She's a well-loved and respected icon in the community—the funny, entertaining person whom everyone wants to be the mistress of ceremonies at their galas.

Growing up around show business in Beverly Hills, Jan saw the pain that comes when a talented person is yesterday's news. She knows countless scenarios of disappointment in Hollywood: the child actress who couldn't get work and pretended it didn't matter; last season's sitcom star who puts on a brave face and says, "I'm taking meetings for multiple projects"; the actor whose fifteen minutes of fame now come only in the grocery store line, when someone says, "Didn't you used to be...?"

Jan saw early on that the business was based on fear. She says, "People who work in television and films desperately want to be in the spotlight or to stand next to someone in that light." Reality shows prove that people will suffer public humiliation, live for a month without a toilet or a toothbrush, and eat worms to be on TV. It's almost as if we don't think we're real unless we are on the tube. It is the business where everyone wants in.

Jan says, "The actors, directors, writers are all afraid of not being seen or heard. And when they get the coveted spot, they're afraid of being squeezed out by the next wave. So many actresses have said, 'Some new girl is always coming up, who's younger, blonder, skinnier...just waiting in the wings to take my place.' Many actors think that the last picture they did is literally their last, that it's been a quirk of fate up until now, and they won't work again."

But this anxiety-ridden atmosphere doesn't scare Jan. She's a delightfully mouthy broad willing to speak her mind: "I am willing to completely trash that which is popular, glad to put myself out of the party-line loop with a point of view that comes from a place of honesty. The public reaction to me is often one of support and kindness. Once in a while there is the opposite, sometimes quite virulent. Over many years of doing this work, I find that those most upset by my media existence (I'm also on radio and in print) are people who aren't used to women, especially women over forty, being so outspoken."

Jan speaks out on the violence in film and television. She gives 'em hell about the depiction of cruelty to animals. She tells audiences they should demand more creativity and cultural enrichment in their viewing. Women love her because she tells it like it is for women in the business. Jan reminds audiences that when male actors age they're said to have "character," while older women are thrown on the scrap heap in this very disposable business.

Jan tries to bring some sense to a world where people are judged solely on looks, connections, and the cost of their designer purses. She believes that a lot of bad films are being made today because everyone sucks up to the powerful and won't tell the Emperor that he's naked. Jan says, "This generation doesn't know anything but itself. Everything is so five minutes ago. There's no curiosity about the past."

Reviewers often go on junkets to interview stars of forthcoming films face to face. The reviewers are flown to the movie location. The stars are seated in a hotel suite, and the reviewers come and go, each getting only five to six minutes to ask questions that have been preapproved by the film's publicity department. The reviewers leave with a video of the interview to play on their local station. Jan has recently stopped doing junkets, but she knows that she'll be replaced and her access may be cut until she has no more currency than "yesterday's mashed potatoes."

But Jan finds freedom in not having to fit the mold. Today, she feels comfortable and serene about her looks, her talent, and herself. Jan sums up, "Through it all I get to look in the mirror and see a fearless woman looking back. It's worth the long hours, headaches, and heartbreaks."

Jan proves that any damn fool can be ordinary; it takes nerve and guts to be an original.

"I realize that if I wait until I am no longer afraid to act,
write, speak, be, I'll be sending messages on a Ouija board,
cryptic complaints from the other side."
AUDRE LORDE

☆ LIFE CHALLENGES ☆

Ask yourself, "Who do I want to play me in the movie about my life?"

Start today and write a new role for yourself.

Speak your mind, even if your opinion is not popular.

The Butterfly Farm

"Follow the path of the unsafe, independent thinker.
Speak your mind and fear less the label
of 'crackpot' than the stigma of conformity."
THOMAS J. WATSON

When I hear about a person who rides a hot air balloon across the ocean or goes on a vision quest in the Sahara Desert, my imagination soars but these brave endeavors are not really things I will attempt. These adventurers are free spirits, the rainbow chasers who can no more settle into a nine-to-five life than the cautious person can contemplate a life outside the lines.

Most of us probably have dreams of living an alternative life, of doing something bold. However, frequently when we relate a dream or scheme, others give us "the look," along with the words "Are you nuts? That won't work! Get practical." I'm sure Columbus and Amelia Earhart heard these very same comments.

Wild ideas, silly plans, and nutty inventions have changed our world. There is power in thinking original thoughts and in refusing to live the safe life. We aren't all adventurers, but we can nourish the free spirit within. Relish your wild self, and don't give negative comments free reign in your head.

William and Karin have wanderlust in their blood and saltwater in their veins. Originally from England, they love to travel—it must be the DNA from ancestors who never let the sun set on the British Empire.

Living on their sailboat, they bummed around exotic islands from the Mediterranean to the Caribbean for five years.

During a few months on St. Martin, the half-Dutch, half-French island, Karin—who had not conceived in eight years of marriage—got pregnant. They knew that their vagabond life was going to undergo an interruption, and this impending change made them afraid. Could they handle the prospect of settling down after years on the high seas? How would they adapt to a life in which they might have to work in one place?

William went to Fort Lauderdale to sell the boat, and while there he visited Butterfly World. Right then, something clicked and he thought, "I could make a living at this." It took months of planning, research, finding investors, and sheer physical labor. William and Karin constructed a large wood-and-mesh enclosure for the butterflies they planned to house. Karin did the landscaping using butterfly-friendly flora and created gentle paths and pools with small waterfalls.

On December 26, 1994, La Ferme des Papillons (The Butterfly Farm) opened its magic to the world on St. Martin. The butterfly

farmers carefully tend the pupas, caterpillars, and the fragile butterflies, which live only about two weeks. William passionately edu-
cates the public during tours. He explains that the clear-cutting of
rain forests and other environmental dangers are causing the extinction of some butterflies.

Eight months after the opening, a Class Four hurricane, Luis,
struck the flat, unprotected island with devastating winds. The island
was ravaged. In the eerie aftermath the only items remaining at the
Butterfly Farm were the two barrels that had marked the entrance.
All of William and Karin's hard work was totally destroyed, and Karin
and their partner, John, were ready to call it quits. William, the opti-
mist, saw this as a marvelous opportunity to rebuild bigger and better.
After begging and borrowing money from friends and family, they
all worked nonstop for three months and reopened.

Seven months later, hurricane Bertha struck and all was lost
again. The battle-weary team built back and opened anew in three
months. There were no storms in 1997, and the gardens and butterflies flourished.

Two more hurricanes have struck since, but the team has become
so good at rebuilding that their turn-around time has shrunk to
only three weeks. William and Karen "import" people from their
home village in Surry to help out. One young man was especially
grateful for this chance to live on an exotic island; to go from the

cold climate of England to a tropical paradise was an adventure he will never forget. That's the thing about people who live bold lives— they often bring others along. One person daring to live his or her dreams affects many others.

> *"The saddest summary of a life contains three descriptions: could have, might have, and should have."*
> LOUIS BOONE

☆ LIFE CHALLENGES ☆

Dust off a wild scheme you've put on a shelf somewhere, and begin it.

List all the ways you are daring.

Think about the hurricanes of the heart you have survived. What can you do to help speed your recovery in the future?

Roll Call

"All I was trying to do was get home from work."
ROSA PARKS

Fear of rocking the boat, fear of being unpopular, or even fear of physical risk can keep people from attempting to stand up for change. Things don't change until people change. Those who effect change sometimes set out to do so, but at other times change begins unexpectedly, when a single person, in a single moment, says, "I can't take this any longer." Thank God for the Rosa Parkses of this world, as well as for the unknown people who have bought our freedoms with their daring. There's an old Southern spiritual that goes, "When the roll is called up yonder, I'll be there." A good question to ask ourselves is, "What roll do I want to be on? What do I stand for?" We can choose the safe path or choose to stand up for what's right when it is hard and unpopular.

"I want to live life, not read about it." says Louette, a Harley-riding lesbian. "It makes me feel stronger to confront my fears head on. On a motorcycle you can't dig in your purse or apply eye shadow; you have to be totally focused. It's the only time I'm completely in the moment. If you aren't, you're gonna die."

Louette was one of the founders of Dykes on Bikes for the Gay

Pride Parade. This spirit of daring is what led Louette to become one of the first female police officers in San Francisco.

Like any pioneer, Louette faced many hurdles. As one of the first groups of women to graduate from the police academy, the new female recruits found that no one wanted to partner with them, and at first they were not allowed to work together. In spite of the hurdles, she excelled in the job and was very well liked by fellow officers, both male and female.

She loved police work, and in her years on the force she worked as an undercover narcotics agent and participated in many sting operations. On one assignment, she went undercover as a cocktail waitress, employed by a bar owner the police were investigating. A bully, the owner made life hell for Louette and the other women at the bar. When he saw her badge after he'd been arrested, Louette thought the look on his face was worth all the misery.

Another time, she and her partner received a call for a burglary in progress. The two suspects surprised Louette's partner and put a gun to his head right between his eyes. The crooks did not see her standing behind him. She pulled her gun and reached around the officer and fired a shot. Her quick thinking probably saved her partner's life. She was given a medal for valor.

Throughout Louette's career she witnessed the ongoing harassment of female officers. She and her fellow women cops had to take it in stride because of the code of silence among cops and the feeling that no one would listen if they complained. It was the perfect Catch 22: if you complained you were called a whiner, but if you didn't complain, you got harassed anyway. In Louette's opinion, many of the male officers were really good people trying to do a good job, but there were also a couple of pain-in-the-butt ones who could make women's lives on the force miserable.

All of Louette's daring and bravery had not prepared her for what occurred in 1984. At a graduation party for new recruits (many of whom she had trained), a woman came into the restaurant, and the crowd thought she might be a stripper someone had hired. Everyone was laughing and clapping until some officers grabbed a graduate and handcuffed him to a chair and the woman began performing a sex act on him. This was the final straw for Louette. Without thinking, she reacted. She and her male partner physically put a stop to it. The woman said, "The vice cops brought me." Louette was sick of women being treated as objects that didn't deserve respect.

The other cops' behavior enraged her: "They were breaking the very laws they had sworn to uphold." Her superiors, her union representative, and everyone else up the chain of command told her to forget it. When she couldn't get anyone to take action, she called the local newspaper.

After the news broke and stayed on the front page for days, the department was forced to do an investigation. Everyone present pretended not to have witnessed the incident, claiming that they must have been in the bathroom at the time. But, as Louette says, "It would be hard to fit two hundred people in a bathroom at one time."

Louette was up against a wall of silence and she was the enemy. Within ten minutes of her admission that she had been the whistleblower who called the paper, word spread. "Snitch" was written on her locker, her car was vandalized, and most coworkers would not talk to her. She went from being a popular colleague to being the most hated person in the department.

Louette got support from the media and civil right groups but not her peers. She left the department because the atmosphere became unbearable, and she filed suit against the city for violation of her constitutional rights and sexual harassment. Because of her actions and her suit against the city, things began to change. New department guidelines were instituted to prevent incidents of sexual harrassment. *Hill Street Blues*, a popular television show at the time, did an episode depicting Louette's whistle-blowing.

Louette could not have foreseen the emotional toll that her brave act would take on her, but she'd still do it all over again. "I could not let it go," she says. "It was wrong and someone had to stand up. I had become so sick of the mistreatment of women."

The personal price for standing up for what she believed was steep, she notes. "I never cried when I was on the force, even though we see every horrible thing imaginable, but after I was off the force I cried all the time. But what doesn't kill you makes you strong."

Louette was appointed by the mayor to an Equal Rights Advocates' Commission on the Status of Women, where she served for four years. She worked on hearings that investigated domestic violence, discrimination, and sexual harassment in the police department. Today, Louette says, "I have faith in my belief that I will get through." She believes that what Franklin Delano Roosevelt said is true: "The only thing we have to fear is fear itself."

✬ LIFE CHALLENGES ✬

Make a list of changes you'd like to see in the world and ask yourself if there's anything you can do to help the changes happen.

Be your own authority on what is true and what is not.

Speak out about injustices you see around you.

CHAPTER 7

Take a Chance

*"A ship in port is safe, but that's not what
ships are built for."*

GRACE MURRAY HOPPER

Permission Slips

"Progress always involves risk, you can't steal
second with your foot on first."
FREDERICK WILCOX

Many of us wait for the right time, the perfect circumstance, or the alignment of the stars to take a chance, begin a new life, or jump into an adventure. All we really need is to make a decision and act on it. In first grade we had to get a hall pass to go to the bathroom and a permission slip to go on a field trip. In later life we may get stuck waiting for a permission slip to inhabit the life we were meant to lead. It's almost as if we are waiting for some mystical time when it is okay to be bold, to strike out and take risks.

People occasionally look shocked when I ask them, "What would you do if you had no fear?" They say that no one has ever put such a question to them. One person said, "I didn't know I was allowed to think about what I'd do." The question may seem foreign because we've become conditioned to be cautious. Life gets rough and we go into survival mode and forget what makes us feel alive. Pretty soon we begin thinking we don't have the right to dream or that our dreams are arbitrarily out of reach. We become stuck in the first grade of life waiting for our hall pass.

A fellow in the computer store related a bit of wisdom that his Catholic school teacher told him: "It's easier to ask for forgiveness than permission."

Right here, right now, give yourself permission to be bold and to make mistakes. Also, give yourself permission to wake up your dreams. Authorize yourself to try on new lives.

The following story appeared in the March 6, 1929, issue of the *San Francisco Chronicle*: "Hazel Cooke, 18, a San Francisco society girl, member of a prominent family and a student at an ultra-fashionable finishing school, has been caught as a stowaway aboard a vessel now on the Pacific bound for the South Seas. When informed of their daughter's adventure, Cooke's parents told the captain of the Union liner *Tahiti* to make her work for her passage." This gutsy flapper embraced the do-it-first-and-ask-questions-later attitude.

Brad said, "I have a good voice and I love to sing. For my whole life, forty years of it, every time I thought of something bold I wanted to do, immediately a voice in the back of my head would start, 'You can't do that, you'll look stupid, you'll embarrass yourself, forget it!'" Like a reverse abracadabra, the desire would be wiped away, stuffed down, and stomped. The voice might as well have been on a PA system like the old air raid signals squawking a warning: "Duck and cover, he's dreaming again!"

One day Brad finally had the nerve to declare his independence from fear long enough to call the San Francisco Opera for an audition. Today he sings in the chorus. In one moment Brad gave himself permission to take a risk, and the desire spoke louder than the fear. We don't have to wait for fear to vanish altogether because that moment will never come; all we need is a moment of daring that can change a whole lifetime of waiting.

> *"Do not fear mistakes—there are none."*
> MILES DAVIS

✡ LIFE CHALLENGES ✡

Write yourself a permission slip.

Give yourself authorization to succeed beyond your wildest dreams.

Look for moments of inspiration and act then.

The Citizen

*"It's when we're given choice
that we sit with the gods and design ourselves."*
DOROTHY GILMAN

For some, permission slips can be tangible documents such as visas, which can pave the way to freedom or deny it. Rory knows the value of slips of paper. He has a quirky, soft sense of humor. He's an ad man by day who has made commercials with B. B. King. When he's not working, Rory paints and surfs. Sometimes he'll spend two weeks in Hawaii on his surfboard waiting for the perfect wave while being lulled by the rhythms of the ocean.

Rory grew up in Durban, South Africa, on the Indian Ocean, a hometown he describes as a "colonial backwater." Two vivid memories of people he met as a child would shape his life. They planted the seed of a dream in young Rory.

The first influential person was a friend of his English, ex-patriot mother. The friend had moved from Durban to New Orleans and returned to visit Rory's mother. As the woman related how glorious life was in the United States, she bragged that she had *two* jobs, as if that were the height of luxury. "It's what everybody does in America," she said. Rory had never doubted that America was the land of opportunity, but now it was confirmed. Two jobs!

Then one day he was playing down by the docks where ships from all over the world stopped to load and unload. He saw some Americans playing baseball. "The thing that stuck me was their sneakers. They were beautiful and perfectly stitched, and the soles were sealed so they'd never fall apart. Not at all like the junk being sold in our stores.

"A fly ball was hit in my direction, and a black man came running over to get it. He was laughing and shouting something to the other players. He was so confident. He smiled at me. He was so different from the South African blacks, who were forced by apartheid into a subservient role and seemed passive. But it wasn't about his color; it was that all the Americans had an attitude. It was cool, optimistic, almost a swagger. That black man in his white T-shirt and blue jeans seemed so superior." Rory thought, "So this is an American. I was smitten."

Rory knew that America was the place for him, and he moved here twenty-five years ago but never applied for citizenship. He put it off because, he says, "once you take the first step towards citizenship you realize how vulnerable you are. What if there's a snag and they decide to throw you out."

He finally went to the Immigration and Naturalization Services Web site and found that the department was now called the

Department of Homeland Security and Immigration. "Yikes!" Rory thought. His middle-aged search for security had pushed him into the heart of the country's post-9/11 paranoia about "foreigners." Rory realized that "from the John Ashcroft view, we were all fair game."

After seeking advice from an immigration attorney and filling in the forms, Rory got a letter from the Department of Homeland Security. "Just the envelope was enough to get me panicked," he says. The letter told him that he'd be scheduled for an interview in the next 380 days. He thought the number was a typo, but it just reflected government slowness.

His appointment was scheduled, and he was interviewed by a Hispanic woman we'll call Marcella. Rory wanted to impress this person, as she might hold his future in her hands. He turned on the charm, and the lovely South African accent helped. During the pleasant interview, the two talked of singing and art. In Rory's words: "We bonded." Only when he got home did he realize that she had not signed the receipt that confirmed his "pass" grade. He went into a tailspin, expecting the worst. "If I called her I'd seem paranoid," he feared. He stewed for a few days and then Marcella called him—she wanted to know if they could go out on a date! Rory's fears ran rampant; he had to tell the one person in the entire county who could ruin his life that he was otherwise engaged. He worried, "Can you be deported for refusing a date?"

Two weeks later he received the letter telling him to come to the Masonic Auditorium for the oath-signing ceremony. What relief!

On April 22 at eight o'clock in the morning, Rory sat with 1,500 other "aliens." He found himself seated between a small Korean woman and a Mexican woman. All had just handed over their green cards, which had symbolized their permission slips to be in America. "We were nervous as rats and as vulnerable as babies," Rory says. "Some of the people who became citizens had come from countries that were corrupt." Trust was not something that came easy; therefore, giving up one piece of paper for the promise of another was a scary proposition.

They sang "The Star-Spangled Banner" and cried; they said the Pledge of Allegiance and cried; they studied their certificates and cried. Rory comments, "Believe me, nobody in this place says the words 'American dream' with the slightest bit of cynicism."

But Rory and his new certificate of citizenship were soon parted. He remembers, "At the ceremony you can apply for a U.S. passport immediately, right there. The catch is that along with the form you have to send your *original* certificate of citizenship, which I'd only possessed for less than half an hour. It seemed so unfair. All of us new citizens once again were worried, but we handed them over to the nice man from the State Department."

Rory continues, "I realized that I'll always be worried about losing what I have. Whether it's my citizenship, a job, or my IRA, it'll always be something. But it's possible to walk through the fear that freezes me out of good things."

✬ LIFE CHALLENGES ✬

Write a pledge of allegiance for and to yourself.

Believe in your childhood desires.

Ask yourself, "Who has inspired me this week?"

Alternative Medicine

"The policy of being too cautious is the greatest risk of all."
JAWAHARLAL NEHRU

Kenny's French accent could make a recipe for a peanut butter sandwich sound like a sonnet. But his voice tells a harrowing story: "I was walking down my driveway to get the newspaper, and my legs could hardly move. Every step caused pain. I felt eighty years old and I'm only forty." More painful than the actual pain was Kenny's fear of spending the rest of his life like this. His hands, shoulders, and feet were crippled with arthritis.

Doctors prescribed the usual treatment, a regimen of anti-inflammatory drugs and painkillers. Most people who live with arthritis have nothing to look forward to but years of drugs and a worsening condition. The medications are only partially helpful.

Kenny did not want to surrender to a life of pain and decreased mobility, so he became proactive in his search for information and relief. He researched every alternative medical avenue. He tried acupuncture and changes in his diet. He went to Canada for specialized laser acupuncture. Nothing worked, though, and walking was increasingly painful.

Kenny went to a new physician who prescribed more drugs, but these did not work either and the doctor had nothing else to offer him. Then the doctor said, "Why don't you try an old remedy? Some people get relief from the sting of bees." The doctor told Kenny that he'd have to find someone who could teach him how to do it. Kenny thought this plan sounded very bizarre—it seemed odd to inflict pain to relieve pain. He was afraid of bees, but the fear of being crippled was greater than his fear of bees and stings. He was brave in his resolve to try anything.

He did research on the Internet and found a woman in his own backyard who kept bees and who knew the procedure. He went to her home, and she took him to her backyard hives.

Kenny says, "She picked up a bee with tweezers and with the speed of light placed the bee on her forearm and let it sting her. I was shocked, and wondered if I would have the nerve to do it myself." It was tricky to learn how to handle the bees with tweezers, and it took many tries before Kenny got it right. Willfully inflicting pain in an effort to avoid more pain calls for major fearlessness.

Kenny benefited from the woman's help: "She told me where to order the bees, and they were delivered to my home. Soon I was stinging myself twenty-five times in one session with an average of three to four sessions a week. Yes, it is very painful, but the sting only lasts about one to two minutes."

He soon saw positive results: "It reduced my arthritis pain considerably. I was not totally out of the woods, but it catapulted me to a new plateau of much less pain." Kenny was able to resume normal movement at last. Today, he continues to be proactive, researching new solutions and telling others of his finds.

"Life is a risk."
Diane von Furstenburg

☆ LIFE CHALLENGES ☆

Ask yourself, "Can the pain of one sting free me from a larger pain?"

What do you think is hopeless? Look again.

Research alternative lives, and methods of coping with your pain.

Passion Defeats Fear

*"I think, at a child's birth, if a mother could ask a
fairy godmother to endow it with the most useful gift,
that gift would be curiosity."*

ELEANOR ROOSEVELT

If you want to fight fear, be passionate—it's the express lane to your dreams. Passion and fear are not compatible, but curiosity is the second cousin to passion. If we are curious about life, we tend to follow this curiosity where it leads without thinking of obstacles in the way. Some people just have an attitude that won't take no for an answer; these are people for whom "No Trespassing" signs mean "Come on in, Welcome to the Party!"

I interviewed two women named Janet, and both were adventurous. The Janet who sails is a self-proclaimed tomboy. The other Janet is more of a glamour girl; she enjoys wearing short skirts and high heels. She discovered she loved to travel when she was young, and she's created a life that reads like a whole shelf of Rick Steves' travel books.

She explains her life this way: "I don't really have much fear because I'm so curious. I have a fire inside that gives me a passion for life's experiences. I'm not sure I was raised with a 'try everything' philosophy but I sure developed it as I traveled."

She'd been to forty countries by the time she was twenty-five and sampled adventures everywhere. When talking to Janet, I'm reminded of the saying, "If you want to G-E-T, you must A-S-K." Janet says, "I always ask for what I want. All they can say is 'No,' and if they do there's always someone else to ask."

Because she asks questions, she has had experiences that most people will never have or even dream of having. A whole world of adventure can begin with Janet's requests, such as: "Can you teach me that? Can I try? Can I come along?" She acknowledges the fear and risk, but she does what she wants to do anyway.

Janet is not just a collector of travel experiences—she gets involved when she sees a need and gets her hands dirty helping. She says, "I want to look back and say I did something that improved the quality of someone's life."

While traveling in Mexico, she discovered orphanages that needed help. She used her personality, contacts, and moxie to raise money. She solicited donations of mattresses, pillows, blankets, and clothes. She organized friends to be on work crews that painted and repaired the orphanages. Once she took 400 kids to a water park for the day. Because Janet goes after what she wants and needs with a vengeance, she was able to ask for and get things to enrich children's lives. Her passion and curiosity make her a dynamo for good.

> *"People say: idle curiosity.*
> *The one thing that curiosity cannot be is idle."*
> LEO ROSTEN

✧ LIFE CHALLENGES ✧

Go out today and ask, "Can you teach me that? Can I try? Can I come along?" Tell 'em Janet sent you.

Figure out what need in the world you can help meet.

Make a list of what you're curious about. Explore those things.

CHAPTER 8

Begin Again

*"Courage can't see around corners,
but it goes around them anyway."*

MIGNON McLAUGHLIN

Sick and Tired

"If you have made mistakes, even serious ones,
there is always another chance for you. What we call failure
is not the falling down but the staying down."
Mary Pickford

We all hate to get to that excruciating point where a part of our life just doesn't work anymore. It could be that we've gone down a road that we were assured was paved with gold. Maybe we've gone into a profession that parents, teachers, counselors, or mates thought would be just the ticket to fulfillment. It could be that the relationship we'd counted on to last till death do us part was ripped away in an instant. In one way or another, at one time or another, we hit the wall and realized that the good life isn't so good anymore—sometimes it's downright toxic.

It's scary to confront failures, endings, and heart breaks. But frequently these life smackdowns offer the opportunity for a new life and a new freedom. We are rarely ready for new beginnings and new relationships and hardly ever ready to let go when the old, familiar relationships end. When those proverbial doors shut, my fingers are usually smashed trying to keep them open.

But take heart: there is immense power in being sick and tired of being sick and tired.

Admitting that we just can't take it anymore (whatever "it" is) brings us to an internal ground zero. From the ashes here, tiny sprouts of new beginnings spring up eventually. I'm always encouraged by the way little green plants make their way through cracks in concrete. We can pave over paradise, but there is life underneath.

Many times the way out and up is not immediately apparent, and we must wander through the scary hallway of life. There's that old saying, "When God shuts one door, he opens another." A wisecracking friend once said, "Sure, but I hate the hallways." Being willing to spend some time in the corridor of "not knowing" can ultimately lead to magical new roads.

Often, the first instinct we have when we are ripped away from the familiar is to jump back in. But if we linger in the space of our loss, we may be shown new, unexpected and uncharted vistas. We may hit the wall, then hit the road.

Sitting in a trendy, New York City bistro, Porter felt like a nervous breakdown waiting to happen. She complained to her friend that she was miserable. She was a driven workaholic, full of fear and desperate for change. For ten years she'd been trapped in the "golden handcuffs," slaving as an account executive for a top advertising agency. She worked on liquor ads and coped by drinking huge amount of same. As Bill Murray said in *Lost in Translation*, "At least the liquor works."

That day, in that bistro, Porter had no idea what would come next in her life, only that she was sick and tired of the corporate craziness. Her friend leaned across the table and said, "I'm going to bike across the country. Want to come?"

Porter quit her job the next day. Four months later she climbed on her bike in the Seattle rain to start across the country. That first day, covered in rain gear and loaded down with a full pack, she thought, "What have I gotten myself into?"

Before she left, she used the four months to dive into a project. She wanted the ride to have a purpose. She put together a campaign to promote breast cancer awareness in women under the age of thirty-five. She filmed young women who were fighting breast cancer all across the country. The youngest survivor was a nineteen-year-old. Porter started a Web site and held educational events across the country. With some backing from Microsoft, she raised $100,000.

The 5,000-mile bike trip passed through eighteen states—this mammoth task accomplished by a woman who didn't consider herself the athletic type.

Since the ride, Porter's film, *2 Chicks, 2 Bikes, 1 Cause* has been shown on the Lifetime cable network in the United States and Channel Four in London. Porter found that she loved putting people's struggles and triumphs on film, and she was hot to start another documentary.

She coped with her old fears by reminding herself that doubt is a killer of dreams. Today, when she starts to second-guess herself or her projects, she trusts that if she does what she loves the way will open.

Porter applied to Stanford University for a master's degree in documentary film and was one of only eight students accepted that year. Today, she produces, directs, and films projects she has a passion for. She's made five films. The last one was shown in film festivals around the world.

Porter took a leap of faith in a bistro in New York, surrendering to the fact that her life was not working. Her amazing, expanded life now tells the stories of people who cannot tell their own.

☆ LIFE CHALLENGES ☆

Write a new life story.

Give a title to the film of your life.

Ask yourself, "Whose story would I like to tell?"

A Reborn Virgin

"Before I met my husband, I'd never fallen in love,
I'd stepped in it a few times though."
RITA RUDNER

A sign at a copy shop read, "If it wasn't for the last minute, nothing would get done." If it wasn't for crash-and-burns, my life would not be as rich as it is.

A number of years ago, after a period of dissatisfaction, I took stock of my life and saw that it was no surprise I was unhappy. I was living in the desert, where I'd moved on a whim and gotten stuck for seven years! I didn't like my job or my apartment; I didn't even like the kind of flowers that grew (barely) in the arid landscape.

I'd come to San Francisco to see friends and—bang!—I felt at home. I loved the hills, the water, the bridges, the trees, the purple irises, and the heavenly, cool fog. I drew up a list of things I'd need to do to move and made a collage of trees, water, and sailboats. I looked at the collage every day and took heart from the positive visualization it gave me.

Finally, I made up my mind to go for it, but I didn't have much money. My wise friend Gene said, "Honey, my sister just dropped dead and she never did much of anything, never took a risk, never really lived. My advice is, don't wait—leave today!" Gene added, "Besides, Diane, you've dated every dysfunctional man in Arizona." Gene knew how much I wanted someone to share my life with, so when she said that, she got me right in the heart.

Gene was right: my prince-picker was broken. I could enter a room and zero in on the wrong guy. I'd been on so many first dates in my thirty-plus years, and I was tired!

I had a vision of opening the door to a new date in my dirty chenille robe, with pink plastic curlers in my hair and a gooey mask on my face. I'd say, "Do you want it or not? It might not get any better than this."

When I got to San Francisco, I embarked on a spiritual and emotional housecleaning. I wanted to get rid of the things in myself that were holding me back from living my dreams. I did affirmations and healing work and fearlessly looked at myself. It was painful, but I was determined to heal. One day I felt a divine click, like a light going on. In that minute I knew that I was going to have a loving mate.

Brian came along like fresh water. He'd just moved from New York, so we were both new to the area and started exploring together as friends. I was very attracted to him but knew he was younger. Twelve years younger, to be exact. Also, I was afraid of getting my heart broken again. A friend said, "If it is right, nothing you can do can screw it up. If it's wrong, nothing you can do can fix it. So relax and have fun." That comment shook something loose in me, and I was able to trust in the process.

Brian and I were honest and open with each other, and this relationship offered me the most support I had ever felt. The day we married, I thought back on all the prayers I'd prayed, the tears I'd cried to get to this day. When you grow up in South Carolina, as I did, you start praying for a mate, on your knees, at about age twelve; I think it's a state law. "Now I lay me down to sleep, send a man and don't make him a creep or a cousin."

At twenty-four I was confident: "Okay, I'm ready, gorgeous and luscious. Send my millionaire and make it snappy."

At thirty, the prayer was horribly humble: "Oh please, please. Hurry."

At thirty-five: "Are you deaf up there? Haven't you heard a word I've been saying?"

As I was walking down the aisle, I realized that all these years my higher power must have been looking down and saying, "Be patient, Diane. He's growing up as fast as he can. He's only in the sixth grade."

Oh, yeah, this worldly woman wore white because my philosophy is: if you have a new attitude, you become a reborn virgin.

The fairy godmother told Cinderella, "No matter how your heart is grieving, if you believe, the dream you dream will come true."

Believe in second, third, and ninety-ninth chances. Don't quit before your miracle.

> *"The material for this book was collected directly from nature at great personal risk by the author."*
> HELEN ROWLAND, *GUIDE TO MEN, 1922*

✬ LIFE CHALLENGES ✬

Never give up on yourself.

Make a needed change today. A new life is waiting for you to move in.

Remember, the love you seek is seeking you.

One Step at a Time

"Freedom's just another word for nothing left to lose."
JANIS JOPLIN

"My cell was my sanctuary. I was in with the cesspool of humanity but I had no other life. Prison was my life. The prison system and the warden took care of me. Life on the outside scared and baffled me. I had no coping skills." Don spent most of 1959 to 1989 in San Quentin for armed robbery.

Given up at birth by his Russian mother, Don was locked in a closet by his first foster parents. His elderly grandparents rescued him. In their care, when he was five years old, he became a little wanderer, walking all over San Francisco alone.

When Don was nine, his grandfather died and his grandmother became too ill to care for him. His mother took him back briefly and then turned him over to juvenile detention. Freaked out, the little wanderer planned his first escape. Although his small heart was pounding, he crossed over the barbed wire and escaped to freedom.

With no one to guide him, Don slid into the lawless world where crime equals survival. The jail system became a revolving door for Don: he couldn't stand being incarcerated, but he couldn't stay straight. Every time he gained freedom, he did something that put him back in a cell.

On his first trip to prison, Don sought out an old timer for guidance: "He showed me how to do time. Stick to yourself and stay out of trouble." He did the best he could to cope with being behind bars. "As long I knew the date I'd be released I could do time, I know how to do time," he says. But one day the warden told him, "Next time, it's for life." He made a decision right then to straighten up.

At one time, Don says, "the world was not safe with me out there." Much has changed. Today, he's a friend to everyone he meets and, oh boy, is he out there.

Don is leaving soon on his second walk across the United States, and this time it'll be a roundtrip journey. His first cross-country trek, in 1998, took him from Boston to San Francisco. He embarked on Mother's Day (May) and arrived on Election Day (November). "The politicians walked with their mouths; I walked with my feet," he says.

What impressed him most about trekking across the country was "the hugeness of creation." He reflects on the scale of the landscape: "The human body is this little speck. It was so vast, so hot, so cold and [there were] bugs, lots of bugs. You have to be right in your mind, because if you get something swirling up there when you are alone it's not good."

When Don is on the road, he usually sleeps in a sleeping bag, without a tent. Once a week he stays in a motel, washes his clothes, and stocks up on supplies. One day, he was walking down Highway

2 in North Dakota, thirty miles from a town. Don was almost out of water when a highway patrolman rolled up. Imagine what this patrolman saw: a tall, muscular man with a gray ponytail and hands like bear claws walking down the highway in the middle of nowhere—pretty much the physical antithesis of an officer of the law.

After they talked awhile, the patrolman drove the thirty miles to get Don fresh water. The patrolman told him, "I'll come find you after my shift. You can spend the night with me and my family." Two hours later he rolled up and took Don home.

Don had a home-cooked hot meal with the patrolman, his wife, and his two boys. He washed his clothes, entertained the family with stories of the road, and got to sleep in a bed with sheets and pillow.

The next morning he had breakfast with the family, and the patrolman took Don to the exact spot where he'd left off his journey the night before. Committed to walking the whole way across the country on foot, Don is scrupulously honest. Determined to experience every rain storm, every bug, he never hitches a ride.

Don says that the people out in the Badlands were incredible; he saw their genuine concern for each other. All over the country he'd walk into diners and notice a table of old farmers who would look at him with his ponytail and road dust and give him the dubious eye. Thirty minutes later they were friends.

For Don's upcoming, roundtrip walk, he'll take a small tent and a cell phone for the first time. He says, "What I've learned is, the ordinary person is the most extraordinary, and maybe somebody can use my experience out there on this planet." He's an ordinary person himself; he just knows this earth a little more intimately than most of us.

His lingering fear, he says, is of "getting old, not being able to finish all I want to do." He notes that he has only twenty-six years to go before his ninetieth birthday: "I have no time to waste and no time to be miserable anymore. I'm at the point where I have to chase my dreams to the fullest."

"I'm a man of means by no means, King of the Road."
Roger Miller

☆ Life Challenges ☆

If there are any bug bites keeping you from your dream, slather on the bug repellent and brave the wilderness.

Ask yourself, "What thoughts keep me in my own prison?"

Look around. How big is your world? Can it be bigger?

Wakeup Calls

"There is often in people to whom 'the worst' has happened
an almost transcendent freedom, for they have faced
'the worst' and survived it."
CAROL PEARSON

Sometimes we make life changes through planning and careful thought, but sometimes change comes through a cosmic wakeup call. Richard says, "I was a nice Jewish boy from New York." He came to free-wheeling California and managed a nightclub that became the favorite hangout of visiting rock stars. It was the place to party in town, with a predictable abundance of cash and drugs. Richard got in on the drug action, but he wanted to be a "careful" drug dealer. He picked low-risk clients like doctors, lawyers, and the idle rich and did well for himself. Dealing cocaine in the 1980s was like shaking a money tree.

One morning, when Richard was at home with his girlfriend, armed men broke down his front door and put guns to their heads. The gunmen wanted money and drugs—it was a classic no-brainer crime to rip off a dealer, since the victim was unlikely to call the cops and report that his stash of coke and hundred-dollar bills had just gone missing.

Richard says, "Having a gun to your head, in that instant you know you've screwed up real bad and would do anything to reverse the damage. You'd make any and every change necessary."

That morning, Richard's girlfriend, who had been worried about his drug use, had called a twelve-step program for help. She was in despair, watching him destroy himself. Someone from the recovery program promised to come talk to her. She said to the robbers, "Some people are on the way over here right now to take us to a meeting. They will be here any minute so you better get the hell out of our house." As unbelievable as it sounds, the thieves were convinced they'd get caught and they left.

It was a "Come to Jesus" moment for Richard—he never did drugs again. There's nothing quite like having a gun aimed at your head to make you consider amending your ways.

A few months later, Richard was visited by the police. They said, "We've been watching you for some time, but it looks like you've cleaned up your act. If you keep going in this direction, we'll leave you alone."

After lots of recovery work, Richard went back to school and became a therapist specializing in alcohol and drug addiction, and he has gone on to help many people on the road to recovery. This drug dealer had the opportunity to change thrust upon him, and he took it in an instant.

*"The need for change bulldozed a road down
the center of my mind."*
MAYA ANGELOU

✦ LIFE CHALLENGES ✦

Take steps to curtail an addiction or bad habit that's stealing your energy. Make a call for help.

Ask yourself if there are any parts of your life that could use a wakeup call. Where would the call lead you?

If there's something in your life you'd like to do over, consider how you might do so.

Never Give Up

"Diamonds are only chunks of coal that stuck to their jobs."
MINNIE RICHARD SMITH

If you're a writer, one recurring thought can grab you by the throat and shake you silly just as you're drifting off to sleep: "What if I lose my data? What if my computer crashes? What if my backups fail?" It is the vulture on the bedpost, and it likes to take its time before it flies off and lets its prey, the pitiful puddle that the writer has become, go to sleep, perchance to dream of software viruses.

I once bought a data-storage device that I was suspicious of. I'm suspicious of most technology, but what are you going to do? Store reams of paper all over town? (Writers used to put their paper manuscripts in the freezer—that way, if the house burned down, the masterpiece might survive.) As it turned out, my suspicion was warranted: even though the data-storage device has worked well for lots of people, mine became defective after a month. The little bastard was holding my data and wouldn't give it back; luckily, I've had enough "vulture visits" that I've learned to backup files nine ways to Sunday. But this particular method had failed. When I complained to the manufacturer and the store, I likened the experience to being attacked and finding out that the canister of pepper spray you'd bought to protect yourself contained only plain water.

After I got over my shock and anger at the device, a different thought surfaced: "I don't care how many setbacks, crashes, and delays I have, I am going to finish this project." It felt great to declare my independence from the little devils that lurk around and try to impede progress on works of art or love or anything.

Persistence is an attitude that says, "I believe in this, I believe in myself, and I will not quit." Interestingly, this attitude pops up right when we need it—after adversity.

> *"When you get in a tight place and everything goes against you till it seems as though you could not hold on a minute longer, never give up then, for that is just the time and the place the tide will turn."*
>
> HARRIET BEECHER STOWE

LIFE CHALLENGES

Be a warrior when guarding your dreams.

Pick up the project you have abandoned and look at it with fresh eyes.

Shoot the vulture.

PART 3

Living the Fearless Life

"What would you do if you had no fear?"

"I would quit my job."—NUMEROUS PEOPLE

"Take a round-the-world cruise. See it all."
—PASSERBY ON THE STREET

"Skydive."—FAN AT A BASEBALL GAME

"Paint my living room red."—CUSTOMER IN PAINT STORE

"Adopt a baby from Africa, where so many children are orphaned
by AIDS."—RUNNER IN MARATHON

"Run for mayor."—SHOPPER AT FARMERS' MARKET

"Open a secondhand store in a small town."—BUSINESS EXECUTIVE

"Everyone thought I was bold and fearless and even arrogant,
but inside I was always quaking."
KATHARINE HEPBURN

It doesn't matter if we think we're fearless or if we do things while quaking. The important thing is to be true to our dreams and live authentic lives. We all have fears, and victory lies in facing them. I think angels cheer when I finally break through some of my self-imposed limitations: "Hallelujah, she's up and running at last!" The next two chapters offer insights on combating common fears, as well as the unique thoughts of those who face fear for a living.

To get you up and running, I've listed antidotes for some top fears. The ones that seem to cause the most terror are fears of rejection, of the future, of getting hurt, of looking bad—not to mention the nebulous "what ifs." Once we face these fears, the boogey man under the bed scurries away, ashamed, and the angels applaud.

To end the book, I've described the three best tools I know for coping with the fears that do come true: laughing at ourselves and our plights, "wandering" when we need to clear our heads and make new plans, and expressing gratitude for all of our experiences, even the negative kind. You never know, after all, what fabulous new vista lies around a nasty bend in the road.

CHAPTER 9

Facing Our Fears

"Fear is the beginning of wisdom."

EUGENIE DE GUERIN

Fear of Rejection

"Losing is the price we pay for living.
It is also the source of much of your growth and gain."
JUDITH VIORST

Everyone gets rejected. The most "together" people you have ever known—Oscar winners, rock stars, truck drivers, and people named Maurice—have all been rejected. The only people who never get rejected are the ones who refuse to take risks. Not risking is permanent rejection.

When we are faced with the big R, we usually feel acute pain and a sense of foolishness for having cared so much. We may feel slightly or hugely embarrassed for having been willing to risk. Most of the time we think that we're the only ones to feel this way.

We are not alone, though—in fact, we're in great company. The music industry, for example, would go broke without "they done me wrong, and they done gone" songs. If you've been rejected, pick up the *National Enquirer* or *Vanity Fair* and you'll read about the heartbreaks of the stars.

Many great love affairs have come about because another relationship did not work out. Like the saying goes, be careful what you pray for because you might get it. If it's not for your highest good, you may be miserable and it will take you forever to get rid of it. Let's take a moment to be thankful for the ones that got away. In my case, I should have been committed for some of the situations I've been committed to.

When you get rejected—whether it is love, a creative project, or not getting a job or assignment you desire, don't abandon and reject yourself. When we face rejection, that is the time when we must send love to ourselves, when we must be gentle with ourselves. Self-love is usually called for when we are feeling the least lovable and worthy. Caring for yourself, treating yourself as you would a heartbroken child, is the quickest way to get over rejection.

You might curl up on the bed, hugging your dog and soaking Fido's fur with your tears. You might ruefully laugh at how horrible and earthshakingly unfair it all is. Regardless of what you do, if you can manage to be on your own side, what usually happens is that a stinking rotten ray of hope will come shining through. I say "stinking rotten," because we don't really think there is any reason for hope. But it comes through nonetheless and says, "Honey, you won't always feel this bad."

It may be only that you can ruefully laugh at how horrible and earthshakingly unfair it all is. But the laughter will produce a little victory over the disappointment.

When you are rejected or unfairly treated, put a note on your mirror, in your car, or anywhere you'll see it: "I will love myself through this and trust my heart to heal." Remember, tomorrow is another day even if you aren't looking forward to it.

Dark times can create new beginnings, and it all starts with that rotten little ray of hope.

> *"When you have come to the end of all the light you know and are willing to take one more step—either you will be given solid ground to stand on or you will be taught how to fly."*
> GORDON PAUL

Fear of Heartbreak

"If you can't live without me, why aren't you dead yet?"
CYNTHIA HEIMEL

What could be worse than the fear of heartbreak? Actual, right now, immediate heartbreak, that's what!

In life we've all seen our poor little hearts dragged through the mud, put through the wringer, and served up creamed on toast. No matter how cautious we are or how we plan, people can obstinately ignore our happy-ever-after dream and refuse to move into the rose-covered cottage.

Heartbreak is not the time to isolate ourselves. It is the time to round up the posse. Let friends bring over takeout Chinese and boxes of tissues and candy. People who might say, "I told you so," need not apply for this emergency mission. Only invite buddies who will tell you that you have every right to feel awful. These buddies will agree that the offending party is a world-class jerk whose picture should be on billboards with a warning.

Many times we just need to vent, to talk it out; we don't need advice, just someone to listen. Then, after our friends have heard the sad story about a hundred times, they might gingerly suggest we take a shower, get dressed, indulge in retail therapy, and begin again.

After a period of heartbreak, before I met my husband, Brian, I was so afraid to open up again. I wrote a mating manifesto for myself. I offer it up here, because maybe you can use it: "Being sick of being alone and staying home playing solitaire, I now am ready to risk. I realize that this risk may involve falling in love, with side effects of giddiness, lightheadedness, and hearing sappy wedding music. I realize I may risk finding my soul mate, and together we will have a soft place to fall. I accept that this process may also entail some dating duds and washouts. During this process I may get hurt, but I'm sick of solitaire."

Fear of Looking Bad

"What an interesting life I had.
And how I wish I had realized it sooner."
COLETTE

Once I was having a few too many cocktails with some people at the Rosarita Beach Hotel in Mexico, and one of the women wanted to talk about something sensitive. I can't remember what the subject was, and she probably wouldn't either, but at the time it must have seemed very important.

She sat inside a huge armoire and was able to completely express herself, partly because we couldn't see her but mostly because she couldn't see us. I don't drink anymore or listen to people talk behind closed doors but it made sense at the time—we're afraid of speaking and being seen.

People fear speaking in front of others—it's universal. I read somewhere that this fear is greater than the fear of death. What is behind this fear? For me, it is the fear of looking bad. A friend related that she stumbled into the wrong meeting at a conference and sat there for two hours because she was afraid of getting up and leaving. "They might think I'm odd," she fretted. These were total strangers who she'd never see again! Such is the power we give to what others think of us. One thing we can do when we feel vulnerable to another's impressions is say to the other person, silently, "What you think of me is none of my business."

A friend once told me, "Sweetheart, in life, five people will love you no matter what, five may hate you no matter what, and four hundred million don't give a damn one way or the other." People are lost in their own world worrying more about what you're thinking of them, as opposed to thinking bad things about you.

The fear of looking bad or appearing foolish (even for a minute) can prevent us from doing what will make us giddily happy and ecstatically fulfilled.

The antidote to the fear of looking foolish is to do something foolish on purpose. You won't believe how free and powerful you'll feel. Laugh at yourself before someone else gets a chance.

My town holds a rather pitiful Fourth of July parade, but we all adore it anyway. Every year we jockey for a position to watch and wave. I've stood there kicking myself for not marching or making a float. Last year I decided I couldn't wait any longer. I had to be in at least one parade in my life.

My friend Rudy volunteered his ancient flatbed pickup truck, and Johnny said he'd paint it. Since we live in Sausalito, on the water, I picked a mermaid theme for the float. Thankfully, the standards for this parade aren't real high. Case in point, some alumni of the

University of California have a marching band. While marching down Main Street, midway through the parade, they all take a sharp right and march into the local watering hole. The rest of the parade continues and then about an hour later, give or take, the band marches back out of the bar and joins the parade in progress.

I asked several women friends to be mermaids with me, but most declined; they were afraid of appearing foolish. I found one who was game, and my husband, Brian, felt sorry for me when someone criticized my concept. He said he'd be on the float.

On July 3, we bolted our deck umbrella to the truck bed and stapled grass skirts around the umbrella to make it look like a tiki hut (actually I wanted shade, so the construction of the tiki hut was driven by self-interest). We bolted plastic lawn chairs on the truck (we're also lazy and want to sit). We had a great decorate-the-float-and-eat-pizza party. I made mermaid costumes, got fun wigs, and created a King Neptune getup for Brian.

Here we were, on July 4th, two mermaids, me the middle-aged one, outfitted with a long red wig, green tail, and purple sequined top. Brian was arrayed in a shiny green toga with a Neptune crown and scepter. We smiled and waved and threw candy and plastic necklaces to the kids. One little girl followed us the whole route. We squirted the crowd with water pistols. People cheered and screamed because we were so silly. A friend took pictures; in one of them, five little girls about six years old are looking up at me in wonder.

My friend Channing said, "The look on their faces was priceless. I can just see one of the girls grown up and saying, 'I was inspired to run for President because I saw a red-headed mermaid who was willing to stand out from the crowd.'" It was the best compliment I've ever gotten. And, oh, our float won first prize.

I almost talked myself out of the parade several times, and I would have missed this completely zany, liberating experience of doing something for the sheer joy of it. So much in life is serious, but allowing ourselves to do something just because we want to is its own reward.

Go out and be silly on purpose—start a parade, be fearless. The only thing you have to lose is your fear. So what if you fall on your face? In the process, you've defeated one of your greatest fears and won. Get on the float!

"Some of my worst failures have been successes."
PEARL BAILEY

Terror of the What Ifs

"Don't let the fear of striking out hold you back."
BABE RUTH

What if my favorite lowfat ice cream isn't really lowfat? What if I buy a house and a heavy metal band moves in next door? What if I like him and he likes her? What if I paint a masterpiece and no one buys it?

Most people have a list of personal "what ifs" that bedevil them. Yet, life being what it is, refuses to serve up only what we fear and instead randomly dishes out the unexpected.

A couple moved into their "almost" dream house and had it remodeled to be *the* dream house. As they went to sleep in the bedroom of their gorgeous home in the hills, their only worry was about spending too much money. That night, a teen driver careened around a curve above the house, lost control, and barreled through the newly landscaped garden. The new trees broke some of the momentum, so the SUV only crashed through the bedroom wall but missed their king-sized bed. The couple was not hurt, and their previous fears about money were wiped out. They were just grateful to be alive.

Living a life defined by the awful "what ifs" is crazy-making. Fearing this, that, and the other, though, is a national pastime. The news media would all have to go out of business if they didn't hype fear. You can tune in any hour and hear the same disaster story repeated every fifteen minutes ad infinitum. Fear of things you can't control will wreck your serenity and peace of mind. The best policy is to realize that FEAR is frequently False Evidence Appearing Real. Consider the reasonable risks in any new undertaking and then pray and hope for the best.

A woman in her fifties mused, "I'd love to go to Africa and see the elephants and lions, but I'm afraid to fly in a small plane. And if I survived the plane crash, what if lions found me and I was on the menu? When I was a little girl I saw a film about a train breaking down in Africa and the passengers got out and lions savaged them."

Our fears get funny sometimes. People living or traveling to Africa might have reason to fear lion attacks, but people in the United States don't usually give lions much thought.

Still, unexpected dangers can strike, as on the day when two friends, Ann and Debi, were riding bikes in a wilderness area in Orange County, California. A mountain lion pounced on Ann. It grabbed her by the head and started dragging her down a hillside and into the brush. Debi grabbed Ann's leg and was determined not to let her go, no matter what. She would not abandon her friend, even if that meant playing tug of war with a mountain lion.

In news reports, Debi said, "This mountain lion jumped on her back and started dragging her. He dragged her down about a hundred yards into the brush and I just kept screaming. This guy (the cat) would not let go. He had a hold of her face."

Ann thought she was a goner, but Debi told her she would not let her go.

Two bikers rolled up and threw rocks and their bikes at the animal. The mountain lion finally let go and ran off.

Later in the day the body of a male biker was found. Authorities determined that he was killed by the same mountain lion that attacked Ann. Debi had saved her friend's life.

Neither Ann nor Debi could have predicted the mountain lion's attack. They might be tempted now to stay indoors and not brave the wilderness again. But household accidents injure more people than ever a mountain lion did, as statistics have shown. Anyone who's ever lived has probably learned sooner or later that it's impossible to control every aspect of our experiences, or to plan and plot for every eventuality. Anything can happen, and the best we can do is commit ourselves to coping with what happens as well as we can, just like Debi did. If you try to guard yourself against every unlikely danger, you'll never stretch beyond your comfort zone. Don't let the "what ifs" run your life. Follow your dreams and have at it.

"Worry is like a rocking chair—it keeps you moving but doesn't get you anywhere."
CORRIE TEN BOOM

Fear of the Future and Uncertainty about Tomorrow

"I'd like to live in the now or at least the soon."
ERICA JONG

To be afraid is to put a down payment on something that may happen in the future. Often, whatever we're afraid of isn't happening right now; it's something that might happen down the line. We *might* go broke, we *might* get mugged, we *might* have to jump out of a plane. Fear rears up when we anticipate the future. It's been said that there are two days over which we have no control: yesterday, because it's a cancelled check, and tomorrow, because it's a promissory note.

A funny friend told me, "If you have one foot in your fears for tomorrow and one in your regrets for yesterday, it will make you cross-eyed." There are many times I've put off or abandoned a good idea because I was projecting a year down the road, thinking of all the problems that might arise. Emerson said, "Fear defeats more people than any other one thing in the world." And Einstein said, "You can't solve the problem with the mind that created it." We truly do create our own problems when we worry about the future or about what we should have done in the past. Lord knows how many great works of art, brilliant inventions, or even love affairs might have been started if someone hadn't stopped himself or herself with fear.

Today, I can realize that I have food, shelter, creative ideas, friends, and coffee shops to sit in and write. In the now all is well. When I was chronically worrying about my future, my friend Gordon would say, "Do you have a bed to sleep in tonight? Did you eat today? Are you healthy today? Then what is your problem?" When Gordon was sick of listening to me, I'd complain to my friend Wanda about some future thing that might loom up, and she'd say, "Honey, you can't shovel the snow until it snows. When it does, I'll be right over with a shovel, but I'd like to remind you we live in the desert."

So many people fear financial insecurity. When Jimmy Stewart was standing on the bridge in *It's a Wonderful Life*, the angel said, "You're not going to kill yourself over money, are you?" When I begin to scare myself with money worries, I think of that line. Sometimes I have to joke my silly self out of fear—for instance, I'll remind myself I have all the money I need for the rest of my life if I only live until the end of the week. Imagining the worst-case scenario until it becomes ridiculous is a good way to cajole yourself out of the fear mode.

One way to diminish your future fears is to make plans and then let go. Be aware, though, that when you visit the future for more than the time it takes to make a concrete action plan, you may be on the verge of obsessive plotting. Don't go there! Put a big fence up and don't open the gate to tomorrow until it is tomorrow. You'll be much more productive today if you take practical actions for the future but then let the future take care of itself. Don't stop yourself from beginning something, whether it's enrolling for classes, putting a deposit on a trip, or accepting a date, just because you don't know how it will turn out.

So many of the people I interviewed said that they could not have planned the amazing, fun, positive things that happened to them. They just had to keep putting one foot in front of the other and doing the next indicated thing. The only time we can practice trust is in the now. The only time we can practice love and kindness is in the moment.

It cracks me up when I hear someone say, in a news story or in conversation, "I was sitting there minding my own business," or "It came out of the blue." Many of the good things in life happen while we are distracted by the everyday stuff. When we aren't frantically trying to plan ahead, the universe can finally get our attention. Living in the now is about being relaxed and enjoying the moment—not fighting with the future.

"Let us be of good cheer, remembering that the misfortunes hardest to bear are those which never come."
AMY LOWELL

Fear Fighters

"A man from hell is not afraid of hot ashes."
DOROTHY GILMAN

I talked to some people who face danger daily to see what they can teach us.

An FBI agent I spoke with had done it all: three tours in Vietnam as a Special Forces officer and fifteen years fighting fires before he joined the FBI. He freely admits that he's an adrenaline junkie but, like most people trained to handle extreme situations, says, "[I] don't do stupid things." Still, a psychologist once told him that people like himself don't make sense: "You run into situations normal people run from."

A fighter pilot related that his wife thinks he worries too much, but he's only being cautious because he knows the dangers that lurk in the world. He has crashed a plane and survived, but he doesn't want to cross Death Valley by car. When the prospect comes up, he protests, "There's nothing out there and what if we break down?"

Many of the firefighters and police officers I spoke to have saved lives. They rush in to comfort people where angels fear to tread— during the most difficult times in their lives: after violent physical attacks, after accidents and fires. They don't ask the person's religion or ethnic background. Every rescue is an affirmation that all life is important and worth saving. Nonetheless, these rescuers say, "We're not heroes. We are just doing our jobs." It seems that heroes never think they are.

But Charlie says, "Firefighting is not a job. It's a way of life and you never really leave it." In his twenty-six years as a fireman, Charlie has seen twenty-six of his buddies die, including his best friend, who rushed into a flaming old tenement in Jersey City, New Jersey, and rescued two children. This friend tucked the infant under his coat and carried another child; after he got them to safety, he collapsed and died. Despite the heartache of this experience, Charlie cherishes the bond he shares with other firefighters, a bond that comes from facing extreme danger together.

Because of his profession, Charlie lives in closer proximity to death than most people—as everyone who's close to him knows. One day, as he was leaving for work, his son rushed out of the house to kiss him goodbye. A neighbor commented on the kiss, and the boy said, "My daddy might not come home tomorrow. I have to kiss him now."

In spite of the danger, Charlie and other fear fighters would not have it any other way. One firefighter said, "The meaning of life is death. Until you are faced with death, with the nearness of it, the inevitability, you don't appreciate the gift of life."

These fear fighters can teach us to know the risks and to take those risks that matter. They teach us that difficult tasks always look overwhelming until we get the right training and learn the procedures. And they teach us that life is precious.

✵ LIFE CHALLENGES ✵

Ask yourself what you can learn from people who face fear daily.

Appreciate every minute.

Help without judging others when the opportunity arises.

Enroll in a CPR class.

CHAPTER 10

Moving On

"Whatever you can do or dream you can,
begin it. Boldness has genius,
magic, and power in it."

GOETHE

Laugh out Loud

"Comedy is tragedy plus time."
Steve Allen

Humor is the saving grace; it can dispel fear, smooth over tense situations, and facilitate healing. It's said that laughter is the shortest distance between people. Humor can also give us courage when we are afraid. No matter how grim the circumstances, finding humor in them helps us take our power back. When we can laugh at it, we can live with it.

In 1989, during the 7.1-magnitude earthquake that struck the Bay Area of California, some raised, double-decker freeways collapsed and pancaked onto the deck below. A man was trapped in his car, which was squashed to a height of about eighteen inches. An off-duty fireman heard the man yelling for help and crawled through the rubble to get to him. When he reached the car, the fireman comforted the man and even got him laughing. He said, "Hey, buddy I think we'll be able to get you out of here, but we may have to damage the car door." The trapped man went along: "Okay, but try not to scratch my paint job." The man was rescued.

Laughter produces a small window of hope; for a moment, we get a new perspective. Humor is an effective antidote to dispel fear.

When our dreams fall apart at the seams, we can talk with a good friend and eventually we'll laugh about it. After we find some humor in the situation, we are then ready to pick up and start over.

> *"Humor is the great thing, the saving thing.*
> *The minute it crops up, all our irritations and resentments*
> *slip away and a sunny spirit takes their place."*
> MARK TWAIN

Hit the Road

"Give your spirit time to breathe."
DIANE CONWAY

When I was a little girl, I'd see "hobos" and tell my mother, "I want to go live with them and eat beans out of a can and travel around the world." She was probably horrified, but I saw it as adventure. I was too young to know that maybe the people were homeless—to me, they just looked free.

Joseph Campbell, who coined the phrase "follow your bliss," advocates "wandering" as a way to discover our destiny. He recounts that Goethe touted the idea of "bumping" into life. Campbell himself speaks of the virtues of wandering: "Nothing is routine, nothing is taken for granted. Everything is standing out on its own, because everything is a possibility, everything is a clue, everything is talking to you."

Campbell spent eight months rambling around America during the Depression; the trip formed the man and the writer he would become. He writes, "Every detail of those years stands out in my memory. Oh, those were grand experiences. I was just flopping around, sniffing out what I would do and what I wouldn't do. I only wanted to do what made sense to my interior. I don't see how you can live otherwise."

This wandering and discovery may take the form of a lifelong avocation, a month-long sabbatical to Tuscany, or a morning of hooky-playing. Leave the cell phone at home and don't let anyone know where you are. Start out on a field trip and let yourself go where your nose takes you. If you see an interesting road, go down it. If your intuition whispers, "Go into that café," go. Stop and talk to an interesting person. Let the things you bump into determine the journey. Meander without a destination or a particular purpose.

Harking back to the days when I dreamed of the hobo life, I've always seen myself packing a small valise, wearing khaki shorts and a T-shirt, and jumping on a steamer bound for unknown ports. So far I haven't done that, but it is a powerful image for me. I get a taste of this adventure when I hop on the ferry from Sausalito to San Francisco to meet my husband for dinner. I get it when I allow myself to visit a small town I haven't been to. I even get it when I go to art galleries.

This seeming aimlessness is the very way that the universe can guide us, can nudge us toward what will make us the happiest and most fulfilled people we can be. We can allow ourselves small amounts of wandering even in a busy life. These may be the occasions when your heart will feel safe enough to tell you what it wants.

Have a Grateful Heart

"Your attitude will make or break you."

WANDA JOHNSON

My wise old friend who looked like a hunch-backed Yoda from *Star Wars* used to say, "Any damn fool can thank God when things are going good. You need to thank God when they're awful."

I was in a crazy, fearful time, and fresh out of answers. Life was not behaving for me. Nothing made sense, and things I felt I didn't deserve kept coming around, regular as a bus. Of course I was fearful—who wouldn't be?

I had nothing to lose, so I tried to practice "radical acceptance" and began saying "Thank you" for everything. "Thank you that I didn't get cast in the show I had my heart set on. Thank you that my rent went up. Thank you that the jerk never called back." I'd go around saying thank you for red lights—that's how radical it got! But I noticed that this practice took the sting out of misfortune, and pretty soon little miracles happened. This saying-thank-you-for-everything business worked like spiritual alchemy. The day after I didn't get the part in that show I mentioned, a friend called to cast me in his film. Because of the exorbitant rent at my horrible apartment, I decided to leave, and my subsequent move opened a new world for me. My friend who got the guy I didn't get wished she hadn't.

Having a grateful heart and a thankful spirit is the shortest distance to peace. Gratitude is like turning on landing lights for miracles; they come zooming in. When we snatch the power back from the bad stuff by blessing it, we have achieved victory over it.

While in college, I rented a furnished apartment in a complex that had both furnished and unfurnished models. I realized that I wasn't making ends meet, so I told the landlady that I couldn't afford the furniture any longer and she could use it for another apartment. Because I was in the habit of thanking God for everything, when I came home one night and found the furniture gone I wasn't really upset. I pulled my air mattress over to the window by the balcony. Lying there on the floor, I realized that I now had a gorgeous view of the night sky and the stars. It reminded me of a good camping trip. If I still had had furniture, I would have never put the bed there.

Thanking God—or the universe or nature or whatever you believe in—puts us in the flow, the natural rhythm of the world. It gets us back in touch with all the good there is. Turning off the gloom-and-doom news and taking a walk to see the stars will quickly put you in a grateful state of mind.

Open the Door

"Every seed has an angel that bends down
and whispers, Grow, grow."
THE TALMUD

Sometimes the scariest thing we can do is to resurrect a forgotten childhood dream or to rekindle an aspiration we have abandoned. Safety seems to lie in pushing the desire away, thinking we won't get hurt if we don't expect too much. It takes bravery to look at things which we deeply desire and think are out of reach. Many people "settle" and by force of will deny their dreams.

While pursuing my dreams of being a self-supporting artist, performer, and writer, I've taken many jobs. I guided whale-watching tours in Maui, drove a cab, worked in a country-western bar, and performed singing telegrams in various costumes, from Miss Piggy to life-size vegetables. Once I had to deliver a singing telegram to a sailboat from a motorboat, dressed like a bunny. I did pretty much anything to avoid doing a real job.

One day a realtor hired me to get a vacant house ready for sale. The last tenants had moved a month or so ago, and it needed a once-over. The house was on a hillside and had upstairs and downstairs decks. The weather was sweltering, and I had to keep stopping to drink water and cool off. On the lower deck, I noticed a small door about three feet tall. Seeing the door reminded me of the walks I took as a child on the beach in South Carolina—whenever I came upon a plank lying on the sand, I'd think that I might find buried treasure. I opened the door to this storage space and found an unexpected world inside. In this small space there was a tiny room that had been arranged with a bathmat and an overturned milk carton. Little dolls and stuffed animals were placed around the "table." On the table was one book, *The Secret Garden*. I had stumbled on a little girl's secret playhouse world. The family had moved away and left the girl's secret garden, but I found it at a time in my life when I really needed the message. Her hidden world told me that even though I was not at present living my dream, it was still there inside of me.

It seemed as if I'd discovered a metaphysical rabbit hole, a peek into the heart of buried desires and dreams. I will never forget the little girl I never met and the gift she gave me. We can abandon—or be told we can't have—our dreams, but they are not gone, and I invite you to become an archeologist of the heart and excavate yours. It's never too late to journey toward the passion that is calling you.

✧ LIFE CHALLENGES ✧

Hold your dreams to your heart.

Believe in your unique self.

Don't quit before your miracle.

Begin the journey . . .

Come to the Web site www.dianeconway.com.
Make your declaration.
The magic starts the minute you do.
Send your story for the next book.

ACKNOWLEDGMENTS

This book would have not seen the light of day without my friend Karen Warner, who believed in this project when I was letting it languish in a drawer. Karen handed the budding manuscript to Mark Kerr at Inner Ocean. She provided editorial and mental health guidance.

Anne Lamott encouraged me to write but more importantly made me laugh (at myself). Thanks to all the people who awed me with their bravery and humanity during interviews and to the women who have shared their heart's desires during retreats. Thanks to Karen Bouris at Inner Ocean for immediately "getting it" and making me feel welcome to their amazing fold. My editor, Heather McArthur, hung in when I was crazed, cheering me on.

ABOUT THE AUTHOR

Diane Conway is a speaker and workshop leader who lives her dreams while quaking in her boots. She's the author of *The Fairy Godmother's Guide to Dating and Mating*. She lives on a houseboat in Sausalito, California with her husband, Brian, and their two dogs, Lily and Mollie.

WALLACE STEVENS

COLUMBIA INTRODUCTIONS TO

TWENTIETH-CENTURY

AMERICAN POETRY

JOHN UNTERECKER, GENERAL EDITOR

WALLACE STEVENS

AN INTRODUCTION

TO THE POETRY

SUSAN B. WESTON

COLUMBIA UNIVERSITY PRESS

NEW YORK

1977

9 2 9 8 7

Library of Congress Cataloging in Publication Data

Weston, Susan B
    Wallace Stevens : an introduction to the poetry.

    (Columbia introductions to twentieth-century American
poetry)
    Bibliography: p.
    Includes index.
    1. Stevens, Wallace, 1879–1955—Criticism and inter-
pretation.   I. Series.
PS3537.T4753Z94   811'.5'2   77-1594
ISBN 0-231-03990-5

Columbia University Press
New York—Guildford, Surrey

COLUMBIA INTRODUCTIONS TO
TWENTIETH-CENTURY
AMERICAN POETRY

Contents

JOHN UNTERECKER

Foreword

The most single-minded poet of the twentieth century, Wallace Stevens was a man in love with marriages: the marriages not just of men and women but of heaven and earth, of north and south, of idea and image, of the abstract and the concrete, of imagination and reality, of night and day, and of the vividest heres and nows straddling violet thens and theres.

He tried for, and achieved, grand unlikely combinations. The nature of art makes love sometimes to Mrs. Pappadopoulos, sometimes to the man on the dump, and once to an emperor of ice cream. Opening Wallace Stevens' *Collected Poems* is a little like opening the tent flaps of The Greatest Show on Earth. But Stevens' circus animals are not trained bears and tigers but rather warped mirror images of ourselves, ourselves as we might be or ought to be, or in our loftiest, loveliest projections are: the comedian as the letter *c*, perhaps, or MacCullough suddenly become *the* MacCullough. The commonest man, in Stevens' poetry, more often than not puts on the habiliments of a god; an angel surrounded by paysans, on the other hand, turns out to have no angelic trappings but instead to *be* one of the paysans, the "necessary angel of earth," the almost invisible artist whose only function is to permit his countrymen to see earth as it really is, "cleared of its stiff and stubborn man-locked set." Stevens' project is to look so hard at the ordinary that its extraordinary unique- ness, its *is*ness, flares out. He says it in the titles of his poems: "Anything Is Beautiful if You Say It Is," "Two Illustrations that the World Is What You Make of It," "Not Ideas about the Thing but the Thing Itself."

If we look long enough at anything it overwhelms us with its possibilities. The lump of coal in my hand becomes the diamond a little greater pressure might have made. I stare hard at a leaf until petiole snaps free from branch and the leaf is autumn cir- cling in a turning wind. I see your sleeping hand and I become the touch of all familiar places I have never known.

To look long and hard at anything—a rock, a blackbird, the subtlest transformations of an eyebrow or an eye, even the over- and-under motion of a wave—can catapult us into love. Stevens' love poems celebrate both the world and the world as woman loved. At first she is the "fat girl, terrestrial, my summer, my night," who surprises the poet into feelings of pathos as she goes about her casual chores, "bent over work, anxious, content, alone." But seeing her as she is and in love, he discovers she has put on another reality. She is now "the more than natural figure," the "soft-footed phantom, the irrational / Distortion, however fra- grant, however dear." For she is both what she has always been and what she has become: the real woman in anyone's kitchen— including Stevens'—and "a fiction that results from feeling." Caught up, "flicked by feeling," he can at last "name her flatly" but also go on to call her by her other truer name, "my green, my fluent mundo."

Stevens' detractors, bothered perhaps by titles such as "The Pleasures of Merely Circulating," and "Two Versions of the Same Poem," and more than annoyed by Stevens' assertion that the artist is "he that of repetition is most master," fret that Stevens repeats himself. And of course he does—somewhat in the same ways that Shakespeare, Blake, Emily Dickinson, Whitman, Yeats, Eliot, and Roethke repeat themselves. Like any major writer, Stevens early on discovered both a body of congenial imagery (think of Blake's forges, Yeats's birds and trees, and Eliot's rose gardens) and a set of congenial themes (Shakespeare's ideas on the role of order in nature and the state, for example). Out of the intersection of obsessive images and themes comes the writer's poetic "voice": in Stevens' case that of an ironic aesthetician who counterbalances his most deeply held convictions with comedy and wit. "After the final no there comes a yes / And on that yes the future world depends," "The Well Dressed Man with a Beard" remarks. But before we've assimilated his paradox, he transmutes idea into image—"No was the night. Yes is the present sun"—and then sends both sun and moon skidding over the edges of the world to point out to us that the only sustaining, unchanging "thing" is "thought . . . , a speech / Of the self that must sustain itself on speech." But this is too heavy a statement for a poem and Stevens quickly manipulates it into playful language, manipulates that playful language into feelings of affection and perhaps love, and rounds out his tour-de-force with a one-line stanza: the statement that the poem has manufactured:

> . . . Ah! douce campagna of that thing!
> Ah! douce campagna, honey in the heart,
> Green in the body, out of a pretty phrase,
> Out of a thing believed, a thing affirmed:
> The form on the pillow humming while one sleeps,
> The aureole above the humming house . . .
>
> It can never be satisfied, the mind, never.

Satisfied that Stevens has found a form for his uneasy notion, we move on to the next poem, satisfied. For variations please us, give us a sense of order in a world of flux. We know as well as Stevens that the order a work of art creates is artificial: a pure invention, an imposition false as a snapshot of a leaping dancer who must in fact return to earth. Yet memory and artifice are all we have to stop the flow of time. Stevens' generous art, cheerful yet serious, confronts the changes of a changing world and stops them long enough for us to enjoy each transformation: the dancer frozen in the form he must complete, the leaf not quite yet fallen to the ground.

Stevens, who loved clean prose and careful thought, would have been delighted with this good book about his mind and art. Modest and accurate, Susan Weston helps us see the poems as they are: brisk, singing documents caught up in change and changing with the poet's life; words frozen on a page that tumble bare ideas into joy.

Preface

I decided at the outset of this study to keep Stevens' poetry
center stage. Other poets and a philosopher or two make brief
entrances when their voices might be useful for understanding
what the poet John Berryman called the spiffy muttering of Stevens' poetry. Because my assimilation of Stevens criticism will be
obvious to the scholar and unimportant to the general reader, I
have kept the scholarly apparatus to a bare minimum. Those
books and articles without which I could not have written this
book are mentioned in the bibliography.

I want to express my gratitude to John Unterecker for his
boundless patience in reading the manuscript and to John Weston for his boundless patience while I wrote it.

SUSAN B. WESTON

Honolulu, Hawaii
January 1977

Acknowledgments

I want to thank Alfred A. Knopf, Inc. and Faber and Faber, Ltd. for their generous permission to quote extensively from the following works of Wallace Stevens: *The Collected Poems of Wallace Stevens*, copyright © 1954; *Letters of Wallace Stevens*, edited by Holly Stevens, copyright © 1966; *The Necessary Angel*, copyright © 1951; *Opus Posthumous*, edited by Samuel F. Morse, copyright © 1957.

T. S. Eliot, "The Love Song of J. Alfred Prufrock" from *Collected Poems 1909–1962*, copyright © 1963, and "Second Thoughts on Humanism" from *Selected Essays*, copyright © 1960, quoted by permission of Harcourt Brace Jovanovich, Inc. and Faber and Faber, Ltd.

The Collected Works of Paul Valéry, ed. Jackson Mathews, Bollingen Series XLV. Vol. 4, *Dialogues*, trans. William McCausland Stewart, copyright © 1956 by Bollingen Foundation, short quote from p. 81. Vol. 10, *History and Politics*, trans. Denise Folliot and Jackson Mathews, copyright © 1962 by Bollingen Foundation, short quotes from pp. 93, 215. Reprinted by permission of Princeton University Press and Routledge & Kegan Paul.

Table of Dates

The reader interested in a closer look at the order in which Stevens wrote his work might begin with Holly Stevens' chronologically arranged selections, *Wallace Stevens: The Palm at the End of the Mind* (Vintage Books, 1972). The order in which he lived his life is outlined below:

1879   October 2. Born in Reading, Pennsylvania, second of five children.

1897   Enrolled in Harvard as a special student; served as president of the *Harvard Advocate*, in which he published several poems (see Robert Buttel, *Wallace Stevens: The Making of Harmonium*).

1900   Went to New York City to try his hand as a writer; short career as a journalist at New York *Tribune*.

1901–3   Attended New York Law School.

1904   Admitted to New York Bar.

        Met Elsie Viola Moll (born 1886) during a visit to Reading.

1908   After several unsuccessful jobs he joined the legal staff of the American Bonding Co., and shortly after became engaged to Elsie Moll.

1909   September 21. Married.

1914   *Carnet de Voyage,* a group of eight poems, appeared in *Trend:* Stevens' first published work since his days on the *Harvard Advocate*.

1916   Joined the New York office of the Hartford Accident and Indemnity Co. Claims investigations took Stevens all over the country.

       May. Moved to Hartford, Connecticut, the Stevens' permanent residence.

1923   *Harmonium* published by Alfred A. Knopf, Inc.

1924   Holly Bright Stevens born.

1932   Bought his first and only house.

1934   Appointed vice-president of Hartford Accident and Indemnity Co., the position he held until his death.

1935   Limited edition of *Ideas of Order* published by Alcestis Press.

1936   *Ideas of Order* published by Knopf, with a new poem, "Farewell to Florida," as its first poem.

       Owl's Clover (OP) published by Alcestis Press.

       Delivered "The Irrational Element in Poetry" (OP) at Harvard University.

1937   *The Man With the Blue Guitar* published by Knopf.

1941   Read "The Noble Rider and the Sound of Words" at Princeton as part of the Mesures Lectures made possible by Henry Church.

1942   *Parts of a World* published by Knopf.

       Limited edition of "Notes Toward a Supreme Fiction" published by Cummington Press.

1943   Read "The Figure of the Youth as Virile Poet" at the Entretiens de Pontigny, a conference at Mount Holyoke.

1944   Holly Stevens married.

1945   Elected to National Institute of Arts and Letters.

1947   *Transport to Summer* published by Knopf.

       Read "Three Academic Pieces" at Harvard.

       Grandson, Peter, born.

1948   Read "Effects of Analogy" at Yale and "Imagination as Value" at Columbia.

1949   Awarded Bollingen Prize in Poetry.

1950   *Auroras of Autumn* published by Knopf.

1951   Received National Book Award for Poetry.

       The Necessary Angel published by Knopf.

1954   *The Collected Poems* published by Knopf.

1955   January. Received National Book Award for *Collected Poems*.

       April. Operation for intestinal obstruction revealed incurable cancer.

       May. Received Pulitzer Prize for poetry.

       August 2. Died in Hartford, Connecticut.

1963   Mrs. Stevens died.

WALLACE STEVENS

Abbreviations

In the text the following abbreviations are used:

CP   *The Collected Poems of Wallace Stevens* (New York, 1954)

OP   *Opus Posthumous*, ed. Samuel French Morse (New York, 1957)

NA   *The Necessary Angel* (New York, 1951)

L   *Letters of Wallace Stevens*, ed. Holly Stevens (New York, 1966)

CHAPTER 1

Introduction

"We live in a mind-made world."
—Suzanne Langer,
"The Prince of Creation" [1]

"Words of the world are the life of the world."
—Wallace Stevens,
"An Ordinary Evening in New Haven"

Asked for a biographical note, Stevens once replied, "I am a lawyer and live in Hartford. But such facts are neither gay nor instructive" (L 227). For gaiety and instruction, we should take his cue and turn to the poetry, where we find the poet: connoisseur of fine wines and of chaos, iconoclast and upholder, a man of single mind and many moods. As for those "facts," Wallace Stevens spent a lifetime battling with them, trying to incorporate, suppress, or transform them. Not that he had trouble being lawyer and poet: he was good at both and grumbled to the curious that there was nothing odd about being both. His first book of poetry, *Harmonium*, was published in 1923, when Stevens was forty-four and well established in his career in the insurance world. The book was not well received, and Stevens, apparently disappointed by his literary reception as well as busy consolidating his career, stopped writing for a number of years. In 1934, however, when he became a vice-president of the Hartford Accident and Indemnity Company—a position he held until his death in 1955—he began publishing again, and for a man who was modest about his poetic activity, produced an astonishing volume of work.

We should be wary of talking about the "development" of a poet who publishes his first book, and one which for many readers remains his best, in middle-age. Yet the poetry does change: stylistically, as Stevens matured the techniques for rendering his theme, and thematically, as he matured his life-long preoccupation with the process of the mind perceiving reality.

I

Continuity and Change

The last poem in *The Collected Poems* is "Not Ideas about the Thing but the Thing Itself." That is what Stevens was after, early and late: the "veritable ding an sich" of the early "The Comedian as the Letter C" and the "thing itself" of the last poem. From *Harmonium* through *The Rock,* that search for a "new knowledge of reality" is an abiding theme. What changes is Stevens' attitude toward language as a medium for knowing reality. The problem is suggested by the title, "Not Ideas about the Thing but the Thing Itself." Stevens' contemporary, William Carlos Williams, insisted in "A Sort of a Song": "No ideas but in things." That statement, Stevens would reply, is an *idea* about the importance of things. The problem is, how to get the "thing itself" into words that are not merely *ideas* about it.

In a late poem, Stevens proclaims:

> Natives of poverty, children of malheur,
> The gaiety of language is our seigneur.
>   (CP 322)

Our poverty of being is the premise, too, from which most of the *Harmonium* poems begin, but they spin out a luxurious web of words over the void, rendering that "gaiety of language" in the light-hearted pile-up of words before even the most freezing thoughts. But in time, Stevens came to speak *about* that gaiety, rather than to render it. The sense of humor in the later poems takes on a very different quality. Compare the humor in "Bantams in Pine-Woods" from *Harmonium* with "Jouga" from *Transport to Summer* (1947). In "Bantams," one cock shoos off another with linguistic élan:

> Damned universal cock, as if the sun
> Was blackamoor to bear your blazing tail.
>
> Fat! Fat! Fat! Fat! I am the personal.
> Your world is you. I am my world.

This is the fairly confident stance of a lean cock who knows his relationship to reality. But listen to the halting syntax and self-contradiction of "Jouga":

> Or perhaps his guitar is a beast or perhaps they are
> Two beasts. But of the same kind—two conjugal beasts.
> Ha-eé-me is the male beast . . . an imbecile,
>
> Who knocks out a noise. The guitar is another beast
> Beneath his tip-tap-tap. It is she that responds.
> Two beasts but two of a kind and then not beasts.
>
> Yet two not quite of a kind. It is like that here.

If read out loud for emphasis on the stumbling syntax and on the tone of puzzlement, the poem makes us smile when we read that line, "It is like that here." Indeed, it is often like that "here," in Stevens' world.

Once we recognize the humor, we will see it often, and in the most serious and earnest poems. In the midst of the philosophically inclined first section of "Notes Toward a Supreme Fiction," for example, Stevens insists that "the sun / Must bear no name, gold flourisher," and we hear the poet mocking what he has just said. The source of the humor seems, often, to be his own doomed effort to speak in words, to say precisely what the relationship is between reality and imagination. In many of the poems, the words themselves are guilty of the "failure" of the poem to reach that new reality, an interdependence of word with reality. Words themselves elicit either humor or despair—the difference is hard to detect—in poems about the difficulty of words. The problem begins early; Crispin, in "The Comedian as the Letter C," complains that "The words of things entangle and confuse."

After the rout of Crispin's attempts to articulate the "ding an sich," Stevens took a new tack and began to explore the basic disjunction of language and reality. *Ideas of Order* and *Parts of a World* frequently express the dissatisfaction with language and poetry and art:

> Pfft. . . . In the way you speak
> You arrange, the thing is posed,
> What in nature merely grows.
> (CP 198)

Only in the very differently constructed long poems of his later style could Stevens overcome his linguistic dilemma. "Words of the world are the life of the world," he can finally say, whereby words become not separate from but an animating principle of reality.

II

The Supreme Fiction

Forged in the crucible of Stevens' discontent with language is the solution to the linguistic dilemma: the "supreme fiction." To understand this important and persistent notion, we must first erase from our personal notions of "reality" anything but what we can point to or stomp on; we must, for example, try to think of the word "table," if spoken in a room which contains no table, as a *symbol*, because the word "table" has elicited something in our *minds*. As long as a word does not point to an actual object, we are in the realm of the mind: memory, imagination, anticipation, abstraction. And these are traits that set us apart from even the most intelligent animals; we are set apart by virtue of our preoccupation with symbols, "with images and names that *mean* things, rather than with things themselves," as Suzanne Langer says.

Erase, then, all mental activity—dream, desire, religious belief, political conviction, and language—from the blackboard "reality." How stark the world looks! And for how short a time it remains devoid of our meanings! The symbol-mongering mind quickly intervenes between blankness and self. But at least for a moment we have started where Stevens starts: with blankness. Even at his most iconoclastic—"Sunday Morning" or "A High-Toned Old Christian Woman," for example—Stevens is not merely dismissing Christian doctrine as fictive; he is affirming our need for fictions. Creating fictions is the essential gift of the human mind; believing them is its curse.

III

The Poet

For us, poetry is the closest approximation to Stevens' "supreme fiction." For Stevens, I think it was an imagined poet, a potential figure that he sketches again and again: "The Noble Rider" and "The Figure of the Youth as Virile Poet." Stevens' definitions of poetry are often bound up with delineations of this potential poet whose imagination Stevens thinks of as a kind of total faculty: imagination informed by reason. And as a merely "potential" figure, he seems to be a *collective* potential: less Stevens' than ours. Stevens is clear about his role: he helps people "to live their lives" (NA 29). This is, of course, all "make believe"—a supreme fiction. But, as I. A. Richards has wonderfully said, the poet's job is more than make-believe; it is making people believe.[2] And what we find in Stevens' poetry, unique in the age of Eliot and Pound, is that make-believe in ourselves; we read Stevens to find the world robed in imagination's sequined harmonies, and to find ourselves, robing and disrobing the world around us.

CHAPTER 2

The Gaiety of Language

"Man is an analogist, and studies relations in all objects."
—Ralph Waldo Emerson, "Nature"

"The eye does not beget in resemblance. It sees.
But the mind begets in resemblance."
—Wallace Stevens, "Three Academic Pieces"

I want to begin my discussion of *Harmonium* by quoting from two of its poems. First, from "Theory":

I am what is around me.

Women understand this.
One is not duchess
A hundred yards from a carriage.

And from "Tea at the Palaz of Hoon":

I was the world in which I walked, and what I saw
Or heard or felt came not but from myself.

Juxtaposed like this, the two poems act like angry philosophers disagreeing over a premise: do I create reality, or does reality create me? This debate takes place frequently among the poems of *Harmonium*, often to the embarrassment of Hoon's fellow so-lipsists, who are all too easily blasted from their convictions by a hostile environment. In "Valley Candle," for example, the candle of the organizing imagination is snuffed out by the wind; in "Six Significant Landscapes," the ants crawl through the solipsist's shadow, making him realize that perhaps he is not taller than the tree merely because he can reach, "with [his] eye," to the sun. And this debate is the subject of "The Comedian as the Letter C," with Crispin beginning with the conviction that "man is the intelligence of his soil" (CP 27), and ending with the knowledge that "his soil is man's intelligence" (CP 36). "That's better," re-marks the narrator, and we with him, feeling that the exclusions of the solipsist are "unrealistic."

Before dismissing solipsism in favor of the theory that "I am what is around me," however, perhaps I should introduce a mod-erating voice to suggest that neither "Theory" nor "Tea at the Palaz of Hoon" is wrong. "The Snow Man" speaks with the au-thority of controlled syntax and wit:

> One must have a mind of winter
> To regard the frost and the boughs
> Of the pine-trees crusted with snow;
>
> And have been cold a long time
> To behold the junipers shagged with ice,
> The spruces rough in the distant glitter
>
> Of the January sun . . .

The two verbs, "to regard" and "to behold," with their puns on respect ("regard") and embrace ("be-hold"), suggest an accuracy

of perception possible only to a wintry mind; one must have a
mind of winter to see all this

> . . . and not to think
> Of any misery in the sound of the wind,
> In the sound of a few leaves,

> Which is the sound of the land
> Full of the same wind
> That is blowing in the same bare place

> For the listener, who listens in the snow,
> And, nothing himself, beholds
> Nothing that is not there and the nothing that is.

The argument of the poem is that one must be a snow man—
"nothing himself"—in order to perceive reality without thinking
of any misery in it.

The very procedure that the poem recommends for seeing the
world as it is also shows how difficult it is for the human perceiver to separate his perceptions from his thoughts. We would
have to be snow men to remain indifferent to the force of the cold
particulars: the "junipers shagged with ice," the "distant glit-
ter / Of the January sun," and the insistent "sound of the wind."
Although the poem affirms the blankness of the reality out
there—"the nothing that is"—it also affirms the inevitability of
human projection: "Nothing that is not there." By suggesting that
"one" would have to be "nothing" in order to "behold" stark reality, the poem denies the possibility of knowing that reality bare of
human projections.

"The Snow Man" adds a new dimension to the solipsism of
"Tea at the Palaz of Hoon," which, significantly enough, was its
companion poem in the original 1921 publication. The two poems
posit two possible responses to stark reality: reality is nothing, to
which the perceiver can only add himself; and reality is merely

an extension of the perceiver. Hoon's solipsism, in the context given the poem by "The Snow Man," may be nothing more than the projection of his feelings upon an otherwise indifferent scene. Hoon feels himself to be "the compass of that sea":

> Out of my mind the golden ointment rained,
> And my ears made the blowing hymns they heard.

If Hoon does not create the ocean or the sunset, he certainly does create the sense of magnificence he feels in them.

Incapable of becoming a "snow man," unhappy about being a Hoon, Stevens creates these poems and these personae not to stage a philosophical debate, but to dramatize his own unresolved feelings about the nature of reality and how he perceives it. The seeds of the poetry's single subject can be understood biographically, for Stevens early felt that he had to make a choice between his pragmatic instincts and his romantic desires: "I must be all dream or all deed," he remarked in his journal (L 34). And perhaps the most revealing journal entry is one which suggests the solution to this dilemma:

> The only practical life of the world . . . as a bustling merchant, a money-making lawyer . . . is to be if unavoidable a pseudo-villain in the drama, a decent person in private life. . . . I believe, as unhesitatingly as I believe anything, in the efficacy and necessity of fact meeting fact—with a background of the ideal. (L 32)

Written before he had found his life-long career as an insurance lawyer, these remarks anticipate the separation that Stevens maintained between his career as a lawyer and his practice as a poet. Stevens protested to the contrary: "What is there odd," he complained, "about being a lawyer and being or doing something else at the same time?" (L 413) Yet he never mentioned his poetry unless someone else brought it up, and few of his business associates had any inkling of his "secret" life. He had effectively separated the "money-making lawyer" from the poet.

For Stevens, the "background of the ideal" was to be found not in literary or artistic movements—which he joined, enjoyed, and profited from—but in that "private life" of which poetry was to be an important part. His long courtship from 1904 to 1909 of his future wife, Elsie Moll, provides a wealth of letters and journal entries which testify to the place of poetry. He struggled during the day to get his affairs in order so that they could marry, while in the evening his letters to her provided a vacation from the daily world of "facts." For her he wrote a collection of "Songs for Elsie" and birthday poems called "The Little June Book," and his letters to her are full of gay little "jigs" of language. The daily dynamics of this business life and courtship resemble the characteristic division in *Harmonium* between night's moonlit imagination and day's sunlit reality. During the day he drew up agreements "full of 'Whereas' and 'Now, therefore' " and during the evening his letters became the occasion of taking what he called a "fling—to prevent myself from growing *too* sedate. . . . Hey-ding-a-ding.—Now you have a blue ribbon in your hair and I have on slippers" (L 113–14).

Poetry too was to be an evening or weekend occupation, a vacation from facts, a "fling" with language:

> Tum-ti-tum,
> Ti-tum-tum-tum!
> The turkey-cock's tail
> Spreads to the sun.
> ("Ploughing on Sunday")

and

> Chieftain Iffucan of Azcan in caftan
> Of tan with henna hackles, halt!
> ("Bantams in Pine-Woods")

This is a linguistic fling, but not meaningless babble. In Stevens' dichotomy between sunlight-facts and moonlight-imagination, the poetry itself came to be about that separation, and also about the inseparability: night depends on day, imagination on reality. The "fling" with language imitates the imagination's embellishments of reality.

This gaudy use of language went hand in hand with a growing sense of his own masks. Originally part of the epistolary fun with Elsie, those masks were not put on, like Prufrock's, to "meet the faces that you meet," [1] but to respond to things and weather and time of day:

> The sunlight is gone, and I must light my lamp. . . . Ought I not suddenly pull off my black wig and black gown and put on a white wig, full of powder, and a suit of motley—or maybe, the old costume of Pierrot? For when I sit at the window and write, I look out on real things and am a part of them; but with my lamp lighted and my shade down—there is nothing real, at least there need not be and I can whisk away to Arcady.
>
> (L 134)

This letter to Elsie was written in 1909, five years before the publication of even the earliest *Harmonium* poems, and shows Stevens already aware of the dimensions of his subject: "I look out on real things and am a part of them" versus "with my shade down—there is nothing real." How often in *Harmonium* Stevens mocks that day-time black-wigged self, twits "Rationalists, wearing square hats" (CP 75), and lets the lamp of imagination effectively ignore an ugly reality:

> When the elephant's-ear in the park
> Shrivelled in frost,
>
> .   .   .   .
>
> Your lamp-light fell
> On shining pillows,

Of sea-shades and sky-shades,
Like umbrellas in Java.

("Tea")

But Stevens, though he counsels rationalists to wear "sombreros," is just as uneasy about the "unreality" of imagination as he is about the ugliness of untransformed reality. Pierrot, for example, is a stock figure from commedia dell'arte, the valet-lover, clown-hero; given new currency by Jules Laforgue during the French Symbolist movement, Pierrot was a mask for the world-weary artist, Laforgue. Stevens, never a world-weary artist, nevertheless adopts his mask with a good deal of distancing irony.

Perhaps Stevens is uneasy about adopting any single mask because he is aware that one mask is only a moment's choice among many masks: "There is a perfect rout of characters in every man," one letter to Elsie goes; "every man is like an actor's trunk, full of strange creatures, new + old. But an actor and his trunk are two different things" (L 91). Stevens was that single actor; his roles as pragmatic businessman, idealist, Pierrot, art-lover, poet—all these are different costumes he puts on. The hallmark of the poetry in *Harmonium* is its variety of moods and personae. Its subject is actually the single issue of actor and costumes: what costume (language, attitude) does he wear with particular kinds of reality? And who determines his choice of costumes—he or the weather? Stevens explored this subject with unflagging energy from 1914 through 1922, publishing some one hundred poems in a variety of little magazines such as *Poetry*, *Others*, and *The Dial*. Collected together as *Harmonium* in 1923, the poetry provides no answer to the questions: Stevens was not after the *truth* of perception, but its poetry.

Stevens' fascination with the poetry of perception accounts for the limitations of his subjects. We will find neither the mordant social wit of T. S. Eliot's "Portrait of a Lady" nor the more domestic insights of William Carlos Williams' "The Artist" or "This is Just to Say." In place of social or domestic drama is the abstract drama of the mind perceiving. And because he was intellectually and emotionally caught up with the abstract drama, Stevens tended to simplify the problem of active perception by restricting it to a landscape or still life. Henri Bergson, whose studies of perception influenced many modern writers besides Stevens, begins his study of the mind with a similar restriction:

> Let us take the most stable of internal states, the visual perception of a motionless external object. The object may remain the same, I may look at it from the same side, at the same angle, in the same light; nevertheless the vision I now have of it differs from that which I have just had, even if only because the one is an instant older than the other. My memory is there, which conveys something of the past into the present.[2]

That "motionless external object" is the necessary limitation in Stevens' drama, and some readers feel keenly the loss of other actors and emotions on Stevens' stage.

But Stevens' limitations are no greater than those of Impressionism or Cubism: both artistic movements tend to sacrifice the human subject to the search for underlying forms, whether the open-air landscape or the studio still-life. It is no digression to consider the theory (albeit in distressing over-simplification) behind Impressionism and Cubism, for Stevens' interest in art was as great as his passion for poetry; he considered that both were concerned with the re-creation of reality by the imagination. Stevens shared Monet's delight in appearances, in the shifting qualities of things affected by changing light or weather conditions. The Impressionists, greatly excited by scientific findings about color, broke the world into fragments of color; the very use of color in an Impressionist landscape questions the ability of the eye to "see" by showing that a single color "impression" is in reality the juxtaposition of two or more colors. From breaking the world into fragments of color to fragmenting its form is theoretically a short step, but one which revolutionized art. The Cubist considers his still life from a variety of angles, and paints as if he were walking around rather than motionless before his subject. Picasso, for example, will paint a profile with an eye that could only be seen from a different angle. Abandoning pictorial representation of the object for the re-creation of its forms, the Cubist submits reality to total metamorphosis. Stevens attended the 1913 Armory Show in New York, and even dined with Marcel Duchamp of "Nude Descending a Stair-case" fame, but he remained fonder of Impressionism, perhaps because of its translation of theory into wonderfully effective landscapes, perhaps because it was closer than the more analytical cube to the refracting prism of imagination.

Substituting the poet's images and metaphors for the philosopher's discourse and the artist's paint, Stevens had to consider the limits of language for representing reality. It is the play of the linguistic imagination on perception that is, finally, the subject of *Harmonium.* As "The Snow Man" makes clear, we cannot perceive reality without projecting ourselves upon it. This is the meaning of Stevens' curious statement in "Three Academic Pieces" that the eye sees, but "the mind begets in resemblance." What the "eye" sees is transformed by what the "I" sees, for the mind cannot view an object without finding resemblances for it. Language is the tool of the resemblance-seeking mind, and *Harmonium* is Stevens' most self-consciously "linguistic" volume, dramatizing what Stevens articulated only much later:

> Natives of poverty, children of malheur,
> The gaiety of language is our seigneur.
>
> (CP 322)

The poems start with some bleak, black, obdurate fact of existence upon which they embroider with the "gaiety of language." The bleakness of the one motivates the gaiety of the other:

> In Oklahoma,
> Bonnie and Josie,
> Dressed in calico,
> Danced around a stump.
> They cried,
> "Ohoyaho,
> Ohoo" . . .
> Celebrating the marriage
> Of flesh and air.

The gaiety of this poem, "Life Is Motion," emanates from the "stump," which, with eleven words preceding and following it, is the center of the poem. "Life Is Motion" because death is stasis; the stump is the central fact of existence. Bonnie and Josie celebrate the marriage of flesh and air, but they dance around the stump, for it alone makes us dance and gives meaning to our celebration of life.

Whatever the "malheur" or "poverty" that Stevens fastens on—death, process, flux, alienation—he rarely fails to celebrate the imagination's mitigations: "Ohoyaho." Announcing the vitality of the imagination in relation to reality, Stevens put "Earthy Anecdote" first in *Harmonium*; perhaps a better introduction would be a minor poem called "Explanation," for it is indeed an explanation of *Harmonium:*

> Ach, Mutter,
> This old, black dress,
> I have been embroidering
> French flowers on it.

"This old, black dress" is Stevens' sense of the desolate barrenness of reality; the "French flowers" refer, perhaps, to his love

of French diction. Asked by René Taupin about the influence of
the French Symbolists on his work, Stevens equivocated: "The
lightness, the grace, the sound and the color of French have had
an undeniable and precious influence on me." [3] What he loved
was the language itself. The unspoken denial to Taupin about the
influence of the Symbolists is fairly explicit in "Explanation,"
where Stevens disclaims:

> Not by way of romance,
> Here is nothing of the ideal,
> Nein,
> Nein.

No, he wears the black dress of the actual, and speaks the harsh
Germanic dialect of reality; imagination, though it can "embroider," must not deny essential bleakness. At least for Stevens,
"drifting through space, / Like a figure on the church-wall" toward some transcendent realm, is not one of the possible solaces
offered by the imagination.

In this poem, Stevens himself explains what it took his readers
somewhat longer to realize; his highly wrought connotations
cover up—"embroider"—blankness. It is less the picture of reality that gives pause to the reader of Stevens' *Harmonium* than the
elaborate devices he uses to cover it up. Just as his favorite
images are clothes—the wigs, gowns, hats, and cloaks of the
imagination draping naked reality—so too his favorite poetic device is some form of linguistic embroidery: nonsense syllables,
radical diction, wide-ranging analogies, and equivocally adopted
figures of speech. Stevens' verbal pyrotechnics are more often a
stumbling-block than his subject, for they either create an apparently impenetrable surface to the poem or modify the
paraphrasable content with subtle ambiguities. I think it will
prove helpful, then, to consider the several techniques that Stevens consistently uses in *Harmonium*.

Because he explores the relationship between reality and the mind as it "begets in resemblance," his most characteristic habit in *Harmonium* is to pile up analogies. We must exercise some caution in assessing Stevens' attitude toward these multiple analogies, for sometimes he delights in the creative patterns found by the mind, and at other times condemns the mind for imposing patterns. For example, in "The Curtains in the House of the Metaphysician" Stevens offers a series of choices:

> It comes about that the drifting of these curtains
> Is full of long motions; as the ponderous
> Deflations of distance; or as clouds
> Inseparable from their afternoons;
> Or the changing of light, the dropping
> Of the silence . . .

The poem brings up a problem that will plague us throughout *Harmonium:* is this "metaphysician" an ironically adopted persona, and is Stevens thus disavowing these analogies? Or is the metaphysician the mind itself, seeking resemblances for what it sees with what it cannot see? In spite of the cloistered and trivial nature of the occasion—the "drifting of these curtains"—I think that Stevens refers to the movement of the mind from the trivial to the meaningful; the analogies spiral ever outward to the largest and most significant motion, "the firmament, / Up-rising and down-falling."

A parallel use of multiple analogy occurs in "The Load of Sugar-Cane," where the similes do not spiral outward toward the meaningful unseen, but remain embedded in the actual. Each simile short-circuits itself by returning to the actual objects surrounding the "going" of the boat. The wind, for example, "whistles / As kildeer do," but the simile forces the poem back to the real rather than toward the ideal, for those kildeer whistle "When they rise / At the red turban / Of the boatman."

One of the best of the multiple analogy poems is "Domination of Black," which uses a series of comparisons to dissolve everything—bush, leaves, peacocks' tails, and planets—in the assault of darkness and wind. The mind recognizes the change and temporality—"turning"—of all things, and is seized with fear for its own continuity: "I remembered the cry of the peacocks." Resembling the mind, the peacock spins beautiful "tales" of resemblances; its high-pitched, uncanny shriek expresses the terror of the mind perceiving the black unity of all things beyond the mind. The analogies spiral outward until the mind feels the final cosmic anguish: "I saw how the planets gathered / Like the leaves themselves / Turning in the wind." Much of the poem's power comes from the lessons that Stevens learned from the Imagist Movement. Ezra Pound, who published his Imagist manifesto, "A Few Don'ts by an Imagist," in *Poetry* in 1913, wanted poetry to be "austere, direct, free from emotional slither." [4] "Domination of Black" is a masterpiece of Imagist practice, following each of Pound's directives: "Direct treatment [of the object], economy of words, and the sequence of the musical phrase." Stevens uses a two-beat stress instead of an accentual line:

> At night, by the fíre,
> The cólors of the búshes
> And of the fállen leáves,
> Repéating themsélves. . .

And deviation from this two-beat line conveys great tension:

> Yés: but the cólor of the héavy hémlocks
> Cáme stríding.
> And I remémbered the crý of the peácocks.

Rhythm, as Harvey Gross has said, tells us "how an idea feels." [5] "Blackness" is the idea here and its "feel" is dissolution.

These evocative rhythms combine with the powerful use of jux-taposed images in a fairly characteristic Imagist poem.

Time and change are the basis of many of Stevens' poems, and the best of them recognize the indifference of the turning world to the anguish of the central self:

> Death is absolute and without memorial,
> As in a season of autumn,
> When the wind stops,
>
> When the wind stops and, over the heavens,
> The clouds go, nevertheless,
> In their direction.

In this poem, "Death of a Soldier," Stevens can work magnifi-cently with a single image because it so concisely shows the pro-cess of nature with which our fates mingle. But Stevens more often felt constrained by the use of a single image, which may be best suited to momentary perception. Resorting to multiple anal-ogies and a sequence of images, Stevens adapted Imagist doctrine much as T. S. Eliot anticipated it in his early poems, "Preludes" and "Rhapsody on a Windy Night." Unlike Eliot, Stevens is not intent on vividly rendering the psychology of urban distress. In-stead, he presents the sensations that occur to the mind as the eye (I) perceives external reality. In "Thirteen Ways of Looking at a Blackbird," for example, each stanza has the precision of an Imagist poem, but the whole poem adds up to an argument about perception and the function of analogy in perception. No such theoretical framework can be argued for Eliot's early poems. I should add that Stevens himself denied this theoretical freight, remarking crossly to one reader, "This group of poems is not meant to be a collection of epigrams or of ideas, but of sensa-tions" (L 251).

These "sensations" derive from the interaction of what we perforce abstractly call reality and imagination; in no way abstract, "Thirteen Ways of Looking at a Blackbird" dramatizes several moments when the imagining mind is pierced by its relation to a particular reality. It would be convenient to say that the power of the poem to elicit this variety of sensations comes from symbol; after all, most mysterious powers are symbolic, and vice-versa. But the blackbird itself does not seem consistently symbolic, even if we call it symbolic of the most general significance, say "death-in-life." [6] Instead, the blackbird links the observer to what he sees. We can see the remarkable focusing power of the bird in the first stanza, where Stevens uses it primarily as a visual reference point:

> Among twenty snowy mountains,
> The only moving thing
> Was the eye of the blackbird.

The bird contrasts and thereby focuses the multiple, large, blank, and static mountains against the single, tiny, dark, and dynamic eye. But the exact status of the bird as bird is questionable, for Stevens introduces two possible puns, "moving" and "eye." These suggest that the perceiver is an emotionally moved I. This kind of ambiguity melts the eye of the bird with the I of the speaker, and the seen with the unseen. In this way, the bird functions to link the observer to the landscape, at the same time creating the "sensation" or mood of the linking.

Interestingly enough, the image of the bird rarely functions as a metaphor, for it is not linked in a figurative way as in, say, "death is a blackbird." Instead of metaphors, we find, in stanza after stanza, that Stevens uses the copula to make literal links between noun and predicate nominative or adjective:

The only moving thing	Was	the eye of the blackbird (I)
It	was	a small part of the pantomime (III)
The blackbird	must be	flying (XII)

Two comments from Stevens' later prose on the behavior of figurative language are useful and insightful. In the collection of epigrams which he whimsically entitled "Adagia" (linking the plural of adage to a musical term), Stevens says, "The word must be the thing it represents; otherwise, it is a symbol. It is a question of identity" (OP 168). And in "Three Academic Pieces": "Both in nature and in metaphor identity is the vanishing-point of resemblance" (NA 72). Linguistically, then, anything short of identity (X is X) can be metaphoric; imagistically, any word pulling us beyond the thing it represents must be symbolic. In the context of Stevens' later prose, the blackbird must be a symbol, for it certainly represents more than a bird; yet in each stanza, the symbolic significance differs from the others. I think it is most helpful to think of the bird as the "occasion" for a crowd of metaphors, the linking together of "blackbird" and a whole array of disparate things: the observer observes, and what he observes reminds him of a blackbird's possibilities—and of his own. The blackbird is a constantly shifting arc of meaningful analogy between the speaker and some of the significant parts of an exterior world.

"The blackbird is involved / In what I know" because, as one term in a metaphor, it is the perceiver's sole means of knowing. When it flies out of sight, it marks "the edge / Of one of many circles." The mind, that is, has an intimation of its limitations, suddenly realizing that it is not the single center of perception, but one among many. The perceiver can find unity for his own mental division ("I was of three minds") by another act of analogy: "Like a tree / In which there are three blackbirds"; the divided self is like a single tree with three birds in it. The bird also allows the perceiver to recognize the silent "pantomime" of reality's flux: autumn, wind, change. "The blackbird whirled in the autumn winds" is more than synecdoche of reality's change, for it allows the perceiver to feel the implicit threat to himself, also whirled in change. Even attempts at isolation from reality are mediated by the blackbird—or its absence. Stanzas VI and XI, for example, show the perceiver behind glass, but pierced by an anxiety that is metaphorically suggested by the "shadow" of the blackbird. In the first, the perceiver is static, the blackbird dynamic; in the second, some "he" is in a glass coach that travels. Perhaps the journey suggests the passage of time, which makes him think anxiously of the blackbird's shadow. The magic fairytale world of Cinderella's glass coach is no cure for the blackbird's inescapable message of relatedness—to reality, process, and time. So the speaker of the poem contrasts himself in this stanza with the "he" of the glass coach, and in other stanzas with those who would escape observation of reality for some timeless and perfect world. Eschewing "golden birds" for blackbirds "around the feet"—down-to-earth birds—the speaker dramatizes his own contact with reality.

By the thirteenth stanza the bird has been successively involved in—or perhaps even permitted—knowledge of all kinds: of the limitations of the mind's perceptual abilities, the flux of reality and the temporality of the self, the necessity of living with that knowledge, and the right kind of aesthetic response to reality. In thirteen stanzas, the poem moves from a crisp black and white landscape to a black and white chiaroscuro, with the last and ominously thirteenth stanza blending the blackness of the bird into the dark tones of the fading day ("It was evening all afternoon"). No longer an organizing point of contrast, the bird is now an omen of death. This is appropriately the last stanza in a poem about our life in reality. The poem could, of course, go on with an infinite number of momentary insights; Stevens stops on the deadly thirteenth only to show that the infinite variety of stances the mind can take as it perceives reality is circumscribed by time and therefore by death.

The sequence of images, like the pile of analogies around a fact, has the effect of showing the dance of the mind around what it perceives. "Thirteen Ways of Looking at a Blackbird," it seems to me, is an effective poem whether or not a reader is familiar with the theoretical framework of Stevens' poetry.

More hazardous to the reader unfamiliar with the context of Stevens' work are those poems that illustrate some unstated theory. A glance at the table of contents of *Harmonium* confirms his favorite title: "Anecdote." Many of the poems, and not just those so entitled, are indeed "anecdotes," little stories that are apropos of something under discussion. We could rifle Stevens' "Adagia"—probably written a good deal after *Harmonium*—for the abstractions to accompany some of these anecdotal poems. "Earthy Anecdote," for example, might be prefaced: "The imagination is man's power over nature" (OP 179) or "In the world of words, the imagination is one of the forces of nature" (OP 170). In the poem ("the world of words"), the force of nature is represented by the bucks, and the imagination by the firecat:

> Every time the bucks went clattering
> Over Oklahoma
> A firecat bristled in the way.
>
> Wherever they went,
> They went clattering,
> Until they swerved
> In a swift, circular line
> To the right,
> Because of the firecat.
>
> Or until they swerved
> In a swift, circular line

> To the left,
> Because of the firecat.

Stevens said of this poem that he "intended something quite concrete: actual animals, not original chaos" (L 209). The "actual" bucks clatter quite concretely, then, but without any order; the firecat-imagination "leaps" and "bristles," a beast of prey. And "because of the firecat," the "clattering" of the bucks becomes a "swift, circular line"—a pattern. Although the bucks of reality flee the firecat of imagination, the firecat nevertheless imposes its patterns of order. And when the "firecat closed his bright eyes," sated by the day's reality, the poem clicks off like a finished movie film. Without the ordering effect of the bright-eyed perceiver, the poem—another pattern of order—ceases to exist.

"Anecdote of Canna" is another theoretical poem, this one dramatizing the adage, "Eventually an imaginary world is entirely without interest" (OP 175). In a late letter about this early poem, Stevens revealed that it "occurred to me one late summer afternoon . . . in Washington" (L 465). "X" is the President, then, the "mighty man" who dreams. His dreams "fill the terrace of his capitol," suggesting that they take over both external reality (Washington the capitol) and internal reality (the capital as head). His "thought" of the daytime continues at night, but with this important qualification:

> . . . thought that wakes
> In sleep may never meet another thought
> Or thing. . . . Now day-break comes . . .

and with daybreak, reality, which "X" welcomes. The imagination, a "night-time" activity, must be in contact with reality to be interesting and valuable.

"Earthy Anecdote" and "Anecdote of Canna" can be quite adequately prefaced by one or another of Stevens' "Adagia," and perhaps its discredits them that they are so easily "allegorized" into abstractions. If "Anecdote of the Jar" is an allegory, if the jar stands for art, say, the poem is nevertheless difficult to reduce to an abstract assertion. True, there are allegorical dimensions to the two images, with the jar suggesting man, imagination, and art, and the wilderness suggesting nature, reality, and unordered chaos. But this "allegory" evades reduction:

> I placed a jar in Tennessee,
> And round it was, upon a hill.
> It made the slovenly wilderness
> Surround that hill.

"Round upon the ground," the jar governs all the resonant "round" sounds, while the wilderness hisses busily ("Tennessee," "slovenly," "sprawled," "bush," and "else"). The stately jar appeals to our love of rounding off loose ends; "tall and of a port in air," it domesticates the sloppy wilderness:

> The wilderness rose up to it,
> And sprawled around, no longer wild.
> The jar was round upon the ground
> And tall and of a port in air.

But this "dominion" is sterile:

> It did not give of bird or bush,
> Like nothing else in Tennessee.

Everything else in Tennessee prolifically "gives"; the jar—bare, barren, empty—can only "take": "It took dominion everywhere."

But of course the jar *does* give something; what it gives is unlike anything else in Tennessee, that bird- and bush-producing state of nature. It simply does not "give of"—reproduce or represent—birds and bushes. The poem's first line—"I placed a jar"— suggests the importance of the gesture to the speaker: the placing, focusing activity of mind organizing the "wilderness."

These "anecdote" poems all dramatize some abstraction, and the "Adagia" are useful comments for establishing the framework of those abstractions. But only in his poetry could Stevens resolve the inherent contradictions he felt. He concretizes the abstractions—usually imagination and reality—with a particular set of images: firecat, jar, candle, moonlight are some of the figures for imagination; bucks, Tennessee (or any Southern landscape), wind, ocean, sun are some of the figures for reality. In spite of the ease with which we label Stevens' particulars, though, the poems are rarely adequately summed up by a single abstract assertion, for Stevens' ambiguous syntax and his titles generally create a richness not apparent at first glance. "It did not give of bird or bush / Like nothing else in Tennessee," for example, is syntactically created ambiguity. And then consider the title: "Anecdote of the Jar." It is typical of Stevens that he would discredit one of his finest attempts at establishing the value of reality and imagination by shrugging it off as merely an "anecdote," that is, a little unpublished story, a cute tale, a bit of gossip.

There are many "anecdote" poems in *Harmonium*—poems, that is, that seem apropros of some more abstract discussion, with obviously "allegorical" particulars. "Valley Candle" is an example, with the candle representing imagination, and the wind the vaster powers of reality. But nothing I can say about their relative powers can approach the drama of the poem's conclusion:

> My candle burned alone in an immense valley.
> Beams of the huge night converged upon it,
> Until the wind blew.

Then beams of the huge night
Converged upon its image,
Until the wind blew.

And then . . . ? The poem is awesomely silent. Similarly, "Bantams in Pine-Woods," "The Jack-Rabbit," "Disillusionment of Ten O'Clock," and "The Ordinary Women" all illustrate some unstated abstraction about the vying of imagination with reality, but all resist single-minded interpretations. My favorite "anecdotal" poem is the whimsical "Frogs Eat Butterflies. Snakes Eat Frogs. Hogs Eat Snakes. Men Eat Hogs," with the title suggesting two possibilities: that men eat butterflies, or that you are what you eat. Then, in a single extraordinary sentence, the poem reverses the title by having "hogs eat men" and having the man become what eats him (not a hog, probably, but an ephemeral butterfly). This delightful displacement occurs through the simile, "rivers went nosing like swine"; rivers travel to sea, hours pass into days, and the whole process suggests that the "arid being" at the center of the poem is consumed by process, change, and finally death. And the butterflies? Perhaps they are the "quirks of imagery" which, although he does not know them, nevertheless thrive on the planter.

"Frogs Eat Butterflies" is typical of *Harmonium* in several ways: it is anecdotal; its comic surface belies the serious subject matter; it uses particulars that clearly stand for abstractions, but puts the particulars together in a teasing way. Before turning to an exploration of the thematic coherence of *Harmonium*, I want to discuss one more poem, also "typical" in that it forces us to account for Stevens' repertoire of ambiguities: an odd persona, an ambiguous title, and a fierce tension between the connotative language and what that language describes. The poem is "On the Manner of Addressing Clouds," which is in the manner of those early poems that earned Stevens the reputation of "aesthete," and his poetry the reputation of "affected," "precious," and even "mandarin." [7] As the title suggests, Stevens will show us the correct manner of addressing clouds; he does so by addressing the entire poem to "you," the clouds, in language so recondite and syntax so tortured that the "address" requires several close readings.

The first phrase, "gloomy grammarians in golden gowns," is descriptive apposition for the clouds, which meekly "keep the mortal rendezvous": go to their death. They are grammarians because they instruct us in the correct speech for the occasion; they "elicit" or call forth the "still sustaining pomps / Of speech." In another appositive phrase, Stevens talks about philosophers and thinkers: "Funest philosophers and ponderers, / Their evocations are the speech of clouds." The sense of this second sentence is that the mutability of the clouds provides mournful ("funest") thinkers with the foundation (or grammar) for their pessimistic thinking. But there is an odd kind of blotting out at work here, for the poem approaches silence under the roar of its diction. The similes double back on themselves, with "evocations" likened to the "speech of clouds," which in turn elicit "still" (silent or yet?) "sustaining pomps." Again, these "pomps" are like "exaltation without sound."

Perhaps the rationale for the archaic diction and tortured syntax is summed up in the last section, beginning "so." The clouds' processional, though toward death, is "casual," and the seasons across which they travel are "stale" yet "mysterious." The clouds go to their death in "that drifting waste" of constant, casual, and *mute* change. The whole process elicits from us elaborate speech, evocations, and pomp appropriate to funerals. Like so many of Stevens' poems in *Harmonium,* this one uses flux and change as the impelling central fact. Also like many of the *Harmonium* poems—"Cortege for Rosenbloom," "The Emperor of Ice-cream," and "The Worms at Heaven's Gate," to mention a few—

Stevens wields the scalpel of comedy against sentimentalizing or idealizing attitudes toward death and change. These amorphous "grammarians" can instruct us in the "meet" (fitting, suitable) "resignation" to death. More important, the poem rubs its rare words together to suggest that our perception of reality can lead us to a "funest" philosophy: funest, stemming from the Latin *funus*, means mournful or funereal; it also puns on "funnest," or most fun.

Though Stevens does not choose his words out of a perverse pleasure at driving us to large dictionaries, the fact is that he liked them. Once we have consulted them, we find what R. P. Blackmur, Stevens' earliest perceptive critic, found: "In the poem, the language is perfectly precise. . . . [T]he word must be looked up, or at least thought carefully about, before the precision can be seen. This is the precision of the expert pun, and every word, to a degree, carries with it . . . the puns of all its senses." [8] The point of this difficult poem, then, is a point about language and humanity; the poem does not use archaic diction merely as an elaborate decorative device over the surface except to make this essential point: language and human meaning *are* elaborate decorative devices over the surface of a reality totally separate, barren, and, except for our projections, meaningless.

But wait: what kind of person would give a lecture entitled "On the Manner of Addressing Clouds"? If I take him seriously, am I immediately seated at a table full of pompous pedants? For all the seriousness of the subject matter, Stevens will permit neither himself nor his readers any "grand pronunciamentos" for long. He continually undermines single-minded interpretation by some hint of irony: he disowns his persona, tortures his syntax, calls the whole poem into question with its title, or somehow manages to suggest that he is grandly gesturing about "the nothing that is."

These ambiguities of attitude, along with certain stylistic

habits—highly connotative diction, multiple choice analogy, and an almost literal attitude toward figures of speech—are the manifestation of Stevens' thematic dichotomy not only between imagination and reality, but between imagination's language and the reality it seeks to depict. If we explore Stevens' attitude toward metaphor, it will become clear that language is itself a metaphor, a cloaking device incapable of depicting external reality. Even those poems celebrating the separateness of reality finally affirm the imagination by showing that reality cannot be known except through our metaphors. This is the theme of "The Snow Man" and, with the emphasis on the nature of metaphor, of "Nuances of a Theme by Williams" and "Metaphors of a Magnifico." In "Nuances," Stevens quotes Williams' poem "El Hombre" as his first stanza, then elaborates on the "nuances" of the personification in Williams' title: the separateness of that star can only be celebrated with rejected metaphors. "Metaphors of a Magnifico" is spoken by an epistemologist who presumes to define reality without metaphors, and the poem is a joke on him. He observes "Twenty men crossing a bridge" and begins an inquiry into that "old song / That will not declare itself": is the bridge I see the same as the bridge you see, and how do we *know* it is? The magnifico's attempts at definition collapse into tautology:

> Twenty men crossing a bridge,
> Into a village,
> Are
> Twenty men crossing a bridge
> Into a village.

They just *are;* reality overwhelms the attempts to define it, and the poem concludes with the vi   l particulars that overcome the epistemologist intent on philosophical meaning. The title—"*Metaphors* of a Magnifico"—suggests that his attempt at definition reduces to so many "metaphors": like the epigrammatic assertions

in "Thirteen Ways of Looking at a Blackbird," anything short of
identity, X is X ("Twenty men . . . are . . . twenty men"), is
metaphoric.

Implicit in these poems is the notion that language itself is a
metaphor, an act of analogy by the mind. In search of "reality,"
Stevens and his personae find themselves in an odd relationship
to their language. They must either reject the metaphors they
use to grasp reality, or grasp reality as a metaphor. Since the perceiver cannot refrain from projecting himself on the reality he
sees, he might as well give up the tussle, and celebrate language
as the life of imagination. Stevens makes fun of the "magnifico"
because of the magnifico's naiveté about his "metaphors"; yet
Stevens himself resorts to the ultimate projection by the perceiver on the perceived: personification. Stevens' sensitivity to
those metaphors of the magnifico should warn us that he was perfectly aware that his own personifications signify not reality, but
reality as known by the imagination. As if to celebrate the separateness of the reality on which imagination depends, Stevens
personifies reality as a woman. Thus our list of "dependencies"
can be expanded: night depends on day, imagination on reality,
male on female. Like the dichotomy between reality and imagination, the separation between male and female seeks resolution:
the male speakers in Stevens' poetry "court" this woman, glimpse
her, but do not "know" (literally and Biblically) her, for reality is
impossible to know objectively.[9]

Such personification—the humanization by the I of the not-I—
complicates that rather facile division of Stevens' early journal,
between day and night, fact and dream. That early division probably began to break down when Stevens, travelling for the insurance company, received his only exposure to places and climes
outside of the New York-Hartford area. Of these trips, those in
the South—Tennessee, the Carolinas, Florida—were most im-

portant; the lasting impression on Stevens of the Southern climate is registered in those poems that annotate a tropical reality
far more fecund than anything the temperate North had afforded
him. Stevens' response to this teeming tropic was highly ambivalent, for here was a sun-drenched "fact" as prolific as the
imagination itself. The geographical symbols that Stevens introduced into his poetry suggest that North and South stand for
two kinds of reality. North, a reality blank and cold, is also the
place to which Spring and fulfillment come; South, a lush and
teeming reality, is monotonous in its prolific chaos. More important, the physical landscape generates a mental landscape: when
the mind encounters the barren landscape, it cannot refrain from
projecting itself (consider "The Snow Man"). Similarly, when it
encounters the chaotic jungle, it cannot refrain from abstracting
and ordering it (witness the jar in Tennessee). Pushed to its logical implications, this mental geography leads to two symbols for
the mind: to mental North as reason, to mental South as imagination. This is one reason that Stevens recommends the creatively
Southern sombrero for rationalists in "Six Significant Landscapes," and sees the analytical "caliper" of "Last Look at the
Lilacs" losing out to "Don John," identified as "Southern" by his
Mediterranean name.

The trouble with this distinction between mental North and
South is that *any* act of the mind—whether embroidery on nothing or abstraction from chaos—is imaginative. And Stevens implicitly acknowledges the imaginative reaction to the Southern landscape by abstracting it—not with a jar, but with a personification.
Again and again, Stevens personifies the South as a woman whose
nature suggests that Stevens was both fascinated and repelled by
its multiplicity. "In the Carolinas," for example, originally part of
a group significantly entitled "Primordia," shows Stevens' reaction to the generative aspects of the Southern soil:

> Timeless mother,
> How is it that your aspic nipples
> For once vent honey?

Aspic nipples! Does he mean a gelatinous mass containing hunks of meat? The venomous asp? Or European lavender? Even the sweet nurturing by the mother, earth, is distasteful, for the nipples "vent" like some great pressure-cooker volcano. Again in "O Florida, Venereal Soil," Stevens seems to draw back from the prolific. The Southern soil gives birth to too much, to a "dreadful sundry," and the poet is affronted by the casual combination of life and death (buzzards and live-moss, the Negro undertaker killing time). The personification of the earth is a portrait of a wanton woman:

> Lasciviously as the wind,
> You come tormenting,
> Insatiable.

"Lasciviously," "tormenting," "insatiable," the soil is indeed *venereal:* bringing love and love's disease. The lover of reality, here, is overwhelmed by prolific reality, a generative yet killing earth.

Then, in the flick of a very significant wish, Stevens turns the earth woman into the woman of night:

> When you might sit,
> A scholar of darkness,
> Sequestered over the sea.
>   .   .   .   .
> Donna, donna, dark,
> Stooping in indigo gown
> And cloudy constellations,
> Conceal yourself or disclose
> Fewest things to the lover.

This "mistress," "sequestered" in the night sky, appeals to the speaker because she is barely there. Stevens often invokes her:

> Night, the female,
> Obscure,
> Fragrant and supple,
> Conceals herself.
>   (CP 73)

and

> Be the voice of night and Florida in my ear.
> Use dusky words and dusky images.
> Darken your speech.
>
> Speak, even, as if I did not hear you speaking.
>   (CP 86)

This same set of qualities—desirably concealed and lasciviously present—appears in personifications of spring and summer. Spring is a "paltry nude" (CP 5), a season that comes "slim through the bareness" (CP 63), while summer is a "scullion of fate" (CP 6), a "slum of bloom," a "fat beast, sleepy in mildew" (CP 62).

What are we to make of these two portraits, one of which shows the lover of "reality" recoiling from its presence? Given the characteristics of these personifications, it is clear that Stevens tells us less about "reality" than about his experience of it. With the two portraits of the woman, the one a fecund mother, the other a virginal beloved, Stevens gives us two experiences that have all the earmarks of a Jungian archetype. Introduced by Jung and analyzed at length by Erich Neumann, the feminine archetype is essential for understanding Stevens' mythology of the imagination. Any projection by the male mind of a female figure is a projection of what Jung called the "anima," the female "soul" of the male mind; Jung's warning against "rational" interpretation of this female is an important caution for arriving at the sense of Stevens' woman:

> In the products of unconscious activity, the anima appears equally as maiden and mother, which is why a personalistic interpretation always reduces her to the personal mother or some other female. . . . [R]eductive interpretations . . . put us on a false track. . . . The anima is bipolar and can therefore appear positive one moment and negative the next; now young, now old; now mother, now maiden; now a good fairy, now a witch; now a saint, now a whore.[10]

Like the Demeter-Persephone myth, mother and maiden are inseparable units of the continuity of experience. Neumann, analyzing the many facets of the feminine archetype, suggests that the mind, by an act of analogy, experiences the earth as both womb and tomb, as both life-giving vessel and life-restricting container. So too Stevens, who personifies the earth as a mother figure who both nurtures and threatens. Anything that gives life also confers the burden of mortality; anything that makes us mortal gives us the poignant pleasures of our fugitive existence. "Death is the mother of beauty," Stevens has said most famously in "Sunday Morning."

Neumann's comparison of the growth of consciousness with the growth of vegetation is also helpful:

> Both ways lead always and essentially from darkness to light. This is *one* of the reasons for the archetypal connection between growth symbolism and consciousness—while earth, night, darkness, and unconscious belong together, in opposition to light and consciousness.[11]

If we apply Jung's and Neumann's comments to Stevens' dichotomy between reality and imagination, we see that Neumann's archetypal images are Stevens' personifications: earth, night, and darkness. Stevens' images of reality assimilated by the imagination are, that is, images of the unconscious. Given the archetypal dimensions of the "woman," Stevens' personification has him looking two ways at once: outward toward reality and inward toward the unconscious sources of imagination. As personification, the woman represents the exterior world made interior, or reality assimilated by the self; as archetype, she represents a projection by the mind of all those images which, like the unconscious, threaten the conscious mind with oblivion: seasonal change, darkness, night, and death. The darkness, mortality, and flux, of which Stevens writes so gaily in *Harmonium,* are personified as a woman to suggest the life-giving relationship between reality at its bleakest and imagination at its most protective. The very woman that is the source of imagination is the source also of all that threatens the conscious self; the cave contains both treasure and dragon: conferring creativity, it also threatens oblivion.

Stevens' by and large male observers of reality court a woman—the creative darkness—that will protect them from the hostilities of that other woman—the earth as tomb, the night as death; they turn to the "sequestered" bride of the night sky, exhorting her to confer order and meaning on confusion and threat. Thus the beautifully ambiguous "Homunculus et la Belle Étoile," with Stevens' inversion of Plato's "sovereign idea." Standing Plato's "Allegory of the Cave" on its head, Stevens substitutes sea and star for Plato's cave and sun (the reality we cannot know, according to Plato, because we see only its reflection on the wall of the cave). Unlike the impoverished cave-dwellers of Plato's allegory, those who live in the reflection of "la belle étoile" live as naturally as fishes "going in many directions / Up and down."

Stevens flings out a challenge to philosophers who reason out an "idea" of reality, for they are unaware that the "gaunt, fugitive phantom" of their Idea is, in reality, Stevens' woman:

> She might, after all, be a wanton,
> Abundantly beautiful, eager,
>
> Fecund,
> From whose being by starlight, on sea-coast,
> The innermost good of their seeking
> Might come in the simplest of speech.

"The innermost good of their seeking" suggests the archetypal dimensions of that "belle étoile"—the sought-after reality is found both outside and inside the seeker. This star serves those that "know the ultimate Plato": probably those who recognize that the ultimate impulse behind Plato's allegory was the "torments of confusion." It is, then, the imagination—"la belle étoile"—which tranquillizes, and any philosophical thesis of an ultimate "Reality" is an imaginative construction designed to still the torments of confusion.

"Homunculus" means a little man, a dwarf, or even an artificially produced manikin. Perhaps Stevens suggests by this the smallness of the analytical mind reasoning out reality. But the word brings up the threats to the self, to the homunculus within, of the vigors of that archetypal woman, as ever "fecund" and "wanton." What I am suggesting is that *Harmonium*, though it defends the imagination as an ultimate good, does so in overtones that imply a threat to the conscious male speakers who observe reality and invoke imagination. Though Stevens thinks of the potent imagination as a Southern male—Don John, for example— most of his speakers are wordy, pompous, posturing figures, middle-aged and slightly incapable. They eagerly await Spring, who comes "slim through the bareness," but rebuke Summer as "a slum of bloom." The observer who courts the woman is threatened by her presence, must step back and ask her to "conceal herself." Like reluctant bachelors courting a wanton female, Stevens' speakers cloak reality with their language, relying on imaginative embroidery as a protective covering from naked reality. Their ambivalent attitudes create the kind of tension that we see in "Of the Surface of Things." One stanza personifies the external world: "The spring is like a belle undressing." But the next finds the speaker ducking under his cloak: "The moon is in the folds of the cloak." The speaker's response to the naked woman is withdrawal into the imagination.

The ambivalence of these personae causes an extraordinary undertow in the poetry, for while Stevens celebrates the embroidery of the imagination, he does so in a way that makes it seem false and distorting; while he celebrates the gaiety of language, he manages to deprecate the speaker as a pedant or an aesthete; while he proffers a definition of reality, he shows the definition to be either wrong or distasteful. This self-critical voice is at the heart of Stevens' development, which can be measured from the three long poems in *Harmonium:* "Sunday Morning" (1915), "Le Monocle de Mon Oncle" (1918) and "The Comedian as the Letter C" (1922).

CHAPTER 3

Introspective Exiles

"The death of one god is the death of all."
—Wallace Stevens (OP 165)

"Sunday Morning" is many readers' first acquaintance with Wallace Stevens' poetry, and what an introduction it is! The meditative grandeur and masterful blank verse of the poem—printed in 1915, merely a year after Stevens' first publication—show the hand of a gifted poet, an heir to Wordsworth. But Stevens is no Wordsworth, and "Sunday Morning" is, perhaps, an unfortunate introduction to his poetry: its serenity is tonally atypical of *Harmonium,* and of most of his work. None of the eddies of self-criticism swirl under its beautifully measured tones, no ambivalence undermines its revelation of a secular religion.

The title and the first five lines of vivid description establish the poem's context and theme: the contrast between the woman's sensuous "sun-day" and the darkly religious "Sunday" of "ancient sacrifice." Rejecting that "old catastrophe," Stevens replaces the religious comforts of the "Son" with the secular "comforts of the sun": "Things to be cherished like the thought of heaven." In response to our "need of some imperishable bliss," Stevens argues that transience is the only source of bliss:

> Death is the mother of beauty; hence from her,
> Alone, shall come fulfilment to our dreams
> And our desires. Although she strews the leaves
> Of sure obliteration on our paths,
>
> .   .   .   .
>
> She makes the willow shiver in the sun
> For maidens who were wont to sit and gaze
> Upon the grass, relinquished to their feet.

This life of the senses becomes the premise of a possible "religion":

> Supple and turbulent, a ring of men
> Shall chant in orgy on a summer morn
> Their boisterous devotion to the sun,
> Not as a god, but as a god might be,
> Naked among them, like a savage source.
> Their chant shall be a chant of paradise,
> Out of their blood, returning to the sky.

This stanza, by proposing the "heavenly fellowship / Of men that perish," tries to answer the question posed in stanza III: "Shall our blood fail? Or shall it come to be / The blood of paradise?" But it is a prophetic assurance that Stevens gains only by using a tone quite at odds with the primitive ritual he depicts. "Whence they came and whither they shall go / The dew upon their feet shall manifest," Stevens proclaims: the fellowship of mortality is wonderfully Biblical. Stevens would never again be able to revert to such traditional tones without being wickedly ironical.

All the ironies and ambivalences suppressed in "Sunday Morning" surface three years later in "Le Monocle de Mon Oncle." Many of the images from "Sunday Morning" find their way into

"Le Monocle," where they are transformed by the point of view of one of Stevens' more typical personae: the aging, introspective, and garrulous uncle. The images take on a new life when seen through the uncle's "monocle"—his limited point of view or his improved vision? In "Sunday Morning," for example, Stevens rejects any paradise but the one we have on our changing and—because changing—beautiful earth:

> Is there no change of death in paradise?
> Does ripe fruit never fall? Or do the boughs
> Hang always heavy in that perfect sky,
> Unchanging, yet so like our perishing earth?

Stevens takes that "ripe fruit" image from "Sunday Morning" and uses it as a metaphor in "Le Monocle"; the result is not poignant process, but grotesque age:

> Our bloom is gone. We are the fruit thereof.
> Two golden gourds distended on our vines,
> Into the autumn weather, splashed with frost,
> Distorted by hale fatness, turned grotesque.
> We hang like warty squashes, streaked and rayed.

Proclaiming that "Death is the mother of beauty," Stevens paints a picture of youthful passion in "Sunday Morning":

> She causes boys to pile new plums and pears
> On disregarded plate. The maidens taste
> And stray impassioned in the littering leaves.

And similarly in "Le Monocle":

> In the high west there burns a furious star.
> It is for fiery boys that star was set
> And for sweet-smelling virgins close to them.

> The measure of the intensity of love
> Is measure, also, of the verve of earth.

But Stevens adds the important qualifying detail:

> For me, the firefly's quick, electric stroke
> Ticks tediously the time of one more year.

If "furious stars" burn for "fiery boys," the firefly's light better measures the passion of a fiery boy become middle-aged husband.

The subject of the uncle's meditation is close to the theme of "Sunday Morning," but with none of the earlier poem's assurance or reassurance. A candid look at existence on our beautifully perishing earth shows that before death, that mother of beauty, there is a long process of aging, a steady diminution of verve that makes the sensuous conclusion to "Sunday Morning" unrealistic. The uncle's theme is the "origin and course / Of love"—with the emphasis on its "course." Speaking politely of "love," the uncle is actually considering the nature of sexuality—the ruses and romanticisms we give to our sexual natures, the "quirks" that come with age. Feeling isolated from his aging wife, to whom he continually turns with unarticulated suggestions, the uncle finds himself increasingly introspective, his "amours" shrunk from deed to word, from action to lecture:

> When amorists grow bald, then amours shrink
> Into the compass and curriculum
> Of introspective exiles, lecturing.

The loss of sensuality is the loss of the sensuous comforts of the sun; the uncle is exiled from the comforts proffered in "Sunday Morning."

Because the context of this "introspective" meditation is less clear than that of "Sunday Morning," it is helpful to construct an occasion for the uncle's opening comments. I imagine a morning bedroom scene in which the wife, in her middle-aged disarray ("Why . . . / Do you come dripping in your hair from sleep?"), has just made some comment. The poem begins with the uncle's reply to that comment:

> "Mother of heaven, regina of the clouds,
> O sceptre of the sun, crown of the moon,
> There is not nothing, no, no, never nothing,
> Like the clashed edges of two words that kill."

Could she have said, "There's nothing left"? Then his reply would mean, "There's never 'Nothing.'" [1] But the six-times repeated negative followed by "Like the clashed edges of two words that kill" suggests a larger context of some endless discussion. The rest of the poem is a silent meditation which, although it intimately involves the wife, smacks of the uncle's isolation from her. As soon as he replies to her, he wonders, "Or was it that I mocked myself alone?"

What is it that drives him into this long, bitter, and yet comic meditation on love? Again, we can piece together the context from several of his thoughts about his wife. [2] One of these follows the charming anecdote of the red bird in stanza II, when the uncle acknowledges their middle-age:

> No spring can follow past meridian.
> Yet you persist with anecdotal bliss
> To make believe a starry *connaissance*.

In Stanza v, he again concludes his remarks about his own diminished sexual intensity with a reminder to her:

> And you? Remember how the crickets came
> Out of their mother grass, like little kin,

> In the pale nights, when your first imagery
> Found inklings of your bond to all that dust.

This is not a question, but an imperative: Remember. Once more in Stanza IX: "Most venerable heart, the lustiest conceit / Is not too lusty for your broadening." The context created by these unarticulated remarks to his wife would be a reproach about the way she is accepting her age. Perhaps her "anecdotal bliss" means that she dwells in the past, on anecdotes of "remember when. . . ." He too remembers the past: the "radiant bubble that she was" and "When you were Eve. . . ." But every memory is burst by a present reality.

Or perhaps her "anecdotal bliss" is a different kind of "make believe": that of some future consolation, the "starry connaissance" of heaven and after-life. In either case, the uncle remorselessly reminds her of present realities; the past is gone, and heaven may not exist:

> The honey of heaven may or may not come,
> But that of earth both comes and goes at once.
> Suppose these couriers brought amid their train
> A damsel heightened by eternal bloom
>
> (CP 15)

Suppose, in other words, that there was a female untouched by process, an eternal Eve. The next stanza is an association on that notion of "eternal bloom." The appearance of an ageless Eve would be less than consoling, because "Our bloom is gone. We are the fruit thereof." Its following stanza suggests that the uncle is writing—or trying to write—a "great hymn," "wild with motion, full of din," to that reality of process: he wants to affirm the necessity of an earthly and aging Eve, of the bloom becoming the fruit, the fruit the rotted rind.

This imagery points us toward the heart of the uncle's dissatisfaction:

> When you were Eve, its acrid juice was sweet,
> Untasted, in its heavenly, orchard air.
>
> (CP 14)

The fruit, he implies, is sweet only so long as untasted; the pleasures of sexuality are greatest when anticipated. Consummated, love becomes "acrid." Similarly, love, which once burned like a "furious star," now flickers like "the firefly's quick, electric stroke." Repetition marks the passage of both time and intensity, and Stevens' brilliant metaphor encircles both sexuality and age, as the firefly's stroke "Ticks tediously the time of one more year." Thus it is less the *loss* of sexuality than the satisfactions of it that the uncle bemoans. When youthful passion is satisfied by the regulations of middle-age, one must turn elsewhere for the "verve of earth." At forty the aging lover—a "ward of Cupido"—is too old and too honest to sentimentalize, and he must search for "a substance in us that prevails."

Whatever prevails, the individual does not, and the poem closes with a bird image that has as much poignancy as the expression of individual transience in "Sunday Morning," where "casual flocks of pigeons make /Ambiguous undulations as they sink, / Downward to darkness, on extended wings." In "Le Monocle," the bird also embodies individual transience in its various stages: a red bird that "seeks out his choir" in the vigor of youth; a blue bird that "circles in the blue sky" of imagination; and a "white pigeon . . . that flutters to the ground." The uncle concludes his meditation with the history of that bird:

> . . . later, I pursued,
> And still pursue, the origin and course

> Of love, but until now I never knew
> That fluttering things have so distinct a shade.

Discovering the insufficiency of sex, the uncle must look to himself, a "fluttering thing," for a new theme. And from the beginning of the poem, we sense that the "deep up-pouring from some saltier well' is not just the salty well of sexuality, but the creative possibilities of his own words. For the poem releases a flood-gate of words, with the uncle posing as a "dull scholar" trying to write "verses wild with motion." He speaks in parables, then offers to "uncrumple" them; he apologizes for a "trivial trope," then goes on to another. His search for a substance that prevails has him bemoaning the loss of sexuality that is the verve of earth, but implicitly finding a substitute in his language. Yet out attitude toward him and toward his substitute "verve" must remain equivocal, for Stevens has given him a monocle, a single lens, a limited point of view.

"The Comedian as the Letter C," by contrast, is binocular, the tale of a sophomoric enthusiast as told by a jaded pendant. The point of view puts the narrative events at two removes, filtering Crispin's virtually heroic search for reality through the speaker's detached and ironic indifference, and then again through Stevens' implicit irony toward such posturing comments as "Sed quaeritur." In spite of this narrative distance, "The Comedian" is a deeply personal poem, a retrospective of Stevens' work up to this point.

Because Stevens has embedded Crispin's ambiguous development in highly connotative language, it is important to approach the poem with its narrative simplicity in mind: Crispin travels from his native Bordeaux over a vast sea, through a tropical storm in Yucatan, to the Carolinas, where he finally settles and has a family. Each place constitutes a "reality" which elicits an aesthetic doctrine from Crispin, making the poem not only about his voyage in search of reality, but about poetry. And specifically about Stevens' poetry: each of Crispin's definitions of reality and each of his aesthetic reactions has its counterpart in the shorter poems of *Harmonium*. This specific self-reference probably accounts for the ambiguities of attitude and language that make "The Comedian" such difficult reading; writing of his own poetic voyage, Stevens was rejecting each of the stops on the way. Submitting Crispin to a last comic gasp in the embrace of his "prismy blond" wife and suffocating reproductivity, Stevens effectively wrote himself into a corner: he had ridiculed each of his previous solutions in *Harmonium,* and left himself no where to go.

Crispin is more than biographically rich, however, for his name suggests a complexity of cultures, eras, and themes. He is named for both the comic valet of seventeenth-century French comedy and the third century patron saint of shoemakers. Valet and saint, Crispin also resembles Voltaire's Candide ("Whatever is is what should be," Crispin remarks at one point) and Beaumarchais' Figaro (Crispin has a barber's eye, and his marriage is a significant event in the poem). As the details of the poem make clear, Crispin wears the clothes of all nations and the traditions of many centuries; this makes him a modern everyman, and a Protean figure to be continually reshaped by his environment.

The poem begins with a backward glance at Crispin's native Bordeaux, where Crispin considered himself "principium" (foundation, base) and "lex" (law). We can understand the impact of the sea on Crispin only with this view of his "ancient self," this romantic belief in his comprehensive scope: "cloak / Of China, cap of Spain" and "bellowing breeches." He has an "eye of land, of simple salad-beds," a "barber's eye" capable of artfully rendering all that he sees. Accompanying this portrait of Crispin's myth of himself is a series of puns on his head, his creative and rational faculties: barber's eye, wig, nincompate (Stevens' version of nincompoop). The barber's eye at sea discovers "inscrutable hair in

an inscrutable world." The *pate* of "nincompate" becomes *paté* at
sea: "One eats one paté, even of salt, quotha." This is an apt pun,
for Crispin is "at sea" literally and figuratively; he feels himself
lost:

> What word split up in clickering syllables
> And storming under multitudinous tones
> Was name for this short-shanks in all that brunt?
> Crispin was washed away by magnitude.
>
> (CP 28)

The landsman of "the bellowing breeches" becomes a "skinny
sailor," diminished and dissolved at sea because the sea makes a
"polyphony beyond his baton's thrust": it makes a noise he neither conducts nor understands. Stevens is explicit: "It was not so
much the lost terrestrial," he says, but the "mythology of
self, / Blotched out." Because he can no longer see himself "con-
ducting" everything, his sense of himself and his magnitude is
washed away.

Just as an "ancient Crispin" is dissolved at sea, so too other
myths, of which Triton is an example. This tempest of reality an-
nihilates both Triton and Crispin: myths. What's left of Triton is
the sea; of Crispin, "some starker, barer self / In a starker, barer
world." Like the uncle of "Le Monocle," whose search for the
"course" of love turns inward, Crispin "became an introspective
voyager" (CP 29). Crispin seems to rejoice in bare self and bare
world, thinking that the "reality" he seeks is before him:

> Here was the veritable ding an sich, at last,
> Crispin confronting it, a vocable thing,
> But with a speech belched out of hoary darks
> Noway resembling his, a visible thing,
> And excepting negligible Triton, free
> From the unavoidable shadow of himself.
>
> (CP 29)

"Free / From the unavoidable shadow of himself": the by-now familiar definition of reality as separate, unaffected by the "distortion" of the self, appears in "The Comedian" as the force of reality that the "imagination . . . could not evade, / In poems of plums" (CP 30). Crispin's poetry of the land is an evasion destroyed by the "gaudy, gusty panoply" of wind, cloud, and sea. By the end of this section, imagination and its poetry belongs with wigs, nincompate and barber's eye, the dressing up, covering "ruses" of the imagination; reality, defined now as a thing separate from the self and not susceptible to poetry, is "whole" and "large."

Shorn of both internal and external myths, Crispin arrives in Yucatan "destitute," and quickly hits upon an aesthetic solution: he will use the "green barbarism" of the tropical Yucatan as a "paradigm" for a new aesthetic, "tough, diverse, untamed." But just as the vast sea-reality shattered "poems of plums," so too tropical reality exceeds Crispin's ambitions:

> The fabulous and its intrinsic verse
> Came like two spirits parleying, . . .
>   .   .   .   .
> For Crispin and his quill to catechize.
> But they came parleying of such an earth,
> So thick with sides and jagged lops of green,
>   .   .   .   .
> So streaked with yellow, blue and green and red
> In beak and bud and fruity gobbet-skins,
> That earth was like a jostling festival
> Of seeds grown fat, too juicily opulent.
>
> (CP 31–32)

Dismissing with obvious distaste this "jostling festival," the narrator shrugs ironically at Crispin's rout: "So much for that."

"So much for that" might stand as the narrator's refrain, for these two sections are a paradigm of Crispin's travels. In each section, Crispin is confronted with a new reality; each new reality issues a new aesthetic; each new aesthetic is routed by yet the next reality. Crispin's brief experiment in an aesthetic of parrot-squawks, for example, is dismissed as a "trifle," followed quickly by a no less disastrous exposure to a tropical thunderstorm. The "connoisseur of elemental fate" flees, of all places, to a cathedral, in the safety of which he hears in the storm

> . . . the quintessential fact, the note
> Of Vulcan, that a valet seeks to own,
> The thing that makes him envious in phrase.
> (CP 33)

Just as Crispin was made new by the "speech belched out of hoary darks" at sea, so now he feels freed:

> . . . His mind was free
> And more than free, elate, intent, profound
> And studious of a self possessing him,
> That was not in him in the crusty town
> From which he sailed.

A new reality, a new self, and a new aesthetic:

> . . . the thunder, lapsing in its clap,
> Let down gigantic quavers of its voice,
> For Crispin to vociferate again.

Still in search of a "relentless contact" with reality, Crispin sets off for America, thinking it a place that might give the "liaison, the blissful liaison, / Between himself and his environment" (CP 34). America, in Crispin's mind, is polar North, a reality absolutely clean of "jagged sides" and "juicy" seeds:

The spring came there in clinking pannicles
Of half-dissolving frost, the summer came,
If ever, whisked and wet, not ripening,
Before the winter's vacancy returned.

(CP 34)

Like Stevens writing "The Snow Man," Crispin is now a nihilist
in search of the "fecund minimum" which he thinks he will find
in North America. His mental picture is, of course, totally wrong;
instead of the gaunt and lank reality he was seeking, he finds a
spring clothed in "veils," "Irised in dew." Another inaccessible
reality here, this one full of the decay, arrant stinks, rankness,
and rotting of a climate given to seasonal change. These provide a
new "curriculum" for Crispin, ever willing to learn, ever "renewed," ever concocting new aesthetic doctrine:

It purified. It made him see how much
Of what he saw he never saw at all.
He gripped more closely the essential prose
As being, in a world so falsified,
The one integrity for him, the one
Discovery still possible to make.

(CP 36)

Although it has been clear to us from the beginning that Cris-
pin's ideas depend upon his environment, it is only now that
Crispin himself recognizes that "his soil is man's intelligence."
This becomes the premise of his artistic colony of local colorists:

The man in Georgia waking among pines
Should be pine-spokesman. The responsive man,
Planting his pristine cores in Florida,
Should prick thereof, not on the psaltery
But on the banjo's categorical gut.

(CP 38)

He enthusiastically plans everything, from "broadest instances" to "smart detail." But the failure to grasp present reality by planning a future colony is predictable:

> These bland excursions into time to come,
> Related in romance to backward flights,
>
> .   .   .   .
>
> Contained in their afflatus the reproach
> That first drove Crispin to his wandering.
>
>   (CP 39)

The "reproach" is simply that this colony, like all his other projections of himself upon reality, is fictive, romantic, false—an "afflatus."

Crispin finds himself receding by slow degrees from a philosophical notion of "realism" to the reality of "things within his actual eye" (CP 40). All that is left of Crispin's aesthetic plan ("shall") is "is," life in its particulars:

> The words of things entangle and confuse.
> The plum survives its poems.
>
>   (CP 41)

Who once planned "loquacious columns by the ructive sea" now concedes defeat before a mere plum. Defeated but not tragic, jovial Crispin has travelled from Bordeaux to Carolina to end up about where he began: "quilted to his poll." Though he has gained experience, he has not gained reality, for the head remains covered; the eye, a barber's eye.

Crispin, throughout the poem a passive figure to whom reality has happened, now becomes engulfed in events: a cabin "shuffles up" and a "primsy blond" arrives with no apparent effort on Crispin's part. Stevens envelopes Crispin's domesticity in metaphors of currency that suggest sexual returns as well as financial ones: "the sun, true fortuner / . . . gives a humped return / Exchequering from piebald fiscs unkeyed" (CP 43). The "returns" on this domestic banking are "chits": daughters with curls. Instead of a writer's colony, Crispin has a "nice shady home"; instead of "chits upon a cloudy knee," he has "chits" for his "jigging"—daughters instead of poems. His life becomes a parody of his idea of the colony, for he has so effectively colonized that he is "sharply stopped / In the door-yard by his own capacious bloom." Crispin has subsided into a quotidian existence that "saps philosophers" because it overwhelms them in particulars. His fate here resembles the conclusion of "Metaphors of a Magnifico," rewritten on a mock-epic scale.

Stevens' final pronouncement on Crispin begins with an elaborate conditional clause ("if the music sticks, if the anecdote / Is false, if . . .") which suggests Crispin has been a profitless philosopher who has consistently distorted and falsified the "text" of his life with "glosses" ("Glozing his life with after-shining flicks"). The narrator concludes:

> . . . What can all this matter since
> The relation comes, benignly, to its end?

A pause follows, and then the narrator (or Stevens himself?) comments, "So may the relation of each man be clipped," suggesting the degree to which Crispin is an "anecdotal" character, a compendium, a modern Everyman. Both "relation" and "clipped" bristle with ambiguity, for the "relation" (story, narrative, relation to the world of reality) is "clipped": cut short, curtailed, clipped out (as in a newspaper clipping), shorn (as in the barber motif) or cheated (as in the financial metaphor). Crispin's heroic attempts at contact with reality are reduced to one or another metaphor of distortion: he has been "glozing his life," and viewing the world "from a fancy gorged / By apparitions." But then, each of Crispin's aesthetic positions has been previously denounced:"evasion,""ruse,""whim,""fiction,""afflatus"and"trinket pasticcio" are the products of the imagination.

This, then, is the story of Crispin, "profitless philosopher." Perhaps we should turn away with a puzzled shrug, like the bitterly indifferent narrator. But there is a good deal more than paraphrasable content to this poem, with its strange title, "The Comedian as the Letter C." Crispin is obviously the comedian, having no share in or desire for the dignified tragic fate. The "Letter C" refers to Crispin, cipher for miniscule man. More importantly, however, the title refers to the game Stevens is playing with the letter "c" which clacks and clickers its way throughout the poem. When we consider the sound of the poem separately from its subject, we can understand some of Stevens' diction: "suzerain" over sovereign, "cozener" instead of sly knave, and "fiscs unkeyed" for treasury. For years, the poem was puzzled out on the basis of its content; when Stevens' letters were published, they pointed out what should have been obvious, but was not: "As Crispin moves through the poem," Stevens wrote to Hi Simons, "the sounds of the letter C accompany him. . . . The sounds of the letter C include all related or derivative sounds. For instance, X, TS and Z." In a postscript, he added, "The natural effect of the variety of sounds of the letter C is a comic effect" (L 351–52). Many years later, when he wrote to Renato Poggioli about the difficulty of translating the poem for anything except the *sense* of it, Stevens said,

> The central figure is an every-day man who lives a life without the slightest adventure except that he lives it in a poetic atmosphere as we all do. This point makes it necessary for a translator to try to reproduce the every-day plainness of the central figure and the plush, so to speak, of his stage. (L 778)

The importance of this comment, in so far as so late a comment can safely be applied to so early a poem, is that the plain figure of Crispin moves on an elaborate "plush" stage created by his imagination: the sounds of the letter C are Crispin's additions of himself to the world he views. Each of Crispin's "pronunciamentos," then, is nothing more than a subjective view of the reality he happens to be in at the moment. If Crispin is c miniscule, C magiscule is Sea, the vast reality that remains separate in spite of our imaginative attempts to embrace it. The sound and the sense of "The Comedian as the Letter C" posit two poles of Stevens' theme: the subjectively projected stage of reality that imagination creates, and the sonorous sea, whose "hoary belchings" create a "vocable thing" that mocks our attempts to impose wordy meanings.

"The Comedian" was written shortly before the publication of *Harmonium*, and shows Stevens thoroughly conscious of his own development. The history of Crispin's travels is the history of Stevens' various definitions of reality, from blank nothing to teeming plurality. That he could bring each of these definitions to bear in Crispin's story, and subject each of them to ridicule along with Crispin's current aesthetic doctrine, suggests that Stevens was at a dead end. He couldn't accept Crispin's fate—a nonpoetic existence in a "reality" that clearly set his teeth on edge—nor could he resign himself to the imaginative embroidery that he had shown in "The Comedian" to be a distorting "flick," an "apparition." It is interesting that as he approached this dead end during the composition of "The Comedian," all manner of fine poems resulted: "The Ordinary Women," "Bantams in Pine-Woods," "A High-Toned Old Christian Woman," and "The Emperor of Ice-Cream," to mention only the most famous. Not only do they exhibit Stevens' fondness for the variant sounds of c, they also swing back and forth between "sun and moon," between accepting stark reality and celebrating the imagination.

In spite of the shorter gifts derived from the writing of "The Comedian," Stevens had written himself into an aesthetic corner, both rejecting "mental moonlight" and recoiling from reality. We can sense his growing dismay in the letters; even during the composition of "The Comedian," Stevens seemed uneasy: "I expect that after a while Crispin . . . will become rudimentary and abhorrent" (L 230). Working on the selection of poems for *Harmonium*, Stevens remarked: "Gathering together the things for my book has been so depressing. . . . All my earlier things seem like horrid cocoons from which later abortive insects have sprung. The book will amount to nothing, except that it may teach me something"(L 231). That was, unfortunately, a prophetic remark. Eclipsed by *The Waste Land* and *Ulysses* (1922), competing with a host of distinguished books (among them Cummings' *Tulips and Chimneys* and Williams' *Spring and All*), *Harmonium* received little notice, and that little was largely unfavorable. Stevens remarked to a friend, "My royalties for the first half of 1924 amounted to $6.70. I shall have to charter a boat and take my friends around the world" (L 243). It was not the lack of royalties that hurt, but the lack of acceptance. For whatever combination of reasons—the indifferent reception of *Harmonium*, his growing responsibilities at the insurance company, the birth of his daughter in 1924, or the aesthetic impasse he arrived at by the end of "The Comedian"—Stevens apparently stopped writing altogether for six or seven years.

CHAPTER 4

Hero-Hymns

"As barbarism is the era of *fact*, so the era of
order must necessarily be the reign of *fiction.*"
                                    —*Paul Valéry* [1]

Harmonium effectively ended in North Carolina, with Crispin
settling into a silent domesticity. In the interval between "The
Comedian as the Letter C" and the earliest poems of the next
volume, *Ideas of Order,* Stevens had probably changed little; he
was, if anything, more secure domestically and financially. But
the world had changed drastically, and Stevens reacted to it.
Ideas of Order (1936), *The Man With the Blue Guitar* (1937), and
Parts of a World (1942) show the evolution of a poet who felt
compelled to transform a barbarous reality into a fictive order,
and to transform it not only for himself but for his audience.
Looking back at *Harmonium* from the perspective of the Great
Depression, Stevens declared it "pure poetry" and said that "we
live in a different time, and life means a good deal more to us
now-a-days than literature does" (L 288). "Pure poetry" was not
an adequate response to the political and social turmoil around

him, and Stevens set out to expand the range of his poetry to include more of "life."

Signalling his new direction, he put "Farewell to Florida" as the first poem in the 1936 edition of *Ideas of Order*. In the poem, Stevens bids farewell to the moon, the "oceanic" nights, and the "sepulchral" soil of the Southern landscape that had played so important a role in *Harmonium*. Stevens declares his ambivalence: "I hated the vivid blooms" and "I loved her once." But his voyage North is no less ambivalent, for he travels not toward a pure blankness of "The Snow Man" but toward a "wintry slime." Rejecting his courtship of the symbolic woman as a kind of slavery, Stevens simultaneously proclaims his freedom and his new bondage:

> To be free again, to return to the violent mind
> That is their mind, these men, and that will bind
> Me round, carry me, misty deck, carry me.

With its ambivalent speaker hailing a "slime of men in crowds" and a freedom that will bind him round, "Farewell to Florida" is a fairly accurate log of the distresses Stevens encountered on his poetic voyage North. Intent on making a social commitment and on giving up the symbolic South of imagination, he nevertheless felt that the reality he was embracing was basically disgusting— "slimy."

Stevens' ambivalence indicates his reaction to the social and political turmoil of the thirties. Thinking about the role of the poet in a socially troubled time and poignantly aware that the poet's role might be to provide images of order for mobs of men who were "crying without knowing for what" (CP 122), Stevens nevertheless felt himself a "most inappropriate man / In a most unpropitious place" (CP 120). Poem after poem registers a sweeping sense of disorder felt not only by those "swarms of men" but also by the speaker of the poems. Many of the "order" poems define an order that would, by its very nature, exclude the people Stevens perceived most needed an order, the masses. Such a poem is "How to Live. What to Do." Stevens was particularly fond of it "because it so definitely represents my way of thinking" (L 293). That "way of thinking" was to find nobility in things as they are, uncrowned by myths or gods. Stevens' "man and his companion" find the "heroic height" and it is empty of God and his angels. It is also, we note, empty of people:

> There was the cold wind and the sound
> It made, away from the muck of the land
> That they had left, heroic sound
> Joyous and jubilant and sure.

The beginning of perceived order, then, occurs away from and above "the muck of the land."

Stevens wanted to make a social commitment with his poetry but recoiled from the "mobs of men" and the "muck of the land." His conflict explains much about the growing abstractness of his poetry; he had to "abstract" the "mobs" into the more palatable "idea of man." The first explicit mention of this abstraction occurs in "A Thought Revolved," from *The Man With the Blue Guitar* (1937). The poet who proclaims the "era of the idea of man" will sing for and of man:

> . . . hero-hymns,
> Chorals for mountain voices and the moral chant,
> Happy rather than holy but happy-high,
> Day hymns instead of constellated rhymes,
> Hymns of the struggle of the idea of god
> And the idea of man, the mystic garden and
> The middling beast, the garden of paradise
> And he that created the garden and peopled it.
>   (CP 185)

It is important to an understanding of Stevens' later work to recognize not only the value he attached to poetic imagination, but
the extent to which he insisted it was a capacity in *all* men. "He
that created the garden and peopled it," he says in this poem; he
means not merely the poet of vast imagination, but any man. In
his "Adagia," Stevens calls man "this happy creature—It is he
that invented the Gods. It is he that put into their mouths the
only words they have ever spoken" (OP 167). Similar statements
in "Adagia" and the poetry suggest that Stevens' debunking of
god- and heaven-myths is less an attempt to show their invalidity
than to demonstrate man's myth-making power at its real source:

> God is a postulate of the ego.
> (OP 171)

and

> The mind that in heaven created the earth and the mind that on
> earth created heaven were, as it happened, one.
>
> (OP 176)

These propositions confirm the development in the poetry of a
humanism that respects man because of his imagination, because
of his capacity to create fictions.

Stevens was aware, too, that few people recognized their own
imaginative projections:

> It is easy to suppose that few people realize on that occasion, which
> comes to all of us, when we look at the blue sky for the first time,
> that is to say: not merely see it, but look at it and experience it and
> for the first time have a sense that we live in the center of a physical
> poetry, a geography that would be intolerable except for the non-
> geography that exists there—few people realize that they are look-

ing at the world of their own thoughts and the world of their own feelings.

(NA 65–66)

This activity of the imagination—a faculty in every person— Stevens comes to think of as poetic activity; it does not matter whether it is written down. What distinguishes the "poet" from the rest of us is his "capable" imagination. Stevens' idea of the poet belongs to the Romantic tradition of Shelley's poet as "unacknowledged legislator of mankind." But Stevens' Romantic aesthetic shares a good deal with modern psychology, especially with Jung's "collective unconscious." Jung claims that the artist "is the 'collective man'—one who carries and shapes the unconscious psychic life of mankind." [2] Rejecting any "social obligation" for the poet, Stevens begins to talk in similar terms:

What is his function? Certainly it is not to lead people out of the confusion in which they find themselves. . . . I think that his function is to make his imagination theirs and that he fulfills himself only as he sees his imagination become the light in the minds of others. His role, in short, is to help people to live their lives.

(NA 29)

With such a definition, art could serve a redemptive function without enlisting itself to political banners or social movements.

As he worked out his definition of the poet's function, Stevens also tried to clarify what he meant by "imagination," that faculty he was equating with poetry. His vast aims for the poet depended on a definition of imagination as a total faculty. Consider this assertion in "The Figure of the Youth as Virile Poet":

We have been referring constantly to the simple figure of the youth, in his character of poet, as virile poet. The reason for this is that if,

> for the poet, the imagination is paramount, and if he dwells apart in
> his imagination, as the philosopher dwells in his reason, and as the
> priest dwells in his belief, the masculine nature that we propose for
> one that must be the master of our lives will be lost.
>
> (NA 66)

Stevens' insistence on the "virility" of the poet goes hand in hand
with his notion of the "masculine" imagination: one informed by
reason and belief. By the forties, Stevens no longer mocks sterile
rationalists; he no longer defends poetry against reason. Rather
he unites them in the "masculine" imagination and considers the
man who has such a faculty a kind of hero. He would be heroic
because he would be the maker of beliefs, in the sense that I. A.
Richards meant when he compared "make-believe" to "faith." [3]

The equation of "faith" with "belief in a fiction" was part of the
psychological and philosophical climate in which Stevens lived.
Nietzsche's famous declaration that "God is dead" is less trou-
bling than his idea that error is a condition of knowing and feeling; for Nietzsche, all beliefs and convictions become "regulative
fictions." [4] Ernst Cassirer, whose *Essay on Man* Stevens quotes
in an essay, proposed the principle of symbolic transformation,
whereby the symbol is not an aspect of reality; it *is* reality. In
1941 when Stevens delivered "The Noble Rider and the Sound of
Words" at a Princeton Symposium, Philip Wheelwright had been
the first speaker. His paper was titled "Poetry, Myth and Reality." Like Stevens, Wheelwright was convinced that the symposium was about more than "specimens" of poetry; for
Wheelwright, "What matters is the myth-consciousness of the
next generations, the spiritual seed that we plant in our children.
. . . On that depend the possibilities of future greatness—in poetry and in everything else." [5] Wheelwright's *rational* call to
mythic consciousness is, however, quite different from Stevens'
more Nietzschean notion:

What makes the poet the potent figure that he is, or was, or ought to be, is that he creates the world to which we turn incessantly and without knowing it and that he gives to life the supreme fictions without which we are unable to conceive of it.

(NA 31)

With the wisdom of hindsight gained from Stevens' essays of the forties, we can see the crucial development from *Ideas of Order* to "The Man With the Blue Guitar." The earlier poems seek a fixed order in a harsh reality, while the later one depicts the masculine maker of beliefs. The poem achieves no ordered reality but renders a continual shaping, a continual exchange between those things being shaped and the shaper—the guitarist. Using the guitarist as a symbol of the poet and his tune as the symbol of the ongoing imaginative process, Stevens abstracts an entire generation's needs and desires into a tune: our project is to play "ourselves in the tune as if in space." That abstraction permits Stevens to wrestle with the importance of art in a time of violent reality, not by enlisting art in the service of the "masses," but by considering "things as they are" and how they might be changed by the blue guitar. The guitarist is a wonderfully versatile tool for simultaneously talking about poetic imagination and the role of the poet. Consider canto XII, for example:

> Tom-tom, c'est moi. The blue guitar
> And I are one. The orchestra
>
> Fills the high hall with shuffling men
> High as the hall. The whirling noise
>
> Of a multitude dwindles, all said,
> To his breath that lies awake at night.

With an echo of Louis' imperial "L'état, c'est moi," Stevens replaces the monarch with the artist, who is inseparable from his art. That art, by evoking responses from others, creates an "orchestra" of feelings. Pivoting the meaning on his two-line divisions, Stevens then shows that this orchestration is all contained in the mental activity of the artist, as the "whirling noise" of the multitude dwindles to the "breath that lies awake at night." The ironical guitarist similarly wonders, "A million people on one string?" and the answer is, implicitly, yes, a million people—their feelings, hopes, and dreams composed in a tune. Such music serves a public function only in the sense that the guitarist offers a choice of dreams to a generation whose dreams are "aviled / In the mud, in Monday's dirty light." The artist provides moments when we choose between reality and reality transfigured by imagination:

> The moments when we choose to play
> The imagined pine, the imagined jay.

"The Man With the Blue Guitar" is a successfully "social" poem only because Stevens has retreated from the ideology of the early 30s and returned to his favorite theme: the struggle between imagination and reality. He starts the poem with two "voices," the guitarist's (for imagination) and the people's (for reality). But both voices are so obviously Stevens' own that he quickly drops the pretext of dialogue. It ceases to be a poem about an adversary relationship and becomes a poem about Stevens' own aims and theories. Shaping and defining the interdependence of imagination and reality, he creates another shaper and definer, the guitarist.[6] At one remove from Stevens himself, the guitarist is in turn searching for another shaper: the hero. This "bronze hero" is significant because it replaces the symbol of the woman with a masculine symbol. The object of the poet's search is no longer the alluring passivity of the symbolic woman but the ongoing activity of the masculine. Moreover, the guitarist senses that to reach the hero is to reach "through him almost to man." Thus the heroic figure is a telescoping device whereby Stevens creates both the excellent imagining man and the representative man among men; both the symbol and that which it symbolizes. This "hero" is the first step toward the creation of a masculine figure who will represent the highest imagination, the collective imagination.

In terms of Stevens' later poetry, the important theme of "The Man With the Blue Guitar" is that the guitarist is creator of other people's dreams. He himself must be—or create—a capable "dreamer," a man of powerful imagination. Stevens was to speak frequently in the 1940s of the "violence from within that protects us from a violence without" (NA 36). "The Man With the Blue Guitar" is the first plumbing of that violent self: "It is / An animal." This clawed and fanged beast of the self Stevens offers in contradiction to traditional notions of the mind: "angelic ones / Speak of the soul, the mind." The violent self can only make its existence known on the blue guitar: "On that its claws propound, its fangs / Articulate its desert days" (XVII).

Recreating the anima as animal is the necessary preliminary to the self facing the violent not-self:

> That I may reduce the monster to
> Myself, and then may be myself
>
> In face of the monster.

In this canto (XIX), Stevens is using a monster image to represent reality, but the echoes from the preceding cantos are important, for that monster is also the violent self. The repeated images cause a dovetailing, for the self wishes that its "dreams" were "objects" and that reality (the monster) were itself. The repeated syntax of the two cantos (XVIII and XIX) further suggests the desire to overcome the dichotomy between self and world:

> A dream   In face of the object
>
> Be myself   In face of the monster

Canto XIX struggles to stabilize the relation between "two things" and "two together as one." Stevens begins by reducing the monster to the self and ends by playing not of the self but of the monster:

> That I may reduce the monster to
> Myself, and then may be myself
>
> In face of the monster, be more than part
> Of it, more than the monstrous player of
>
> One of its monstrous lutes, not be
> Alone, but reduce the monster and be,
>
> Two things, the two together as one,
> And play of the monster and of myself,
>
> Or better not of myself at all,
> But of that as its intelligence,
>
> Being the lion in the lute
> Before the lion locked in stone.

The wishful phrase, "that I may," governs this fierce syntactical struggle as well as the alliterated rhythms that suggest a resolution.

In *Parts of a World*, the lion image occurs again, in the poem proclaiming that "Poetry is a Destructive Force." The poem speaks of the beastly forces within a man: "It is a thing to have, / A lion, an ox in his breast, / To feel it breathing there." The poem concludes:

The lion sleeps in the sun.
Its nose is on its paws.
It can kill a man.

Interestingly enough, Jung was at about this time giving a series of lectures at Yale, arguing for the "reality" of the imagination:

Even if a neurosis had no cause at all other than imagination, it would none the less be a very real thing. If a man imagined that I was his arch-enemy and killed me, I should be dead on account of mere imagination. Imaginary conditions do exist and they may be just as real and just as harmful or dangerous as physical conditions. . . . Although the mind cannot apprehend its own form of existence, owing to the lack of an Archimedean point outside, it nevertheless exists. Not only does the psyche exist, it is existence itself.[7]

While Jung is talking about neurosis and Stevens about poetry, both men agree that the psyche is "existence itself." "Imagination," "fantasy," "make-believe"—these terms do not conjure up the power or potentially destructive forces of that second self which Jung is urging his audience to recognize and which Stevens is calling the very power of poetry.

Stevens associated the harnessing of this power with a figure that occurs throughout the poetry and prose of the forties: the "noble rider," the "virile youth," the "philosophers' man." Each of these figures is capable of make-believe: creating belief. "Mrs. Alfred Uruguay" shows how much the creation of this "noble rider" changed the symbolic landscape of Stevens' poetry, for everything associated with the symbolic woman—moonlight, elegant clothes, and the search for imaginatively-apprehended reality—has become suspect. Mrs. Uruguay, elegantly dressed and with a significantly Southern name, quests for a kind of Platonic reality. In her ascent, imagination's moonlight becomes associated with mud:

> . . . "I have said no
> To everything, in order to get at myself.
> I have wiped away moonlight like mud."

Her search for reality—apparently both inner and outer—is similar to Stevens' in *Harmonium;* in this later volume, her imaginative quest is so ridiculous that it dirties the moonlight. Given Stevens' habitual symbols, we can interpret his rejection of Mrs. Uruguay as a rejection of the imagination associated with South, moonlight, and clothes. By contrast, the "noble rider" is poorly dressed, riding toward the sun—symbol of reality—and "phosphorescent" with imagination. Unlike Mrs. Uruguay's nay-saying, which prevents her finding anything more than bare "to be," the noble rider's imagination creates the place toward which he rushes: "the imagined land."

The appearance of the "noble rider" also changes the tone in which Stevens speaks of the "supreme fiction," one of the enduring themes in his poetry. During *Harmonium,* Stevens had two voices for offering the fiction: ironic and sacramental. For example, he uses a wickedly playful voice in "A High-Toned Old Christian Woman": "Poetry is the supreme fiction, madame." But this is an ironic tango ("Palm for palm, / Madame, we are where we began") whose point is less to affirm the speaker's supreme fiction than ironically to show that the widow has one too: "fictive things / Wink as they will. Wink most when widows wince." In "Sunday Morning," by contrast, Stevens uses a sacramental voice, almost unique in his work, to show that divinity resides in the self:

> Divinity must live within herself:
> Passions of rain, or moods in falling snow;
> Grievings in loneliness, or unsubdued
> Elations when the forest blooms; gusty
> Emotions on wet roads on autumn nights;

> All pleasures and all pains, remembering
> The bough of summer and the winter branch.
> These are the measures destined for her soul.

Here Stevens has put on a "grand style," as Helen Vendler says, donning the "robes of Wordsworth and Keats" to buy sublimity at the cost of his typical ironic gesture.[8]

Irony and sacrament are both abandoned, however, in the later "philosophical" tone. Stevens is on the one hand more sure of his supreme fiction and on the other hand less intent on making man a substitute for the gods than on just making for him the "idea of man." "Asides on the Oboe," for instance, in which the supreme fiction is named, has neither the divinity-seeking nor the debunking voice, but rather a serious, matter-of-fact tone:

> The prologues are over. It is a question, now,
> Of final belief. So, say that final belief
> Must be in a fiction. It is time to choose.

In "Asides on the Oboe," the fiction that Stevens proffers is the "impossible possible philosophers' man." A fiction? A "thing" created by the imagination? Certainly, but "real" too in the sense that Jung meant and real also in the sense that this central man is nothing but us—an "idea of man."

Rejecting the obsolete fictions, Stevens offers a new one, the hero, and defends his choice:

> If you say on the hautboy man is not enough,
> Can never stand as god, is ever wrong
> In the end, however naked, tall, there is still
> The impossible possible philosophers' man.

A product of philosophy and reason, as well as of the imagination, this philosophers' man seems a man-myth, the center of man's achievement, yet not a god. He is:

> The man who has had the time to think enough,
> The central man, the human globe, responsive
> As a mirror with a voice.

Clearly ourselves, this "human globe" also seems to be the earth, or the way man perceives the earth, as a "mirror with a voice." He *is* us, at the same time he represents our perceiving; as part of the supreme fiction, this hero is an "identity" for the thing of the imagination.

In "Chocorua to Its Neighbor," another poem in which Stevens creates the central man as hero, the mountain comments that to perceive this hero is "to perceive men without reference to their form" and that to "think of him destroyed the body's form." Like "Asides on the Oboe," the poem creates a representative figure who might be the vast sum of humanity's parts. The time and occasion of his appearance suggest that he is some kind of collective man:

> . . . He came from out of sleep.
> He rose because men wanted him to be.

This "trash of sleep" will disappear with day, and yet remain as man's "common self, interior fons." The vocabulary here, the occasion of the hero's appearance, and the effect—"the feeling of him was the feel of day"—all suggest some version of a lively collective unconscious projected by sleeping humanity. A fiction, this hero doubles back to a belief in man himself.

The mountain that alone "perceives" him is probably the "human mountain" out of which the captain, the cardinal, the scholar, and this hero are all "fetched." The identity of Chorcorua as a human mountain clarifies the relationship between it and the hero. The hero is "cloud-casual . . . / But resting on me, thinking in my snow." The mountain is, perhaps, a collection of humanity, not a collective representative: "large / In my presence, the companion of presences / Greater than mine." The hero grows out of the human mountain, rests on its eminence, the summary of men's wishes. Unlike the mountain, then, which might be characterized as the totality of being, the hero is "rugged roy" of "human realizing," a potential of potentials.

This heroic symbol provides a "largeness lived and not conceived." And yet the poem also insistently rejects those very characteristics that might be perceived; denying substance, form, and element to the hero, the mountain gives us only a "prodigious shadow." If, then, he is "lived and not conceived," we are in the realm of the mind, which deals with the real but not conventionally perceptible. Jung had discussed this very difficulty when he said, "Although the mind cannot apprehend its own form of existence, owing to the lack of an Archimedean point outside, it nevertheless exists. . . . It is existence itself." [9] So too Stevens' hero: "an eminence, / But of nothing." During the day he remains not as a master-father but as

> . . . bare brother, megalfrere,
> Or by whatever boorish name a man
> Might call the common self.

"Megalfrere" suggests his ambiguous status: megalo-frere means large brother; m'égal-frère means my equal brother. Both source (fons) and foundation (fond), he is that very vehicle for dissolving perception and conception together in the nongeography of the self: "Where / He is, the air changes and grows fresh to breathe." Because he is a means of knowing that we live in the center of a physical universe which we see only through our own thoughts and feelings, this hero is "rugged roy"—king of men's realizations, integrator of values and summary of wishes.

Stevens' insistence on a distinction between conception (a mind-invented abstraction) and perception (the mind stimulated by external stimuli) is crucial. A similar distinction occurs toward the end of "The Man With the Blue Guitar":

> And say of what you see in the dark

> That it is this or that it is that,
> But do not use the rotted names.

The poem operates at the level of gesture, pointing out toward the "that," the new thing that must be named and that must, just as urgently, be unnamed. "Say of what you see in the dark" indicates that this new reality cannot be merely pointed out; it exists beyond the realm of the object. In order to talk about ideas or absent things, we rely on language; any naming, however, takes an object out of the "that" world—gesture—and transforms it into a *concept*.

Words represent both man's freedom and his bondage. William James refers to our power to frame abstract concepts as "one of the sublimest of our human prerogatives," but he is quick to point out the seductive danger of this power: "Concepts, first employed to make things intelligible, are clung to even when they make them unintelligible." [10] Not only is the immediate experience a mere "that," it is also in flux. To fix the experience in the act of naming it, to lend it a conceptual frame, is to alter its durational aspect. But naming—or language—is all we have, even to describe that durational aspect of experience.

This is the paradox Stevens finds himself in when he writes a poem like "The Latest Freed Man." The man experiences a moment "at the centre of reality" because he experiences a moment of being without language: "To be without a description of to be." The excitement of "everything bulging and blazing and big in itself" comes, the poem would insist, from a wordless, doctrineless participation in reality—but one that is, paradoxically, wonderfully expressed in this verbal construct. That wordless ephemeral moment endures only in words.

Some philosophers of language argue that speaking brings a thing into existence, that naming a thing makes it real to the perceiver. [11] The project for metaphor, then, becomes a way of naming a thing anew, or of naming a new thing. When Stevens says "the tongue is an eye," he puts himself firmly in agreement with them. But more often his poetry demonstrates or complains about the inadequacies of language to describe either the self or the world.

The insistence on notifying the reader that a poem is "language-bound" might be predicted from a similar preoccupation in *Harmonium*, but the early elegance gives way to this almost palpable wrestle in "The Man With the Blue Guitar":

> The earth is not earth but a stone,
> Not the mother that held men as they fell
>
> But stone, but like a stone, no: not
> The mother, but an oppressor, but like
>
> An oppressor that grudges them their death.

To say that earth is "not the mother" is to reject an old metaphor; to say "not / The mother, but an oppressor, but like / An oppressor" is to reject both the old and the new metaphor in favor of explicit similes that demonstrate the inadequacy of language to define reality.

Convinced, at least some of the time, that the "poses of speech, of paint, / Of music" are merely additions to reality, Stevens begins to play at the edge of language, where the mind plays. In "Autumn Refrain," for example, the presence of the definite article signals the "wordiness" of the concept—that it is a word, and not the thing itself:

> And grackles gone and sorrows of *the* sun,
> The sorrows of sun, too, gone . . . *the* moon and moon,
> The yellow moon of words about the nightingale.
>
> (my italics)

The pedantic speaker of "Extracts from Addresses to the Academy of Fine Ideas" puts the point exactly:

> . . . Compare the silent rose of the sun
> And rain, the blood-rose living in its smell,
> With this paper, this dust. That states the point.

Only in the "difference between the and an" (CP 255) can Stevens find the poetry of the mind trying to live inside of reality.

More and more, Stevens' poetry comes to be about poetry, but about it in the special sense that was taking shape for him: "Poetry is the imagination of life" (NA 65). Poems such as "Poems of Our Climate" and "The Glass of Water" are like glosses on the text of that theoretical poem, "Of Modern Poetry." All of them imitate the "mind in the act of finding / What will suffice." "In the act" is accurate: Stevens' poetry has become increasingly gerundive, mimicking the activity of the mind as it adopts a position, finds it unsatisfactory, and flits to another, then another. If a poem does take a particular stance, Stevens is sure to indicate its ephemeral duration: "It can never be satisfied, the mind, never" (CP 247). And this flitting provides the very rhythms of the long poems; in "The Man With the Blue Guitar," the world-reality provides a rock "To which his imagination returned, / From which it sped, a bar in space."

"In the act" also initiates the theatrical metaphor in "Of Modern Poetry," a metaphor which provides Stevens with excellent mileage. The first use is historical: the old scripts are useless now; the past is a souvenir. Stevens frequently compares the past and present *stages* of life, always suggesting that we have lost our scripts, that the old myths and traditions are useless. He knows they are outmoded in the same way Paul Valéry does when he defines modern men as living "on familiar terms with many contraries waiting in the penumbra of his mind and coming by turns onto the stage." [12] In the poem, the "stage" is both the mind and the poem, each trying to find a script. Improvising, the actor (both mind and poem again) will "speak words that . . . / In the delicatest ear of the mind, repeat, / Exactly, that which it wants to hear." That "invisible audience" hearing what it wants to hear is both the mind and the reader of the poem. The theatrical metaphor thus gives Stevens a telescoping device; he can talk about the modern mind in the same breath that he is talking about his favorite topic of the forties—poet, poem, and audience.

In echoes of "The Man With the Blue Guitar," "Of Modern Poetry" considers the poet "A metaphysician in the dark, twanging / An instrument." The strumming guitarist and the improvising actor suggest that for Stevens poetry is less about "what will suffice" than about the "act of the mind" finding it. The climax of the poem occurs when Stevens suggests the possible contentment of the mind:

> Sounds passing through sudden rightnesses, wholly
> Containing the mind, below which it cannot descend,
> Beyond which it has no will to rise.

Stevens cannot say *what* the mind wants to hear; he must be content to write *about* a poetry that would express what the mind wants to hear, and to render the satisfaction that *might* ensue. Stevens' is a conditional world indeed.

"Reality is not that external scene," Stevens says in "The Noble Rider and the Sound of Words," "but the life that is lived in it"

(NA 25). The intuition that "reality" is simply the life we are living provides some of Stevens' finest moments, coming as they do
after a long struggle with syntax or image. In "The Man With the
Blue Guitar," there is a kind of rhapsody about saying "things are
as I think they are / And say they are on the blue guitar" because
the wrestle between the two has been so terrific. Similarly in
"The Man on the Dump," we receive Stevens' "truth": "the the."
Not "*the* truth," for Stevens knows, along with the philosopher
William James, that there is no such thing as "the truth." And
also not *the* man, *the* object or *the* image; just the *the:* particular
experience unspecified. To provide the concrete experience that
constitutes "the the" might void the poem's power to express the
idea behind the immediate experience. The distinction can be
readily seen in a comparison of Stevens and William Carlos Williams. Williams' famous "The Red Wheelbarrow" is a poem of the
mind, but how different from Stevens:

> so much depends
> upon
>
> a red wheel
> barrow
>
> glazed with rain
> water
>
> beside the white
> chickens. [13]

The banality of the scene hardly strikes us, so sparkling and tense
are Williams' line breaks. The commonplace objects are offered
to the imagination's scrutiny: "so much depends." This is a poem,
then, about the aesthetics of our consciousness; it dramatizes one
moment when the mind interacts with its environment. What
depends, though, and for whom? It matters little whether we

decide that a farmer, a doctor, or a poet is looking at a red wheel-barrow; whether a crop, a life, or an aesthetic relationship derives from the looking. The dynamism of the poem lives in the tension between mental consciousness ("so much depends") and the "dependent" concretions that follow. Stevens, by contrast, rarely risks the intrusion of so concrete an object as a wheelbarrow, rarely risks the reader's too specific enquiry about context. Too suspicious of images or metaphors to allow them to entirely carry a poem, Stevens relies on a comment about the image or metaphor: "the the."

I think this comparison accounts for the difficulties of Stevens' later style. It is the result of both his distrust of language and his theorizing about poetry. In 1935, he wrote to one correspondent, "It is difficult for me to think and not to think abstractly. Consequently, in order to avoid abstractions, in writing, I search out instinctively things that express the abstract and yet are not in themselves abstractions" (L 290). I pointed out a number of Stevens' habitual symbols in *Harmonium:* geographical, diurnal and seasonal images, to name a few. Stevens begins to use these symbols as "code" words, detached from the contexts that gave them their original meaning. We must know something of what Stevens means by sun and moon, for example, in order to arrive at the meaning of this cryptic canto in "The Man With the Blue Guitar":

> It is the sun that shares our works.
> The moon shares nothing. It is a sea.

It is fairly easy to trace Stevens' impulse to pillage his own poetry for these symbols. The delightful "Disillusionment of Ten O'Clock," an early poem in *Harmonium*, depends on the contrast between the "white night-gowns" of the unimaginative sleepers and the colorful zany nightgowns they might have. The contrast is simply between color and noncolor; we would go astray to bring a "thesis" to the poem on the basis of its "green rings" and "red weather." But by 1918, in "Le Monocle de Mon Oncle," Stevens' famous color-coding is clearly present in those birds whose colors insistently suggest something more than mere color: the "red bird" of reality, the "blue pigeon" of imagination, and the "white pigeon" of fading existence. Perhaps the most self-consciously color-coded poem in *Harmonium* is "Anecdote of the Prince of Peacocks," written about the time of the last poems of *Harmonium:*

> . . . "Why are you red
> In this milky blue?"
> I said.
> "Why sun-colored,
> As if awake
> In the midst of sleep?"

We should be prepared, then, for the beginning of "The Man With the Blue Guitar":

> The man bent over his guitar,
> A shearsman of sorts. The day was green.

Although Stevens' guitarist bears a lively resemblance to Picasso's, Stevens is not imitating Cubist technique; he is simply imitating himself. If "green" signifies the color of external reality and "blue" signifies the color of imagination, then nothing could be more clear than a poem about the music of a "blue guitar" trying to sing a tune of "things exactly as they are"—"green" day.

This system of self-reference might almost be diagnosed as a hardening of the corollaries, a dangerous condition because it tempts readers to mechanically "decode" Stevens' poetry. Thus we might "decode" every instance of the word "blue" to the abstraction "imagination," and every instance of the word "red" to the abstraction "unassimilated reality." But while Stevens condemns the man who will not be "touched by blue," he is also capable of condemning those "pale intrusions into blue" as "corrupting pallors." We must remain sensitive to Stevens' nuances and respectful of a shorthand device that permits Stevens' poetry its complexity of thought and emotion.

The greatest complexity derives from Stevens' search for a conjunction of the imagination with the world of reality in a language that does not violate the necessary element of constant change inherent in both mind and reality. In the midst of his skirmish between the mind and the eye, Stevens invents the symbol of the hero, a figure frequently associated with language and speaking. This association suggests just why the hero is so significant a symbol in Stevens' prose and poetry of the forties. Language marks out the boundaries of the encounter between the self and the not-self; it is a bridge between interior and exterior: so is the hero, that "rugged roy" of us and in us. In a poetry full of the difficulty of interpreting the buzz of ocean and the roar of wind, yet just as intent on seeing "notations" and "signs" in them, the birth of the hero becomes a way of articulating the interaction between world as chaos and world as word. Just as important, the hero becomes a kind of bridge between the silent self and the undeciphered world. The articulation of the one is the definition of the other. Naked and tall, the hero is "plus gaudiest vir" or the most joyous—and the most joy-creating—hero.[14]

The creation of this symbol signals Stevens' later style, in which definition of without becomes simultaneously definition of within. Two kinds of chaos keep their durational aspect in a poetry of flux that is also a poetry of fixed words.

CHAPTER 5

"Notes Toward a Supreme Fiction"

"In the beginning was the Word."
—Gospel According to St. John

"It is the theory of the word for those
For whom the word is the making of the world."
—"Description Without Place"

At the end of both "The Man With the Blue Guitar" and the later "Notes Toward a Supreme Fiction" are secular communion images: "the bread of time to come" and "the bread of faithful speech." The two phrases pinpoint the difference between the long poem of 1937 and the long poems of the 1940s: a move from a doctrine of imagination to a doctrine of the word. "The thesis of the plentifullest John," Stevens whimsically calls it in "Description Without Place." Though he seems to be talking about the same dichotomies—real and imagined, world and mind, order and disorder—the later poetry exhibits obvious stylistic changes that indicate a change in attitude. Stevens is right, after all, that a "change of style is a change of subject" (OP 171).

He expresses his new attitude again and again:

> . . . Life consists
> Of propositions about life.
>   (CP 355)

> A sound producing the things that are spoken.
>   (CP 287)

> Natives of poverty, children of malheur,
> The gaiety of language is our seigneur.
>   (CP 322)

And finally, "words of the world are the life of the world" (CP 474). In Stevens' later poetry, word and object, poem and pure reality can exist in the same world:

> The poem of pure reality, untouched
> By trope or deviation, *straight to the word,*
> *Straight to the transfixing object.*
>   (CP 471, my italics)

Stevens has come a long way from Crispin's despair, that "the words of things entangle and confuse." The *ding an sich* that Crispin sought is now married to the seeking mind.

How does one overcome that stubborn Cartesian duality, and where is the marriage? It resides in "A few words, an and yet, and yet, and yet—" (CP 465). The "disparate halves / Of things" are waiting for "espousal to the sound / Of right joining" on the simple wing of metaphor: "as if." Stevens' later poetry becomes what he called an "endlessly elaborating poem" about a "never-ending meditation," and the moments of rapture always affirm an "as if" as if it were true: "It is possible, possible, possible. It must / Be possible" (CP 404).

I suspect that Stevens discovered the doctrine of the word at the same time he discovered his later style; that is why I consider "Notes Toward a Supreme Fiction" so crucial a poem in the development of Stevens' mature style. It is the first of his "endlessly elaborating" poems, written in 1942, immediately after the publication of *Parts of a World*. An extension of familiar themes in *Parts of a World*, "Notes" also discovers a style which allows Stevens to overcome the necessity of choosing *between* mind and world; instead

> He had to choose. But it was not a choice
> Between excluding things. It was not a choice
>
> Between, but of. He chose to include the things
> That in each other are included, the whole,
> The complicate, the amassing harmony.
>
> (III, vi)

"Notes" is the discovery of Stevens' mature technique in the sense that it shuffles back and forth—flits, wings, arches—between the object and the mind. This word-winging creates the poem *as process,* and in that process Stevens can finally abandon the fiction of the "noble rider" and affirm himself—and his own speaking. It is no longer a "potential poet" who *might* grasp reality without distortion, but Stevens himself "almosting" it. This affirmation of his "make-believe" occurs only because of the complex—and sometimes even tortuous—exploration of language that comprises so much of the poem.

Schematically, "Notes Toward a Supreme Fiction" can be seen as a meditation on the implications of "The Sense of The Sleight-of-Hand Man":

> It may be that the ignorant man, alone,
> Has any chance to mate his life with life
> That is the sensual, pearly spouse.

To escape the tyranny of concepts—words—each man, like an eternal generation of Adams, must transform his own seeing into his own naming. The first section, "It Must Be Abstract," is dedicated to creating the "ignorant man":

> You must become an ignorant man again
> And see the sun again with an ignorant eye
> And see it clearly in the idea of it.

The language of much of this section mimics its subtitle: it is abstract, mind-centered. All of Stevens' energies here are channeled toward the creation of "major man," and not toward the world he will marry. Compare the coldness of Stevens' attitude toward the sun with his ecstasy about the hero:

> Begin, ephebe, by perceiving the idea
> Of this invention, this invented world,
> The inconceivable idea of the sun.
>
> (I, i)

and

> . . . he that reposes
> On a breast forever precious for that touch,
>
> For whom the good of April falls tenderly,
> Falls down, the cock-birds calling at the time.
>
> (I, ix)

Dialectically, then, "It Must Change" moves out from this hero to the world of change in which he exists—as part of us. Here the world is introduced not as an "idea" or an "invention" but as the green reality of the planter's island or the booming "bees" of being. But "It Must Change" is cruelly reductive about both human orderings and human speech. The world that Stevens presents in this section is a living and changing world on which man again and again *imposes* his order. "To impose is not / To

discover," he says in the third section; words themselves are part
of the imposition. Even the supreme fiction is necessarily of
words, which, because they do not exist in change, are *almost* incapable of rendering the supreme fiction. Given the three-part
structure of the poem, we might expect the solution at the end:
the "mundo" finally named, and therefore seized, but seized in
change. The world achieved at the end of the poem is a world
transformed by mind. As Stevens says in "The Figure of the
Youth as Virile Poet," "It is the *mundo* of the imagination . . .
and not the gaunt world of the reason" (NA 57–58). If the quest of
the poem is a marriage of self and world which overcomes the self
as Logos in the very act of speaking, what could give more pleasure than its discovery?

At the beginning of "It Must Be Abstract," we are a long way
from any marriage. The language and Stevens' philosophical
stance impart a coldness and distance to the "reality" under consideration. Addressing the ephebe, Stevens has stepped away, at
least momentarily, from the world he once described, to describe
instead the processes by which one *ought* to perceive the world.
From the role of meticulous observer of the world changed by
imagination (think of the observations in "Sea Surface Full of
Clouds," for example), Stevens has put on the academic robes of
the poet-philosopher, to tutor the "ephebe" in meticulous observation. An ephebe is a young man preparing for citizenship, and
Stevens is preparing him for a very ambitious role, for he is none
other than the potential poet, the "Youth as Virile Poet."

Under Stevens' tutelage, the ephebe learns to rid himself of
the old myths that interfere with the interaction of self and world.
The first step is a scrubbing job: "How clean the sun when seen
in its idea, / Washed in the remotest cleanliness of a
heaven / That has expelled us and our images." The ephebe must
recognize the separateness of the sun, and his own impulse to
ease that separateness by projecting gods. "Phoebus is dead,

ephebe," Stevens tells his young initiate, suggesting with his anagram that the young poet replaces the old god, and that the ephebe must refrain from projecting versions of himself on the world. Instead, "The sun / Must bear no name, gold flourisher, but be / In the difficulty of what it is to be." As I pointed out earlier, Stevens' humor allows him to add "gold flourisher," telling us that though the sun "must" bear no names, we *will* give it names. But this old repudiation of "rotted names" has a new shrug: "There was a project for the sun and is" suggests, first, there was and is a project for the sun (namelessness), and second, there was a project for the sun and for *is*—"being." "Being" is constantly emerging and changing, and Stevens is discovering a kind of poetical ontology: a project for "being" that recognizes the mind not as an isolated container, nor as sole creator of reality, but as one pole in an intercourse of realities.

"It Must Be Abstract" starts with one abstraction, "the idea of the sun," only preparatory to developing another abstraction, "the idea of man." There is one sun, to be seen right; there are many ways to look at many men—individually, in the mass, rich, poor, MacCullough, and *the* MacCullough. What Stevens is attempting in "It Must Be Abstract" depends on the "first idea" as it is learned in the first cantos; we can arrive at what he calls "major man" only through the process of abstracting as Stevens shows it in the first cantos. But once reached, major man yields what the sun cannot: an ecstasy, a way of speaking. Major man is part of the "idea of man"; he is the idea's "exponent":

> More fecund as principle than particle,
> Happy fecundity, flor-abundant force,
> In being more than an exception, part,
>
> Though an heroic part, of the commonal.
> The major abstraction is the commonal,
> The inanimate, difficult visage.
>
> (I, x)

Major man, then, is exponent in two senses: spokesman and mathematical factor, as if man were raised to his highest degree, man to the nth power. He is principle, but also part; not an exception, but the whole.

The real purpose of "It Must Be Abstract" has been the creation of the major man. The reason he is important, and the reason that he gives such rapture, is that he allows us to speak and see the "difficult visage. Who is it?" Stevens answers, "It is he," pointing toward the figure in the old coat and sagging pantaloons who is, perhaps, humanity unredeemed by imagination. This figure is the term to be raised exponentially, and for whom we are all initiates:

> It is of him, ephebe, to make, to confect
> The final elegance, not to console
> Nor sanctify, but plainly to propound.
>
> (I, x)

We must pay attention to Stevens' Latin. We have major man as "exponent"; the ephebe as "proponent." The first, *exponere*, suggests the abstraction itself: a placing out of. By contrast, the ephebe *pro*-pounds, places in behalf of, or *for*. Propounding the abstraction, confecting or composing the abstraction of this singular and pathetic figure, is to reach to major man. This is done not to console the poor man nor to remake him into a divine figure, but simply and "plainly" to speak *for* him.

To accomplish this, the ephebe must be able to "abstract" reality. In Stevens' words, "he must be able to abstract himself and also to abstract reality, which he does by placing it in his imagination" (NA 23). Stevens is here speaking precisely, for etymologically "abstraction" means taking something from the external world and putting it in the mind. A moment's fresh consideration—how does one get that table from out there into nonexistent mental space?—reveals a wonder chewed over too much by philosophers and too little by poets. Many of the cantos are exercises in such an effort. In canto VI, for example, Stevens again tries to reach a thing like "*a* sun,"

> Without a name and nothing to be desired,
> If only imagined but imagined well.

The attempt fails, but the effort has its effect: "My house has changed a little in the sun." Although he is back in the world of concrete reality ("the sun"), the attempt to imagine "a sun" without a name—to conceptualize without falsifying—has had its effect. The process of trying to reach this abstraction is like painting ("realizing" is Stevens' word) the weather. Particular weather is not abstract, of course, but what Stevens turns to is an abstraction—"weather." The weather is brushed up: "Wetted by blue, colder for white."

The canto's struggle between the concrete world and the mental abstraction is beautifully resolved as a "seeing and unseeing in the eye," and as

> The weather and the giant of the weather,
> Say the weather, the mere weather, the mere air:
> An abstraction blooded, as a man by thought.

The giant stands for the fiction we project when we form an idea; he is the thinker of the first idea, and he is the *reason* we give to the weather when we abstract. But there is still the "mere" weather. When the mere weather and the giant—who is a symbol for the self-consciously created abstract idea of the weather—come together we have an "abstraction blooded."

Cantos VII and VIII interact with the two kinds of thinking I have just considered: a seeing and an unseeing in the eye. Consider, first, the giant, "A thinker of the first idea" (VII). If "the first idea is an imagined thing," then so is the giant. And in canto VII, Stevens relaxes:

> It feels good as it is without the giant,
> A thinker of the first idea. Perhaps
> The truth depends on a walk around a lake,
>
> A composing as the body tires, a stop
> To see hepatica, a stop to watch
> A definition growing certain and
>
> A wait within that certainty, a rest
> In the swags of pine-trees bordering the lake.

These are almost tender syntactical equations:

a stop to see	hepatica
a stop to watch	definition
a wait within	certainty
a rest in	swags of pine-trees

These equations of states of mind with natural setting prepare us for the statement:

> Perhaps there are moments of awakening,
> . . . in which
>
> We more than awaken, sit on the edge of sleep,
> As on an elevation, and behold
> The academies like structures in a mist.

The "academic" search for truth is mentioned again in the conclusion:

> They will get it straight one day at the Sorbonne.
> We shall return at twilight from the lecture
> Pleased that the irrational is rational.
>
> (XXX, x)

But here Stevens is playing with the "groves of Academe"—the name of the garden near Athens where Plato taught. Is he mocking as "structures in a mist" the academies of learning that get their name from Plato's gardens? Or is he suggesting that Plato's misty "Ideas" derive from similar strolls in similarly real gardens? For Stevens, at any rate, the "truth" depends on a stroll in the "real" weather among real things; it is a truth not imposed by reason but intuited during a moment of heightened consciousness.

Canto VII concerns "composition" as it occurs without the giant. In contrast, canto VIII, also a composing, is an architectural or poetical rendering as a direct result of imagining the giant. In each case, composition involves an architectural ordering of the world, the first into "structures in a mist," the second into a "castle-fortress-home." Stevens is considering ways in which he might discover order, but the composing of canto VIII is not only an architectural structure, but a linguistic one. This reappearance of a linguistic problem suggests why the giant, the major man, and other fictions of mankind in a collectivity are necessary: they concern human speech. Watch the association of the "idea" in the canto:

> The first idea is an imagined thing.
> The pensive giant prone in violet space
> May be the MacCullough, an expedient,
>
> Logos and logic, crystal hypothesis,
> Incipit and a form to speak the word

And every latent double in the word,

Beau linguist.

Syntactical ambiguities enrich the kind of *logos* Stevens offers:

| Giant | may be | the MacCullough | } beau linguist |
| the MacCullough | is | MacCullough | |

With the syntax dissolving the grammatical referents, the identity blurs between the three figures. "The pensive giant prone in violet space" is probably the sun; MacCullough is "any name, any man" (L 434). Between the perceiver and the perceived is the crucial figure: the MacCullough. Like Stevens' other heroic figures, the MacCullough lives in the physical world not as a sensualist nor as an empiricist, but through his mind. The capable man imagines—and imagines metaphysically—the world around him, reconstructing out of the empirical particulars a true structure. Part of the reconstruction bears the name "giant," which represents the thinker's idea of the physical world. The MacCullough is "beau linguist," then, because he provides a "crystal hypothesis." "Hypothesis" is the basis—or foundation, to return to the architectural metaphor—of an argument; the giant is enclosed in a "crystal hypothesis" only in the sense that the physical world is grasped as an idea. The MacCullough is the "beau linguist" because he provides the clarity and excitement of the idea that must precede speech.

He may be both Logos and logic (both word and method for using the word), but the actual speech rests with MacCullough, the man himself, the frail human figure by the sea:

If MacCullough himself lay lounging by the sea,

Drowned in its washes, reading in the sound,

> About the thinker of the first idea,
> He might take habit, whether from wave or phrase,
>
> Or power of the wave, or deepened speech,
> Or a leaner being, moving in on him,
> Of greater aptitude and apprehension,
>
> As if the waves at last were never broken,
> As if the language suddenly, with ease,
> Said things it had laboriously spoken.

What a familiar scene this is! Remember Crispin, "washed away by magnitude" before the sea, "The Doctor of Geneva," and "The Idea of Order at Key West," to name only a few. This scene has a new dimension: it is resolved. MacCullough, imagining, gleans from the sound of the sea a being bigger than himself, a "leaner being." As soon as he has an idea like this, an idea of himself understanding, MacCullough hears the understanding. Things clear. Then we move outward toward "the MacCullough" and the giant.

Stevens himself was quite firm about this interpretation of the canto:

> The gist of this poem is that the MacCullough is MacCullough; MacCullough is any name, any man. The trouble with humanism is that man as God remains man, but there is an extension of man, the leaner being, in fiction, a possibly more than human human, a composite human. The act of recognizing him is the act of this leaner being moving in on us.
>
> (L 434)

The act of recognizing him is the act of this leaner being moving in on us: but what this recognition yields! The acutest speech that Stevens has been hunting since *Harmonium* here seems close to realization. It is not that a great thick voice will speak out of the clouds, but that MacCullough, recognizing something *in himself* that might be bigger than he is, approaches speech. In him is the Logos and logic; in him alone the voice that can speak.

Of course, this triumph is mitigated by Stevens' habitual qualifications. "If" MacCullough read from the sound of sea, he "might" take habit, "whether" from wave "or" phrase "or" power of the wave "or" deepened speech "or" a leaner being. We can see, from these "or's," that the significant leaner being shares a suspiciously oceanic quality with everything else. Stevens almost lulls us with his fluent meter and sudden rhyme into forgetting that MacCullough's recognition is an "as if."

Where does such qualification leave the "beau linguist"? We can note one thing with certainty: the first idea is an imagined thing. We start not with the giant, but with human MacCullough by the sea. From him comes that important "extension of man" that Stevens was convinced could create a meaningful humanism. "The act of recognizing him," said Stevens, referring to the "leaner being," "is the act of this leaner being moving in on us." But who creates whom, we wonder. The canto starts with the giant and moves down to MacCullough; we explicate backwards in order to understand the giant's apparent meaning. Clearly not MacCullough by the sea, but the creation of this leaner being, also called "major man," is for Stevens the important thing.

Between the two, man himself and the "leaner being," we approach the Logos. Only MacCullough can speak the word, but only *the* MacCullough can make the word clear to him. Having created that complex relationship, Stevens considers the *idiom* of the speech. Despite the qualifications in canto VIII, the *word* is evidently sufficiently established for Stevens to turn from Logos to logic in canto IX. Here we see the rejection of the "romantic intoning" for "reason's click-clack." Major man comes, surprisingly enough,

Compact in invincible foils, from reason,
Lighted at midnight by the studious eye,
Swaddled in revery, the object of

The hum of thoughts evaded in the mind,
Hidden from other thoughts, he that reposes
On a breast forever precious for that touch.

The birth of major man, according to this method, occurs only in the conjunction of thought and emotion. The reasoning (an echo of "logic" from the preceding canto) part of the mind must be imported into the romantic part of the self. But it is not that simple, really, for Stevens manages a merging of styles that seems to dissolve the one term, Romantic, into the other, Reason. "The Romantic intoning," for instance, is said to be part of apotheosis, "appropriate / And of its nature, the idiom thereof." Most lawyerly language. And "reason's click-clack" is endowed with a different style: "its applied enflashings" arouse the tenderness of the comments, "Swaddled in revery" and "he that reposes / On a breast forever precious for that touch." In sum, reason's idiom takes on romantic trappings, and romantic clairvoyance is denounced with rhetoric.

By the end of this canto, we have arrived at the destination: major man, born out of us by thought, creation of whom allows us to speak the "acutest speech."

Stevens' injunction that the supreme fiction be abstract seems easily explained; as a product of the mind or imagination, it is necessarily abstract. From "It Must Be Abstract" to "It Must Change," the poem moves from the supreme fiction as mind-created to the supreme fiction as necessarily existing in change. It must change because both imagination and reality change. But Stevens shows how difficult it is to be both changing and changed, for he abandons the triumphs of his first section, along with the ephebe and his own stance as tutor. Consider the majority of figures in this section: the old Seraph, the President, the statue Du Puy, the dead Planter, and Ozymandias. All masculine figures, they share little with the ephebe or major man. They are much more like the old man in the old coat, "looking for what was, where it used to be." They are old, mind-centered, fixed in the desire for permanence, and, in their changelessness, "dead." To the Planter, Stevens is tender; to the statue Du Puy, merciless; to the Seraph, ambiguous; to Ozymandias, ironic. What they all share, at any rate, is man's universal desire to find an order in what Stevens calls a "universe of inconstancy."

The old seraph of canto I is "parcel-gilded," an archaism suggesting that this celestial being is half-gilt, and also that he is a product—a parcel—of the past. He is witness to Stevens' scathing version of the seasonal renewal, which man has taken as a comforting analogy for his own immortality: "the bees come booming as if they had never gone." The seraph lives in his mind, "is satyr in Saturn, according to his thoughts." Like the seraph is that other metaphysician, the President. Perhaps President of the Immortals and therefore another archaism, or perhaps a modern-day statesman dictating that poets remake reality, he "ordains the bee to be / Immortal" (II, II). But, complains Stevens, "Why / Should there be a question of returning or / Of death in memory's dream?" No, each spring is a new beginning; the "bee" is a new become, a being a-new.[1]

Stevens rejects the traditional interpretation of the great seasonal flux: myth, he insists, outworn. Change is constant, but also inconstant. Another attack on man's desire for constancy is the canto on General Du Puy, whose permanence makes him "a bit absurd" (II III). Inhuman, "the General was rubbish in the end." He probably shares his dump with Ozymandias, a figure derived from Shelley:

> "My name is Ozymandias, king of kings:
> Look on my works, ye Mighty, and despair!"
> Nothing beside remains. Round the decay
> Of that colossal wreck, boundless and bare
> The lone and level sands stretch far away.

Borrowing Shelley's figure symbolizing the colossal vanity of human wishes, and the colossal irony to dreams of immortality, Stevens uses only the famous name and one meager reference to the desert: "She took her necklace off / And laid it in the sand" (II, VIII). Stevens probably presumes an ironic response to Ozymandias, but uses him only as another version of the ordering human.

"It Must Change" offers an array of these ordering figures, each symbolizing one version of order imposed on change. In the midst of these is Stevens' version:

> Two things of opposite natures seem to depend
> On one another, as a man depends
> On a woman, day on night, the imagined
>
> On the real. This is the origin of change.
> Winter and spring, cold copulars, embrace
> And forth the particulars of rapture come.
>
> (II, IV)

The origin of change is the interdependency, the embrace of generals from which particulars spring. About more than natural change, though, the canto is also about the mind as it perceives change, for it continues: "The partaker partakes of that which changes him." Winter and spring "change" each other; the imagination changes the real, and the real the imagination. The mind, too, changes as it lives in the changing world; conscious of change outside, it changes.

Although this vision of unity is essentially Romantic, Stevens is nevertheless mocking Romanticism. In canto VI, for example, the sparrow's song is an allusion to Shelley's "Ode to the West Wind." Shelley's incantation for renewal and inspiration provides the poet's path from despair to hope: "Be thou, Spirit fierce, / My spirit! Be thou me, impetuous one!" And Stevens mocks: "Bethou me, said sparrow, . . . / And you, and you, bethou me as you blow." That sparrow is Stevens' way of mocking the Shelleyan desire to merge the self as spirit with the world as spirit. The rejection of Romanticism is the last rejection in a series. Rejecting the old Seraph's "constant / Violets, doves, girls, bees and hyacinths," rejecting the analogy of human immortality in seasonal renewal, and rejecting the myth of immortality in art or monument (General Du Puy and Ozymandias), Stevens turns to and rejects the attempt to merge the self with the world. This last is, for Stevens, the most difficult rejection; his own urge toward this Romantic solution accounts for the fine poetry of the canto's rejection.

His fear of Romantic solipsism explains the conclusion to "It Must Change":

> . . . The freshness of transformation is
>
> The freshness of a world. It is our own,
> It is ourselves, the freshness of ourselves,
> And that necessity and that presentation
>
> Are rubbings of a glass in which we peer.
>   (II, x)

This muted conclusion seems a union, both of subject and tone, of two cantos from "It Must Be Abstract." We remember the lyricism of Stevens' incandescent little poem about poetry:

> The poem refreshes life so that we share,
> For a moment, the first idea . . . It satisfies
> Belief in an immaculate beginning

> And sends us, winged by an unconscious will,
> To an immaculate end. We move between these points:
> From that ever-early candor to its late plural
>
> And the candor of them is the strong exhilaration
> Of what we feel from what we think.
>
> (I, III)

Stevens, at the end of "It Must Change," is again talking about "freshness," a version of "candor," "refresh," and "immaculate." But the conclusion also echoes another canto of "It Must Be Abstract," the one about man's incurable narcissism:

> The first idea was not our own. Adam
> In Eden was the father of Descartes
> And Eve made air the mirror of herself,
>
> . . . They found themselves
> In heaven as in a glass; a second earth.
>
> (I, IV)

At the end of "It Must Change," Stevens returns to his subject, the poetry of the supreme fiction, and remarks quite honestly but very quietly that the poem gives us only "ourselves," and not the world, a mirror and not the "bare board."

His despair—if we can call so whimsical a gravity "despair"— is usually about words, "minstrelsy," seducing hymns of which his own poetry is surely a part. The last two cantos of "It Must Change" find Stevens returning inevitably to his subject—his own poetry, his own perception of relations. Canto IX for example, defines his poetic problem exactly: to go from the "poet's gibberish to / The gibberish of the vulgate and back again," to catch, in other words, both the "peculiar" (particular) which is life and living in change, and the "general" which is the "imagination's Latin." The poet, attempting the "peculiar potency of the general," attempts precisely what Stevens had in "It Must Be Abstract." There he had rendered the man in the old coat (peculiar and particular) into the potent major man, abstract and general. This reflexive canto, this meditation on his own procedures, seems a fine comment on Stevens' love-affair with ideas, and his repeated attempts to get at the *idea* of living in a world through the necessarily concrete language of poetry. Such a speaker speaks "a speech only a little of the tongue" (II, IX).

This raises the question: "Does the poet / Evade us, as in a senseless element?" Yes, he is in a *senseless* element, but no, he does not evade: "Evade, this hot, dependent orator / The spokesman at our bluntest barriers?" Clearly, the poet reaches beyond our limitations ("our bluntest barriers"); he is "exponent by a form of speech," recalling major man in "It Must Be Abstract." The poet is the mediator between ourselves, our limitations, and our finest realizations—our rugged roy of ourselves.

What distinguishes "It Must Give Pleasure" from the other two sections, aside from the voice, is the array of feminine figures. "It Must Be Abstract" has none, "It Must Change," one. In "It Must Give Pleasure," we find the "blue woman," Bawda, and the "fat girl." Despite their proliferation, the last section seems to reiterate the problems of the first two: "the difficultest rigor" of right perception (I, II); the problem of change (III); the marriage of reason and imagination as it affects self and perceived place (IV); the imposition rather than the discovery of order (VI–VIII); another bird song about change and living content in the now (IX); the closing canto about naming (X). But this last section of "Notes" concludes triumphantly—for Stevens; in order to assess the height of the symbolic integration achieved here, I want to give a brief reprise of Stevens' changing symbols.

In my discussion of "Farewell to Florida," I suggested that during the thirties Stevens rejected the Southern woman and all she stood for; in order to make his search for reality "masculine,"

Stevens substituted masculine speakers and masculine ideals: the hero, the possible poet. During this period, the feminine figure remained peripheral or threatening. Two poems in *Parts of a World*—"Oak Leaves Are Hands" and "The Hand as a Being"— show Stevens' indictment of the feminine figure. Both titles apparently find the hand most capable of translating thought into deed, imagination into reality. Like the symbolic woman, then, the symbolic hand likely refers to both inner and outer realities. In "The Hand as a Being," we see the anima figure as a threatening weaver of veils:

> She held her hand before him in the air,
> For him to see, wove round her glittering hair.

There is an interesting tension between two states of mind:

> He was too conscious of too many things

and

> Of her, of her alone, at last he knew
> And lay beside her underneath the tree.

The "I" comprising a multiple consciousness can behold the "naked, nameless dame" only at the risk of obliteration. With the "mi-bird" (or self) flown off, "our man" knows only "her alone." The conclusion is surely a deathly one—though, like the Elizabethan "death," it may provide certain sensual satisfactions.

Similarly in "Oak Leaves Are Hands," Stevens exorcizes the anima figure:

> Mac Mort she had been, ago,
> Twelve-legged in her ancestral hells,
> Weaving and weaving many arms.

She is "evasive and metamorphorid," a portmanteau word suggesting constant metamorphosis and metaphor, as well as phorid—for fly—and the entomological *-ids* of arach*nid* and ap*hid*. That she is the troublesome lady of imagination is clear from the first stanza: "a lady, . . . / For whom what is was other things." Although this spidery weaver of metaphoric resemblances is denounced as a deathly "Mac Mort," Stevens seems to be attempting a reconciliation with masculine Logos:

> So she in Hydaspia created
> Out of the movement of few words,
> Flora Lowzen invigorated
>
> Archaic and future happenings,
> In glittering seven-colored changes.

Stevens has metamorphosed the feminine figure from Mac Mort to Flora Lowzen, a promising if trivial development.

The "supreme fiction" toward which Stevens is working at this time rests on the marriage of the hero (Logos) and the female imagination. And, of course, the mind's "sexes" are projected onto the external world: the woman is the beloved reality and the giant is a man's *idea* of the physical world. Thus we get a configuration like this: "It may be that the ignorant man, alone, / Has any chance to mate his life with life / That is the sensual, pearly spouse." The "pearly spouse" is reality—but the beloved reality known by the imagination. This suggests that at the end of "Notes" we ought to see a marriage of the two principles, male and female, Logos and reality, reason and imagination. But the hero, major man, the giant, is gone; born in "It Must Be Abstract," he does not reappear. Who is it, then, that marries, that speaks? "I"—someone very close to Stevens himself. The passage is remarkable:

> Is it I then that keep saying there is an hour
> Filled with expressible bliss, in which I have
>
> No need, am happy, forget need's golden hand,
> Am satisfied without solacing majesty,
> And if there is an hour there is a day,
>
> There is a month, a year, there is a time
> In which majesty is a mirror of the self:
> I have not but I am and as I am, I am.
>
> (III, VIII)

Apparently the reappearance of the feminine figure allows Stevens to abandon the fiction of the "impossible possible philosophers' man" and become himself the noble rider—commit himself to the desperate project.

When Stevens identifies himself with the noble rider, speaks as an "I," he also discovers the nobility he has been vainly seeking since *Harmonium:* he can be "satisfied without solacing majesty," because "there is a time / In which majesty is a mirror of the self." The majestic angel that he imagines, almost Miltonic in his leap "downward through evening's revelations," is, nevertheless, imagined. Stevens knows that, insists on that, but asks: "Am I that imagine this angel less satisfied? / Are the wings his, the lapis-haunted air? / Is it he or is it I that experience this?" The answer is implicit: the wings, the flight, the experience are mine, because I imagine them.

Stevens' remarks on nobility in "The Noble Rider and the Sound of Words" are relevant here:

> The imagination gives to everything that it touches a peculiarity, and it seems to me that the peculiarity of the imagination is nobility. . . . This inherent nobility is the natural source of another. . . . I mean that nobility which is our spiritual height and depth.
>
> (NA 33–34)

The cantos spoken by "I" strive for that "spiritual height" that is nobility, for the speaker magnificently imagines an angel "serenely gazing at the violent abyss," an angel who "needs nothing," "forgets the gold centre." If he can so imagine an angel, then in the act of imagining, he himself has *expressed* (as in "expressible bliss") the angel's bliss as his own. "Majesty is a mirror of the self," he concludes, because as a register of the "spiritual height" attained, we have the angel. He does not exist—"I have not"—but he is imagined well, and recognizing that power, the speaker is content to say, "as I am, I am."

This is the "fact" that Stevens inevitably ends with, the "fact" of actual poverty. It is the necessary qualification to the noble angel, for to soar too keenly with the imagined angel would be to falsify reality. To imagine the angel is to find majesty; to know that the angel is imagined is to find the "difficultest" majesty. In that recognition we reach the "amassing harmony" of imagination and reality, a harmony which means that the world, rightly perceived, can be named. Such is the union achieved in the last section of "Notes." Having recognized both imagined angel and imagining self, Stevens makes his famous remark: "Perhaps / The man-hero is not the exceptional monster, / But he that of repetition is most master." A statement about himself and his poetry, perhaps it is also a statement about the noble rider; his can be no straight path toward the "phosphorescent sun." Stevens' new look at his "hero" suggests a union of major man with the "old fantoche" (CP 181) in the figure of the poet. In the poet we will find both man and hero, in him the "luminous flittering" between the two symbols and between the imagined and the real.

By the end of "It Must Give Pleasure," we have seen a spate of changes in Stevens' poetry: the reappearance of the feminine figure, the change from the exceptional noble rider to the representative man-hero, the new speaker "I," and the renewed sense of majesty derived from the self when it becomes the noble rider, satisfied at last. From all this follows the conclusion:

> Fat girl, terrestrial, my summer, my night,
> How is it I find you in difference, see you there
> In a moving contour, a change not quite completed?

We can see the shadows of the relationship between this "man-hero" and his world. Like the "origins of change" in "It Must Change," we hear "my summer, my night," and know that the speaker himself must comprise his winter, his day.

The speaker, feeling an "unprovoked sensation," needs to "name you flatly, waste no words, / Check your evasions, hold you to yourself." Of course, to name "flatly" might risk changing the rounded contours of the world, but the speaker, polite and cautious, risks nevertheless. The risk is neither reasonable nor reasoning, but a necessity because:

> . . . You
> Become the soft-footed phantom, the irrational
>
> Distortion, however fragrant, however dear.
> That's it: the more than rational distortion,
> The fiction that results from feeling. Yes, that.

I think we can see the familiar procedure of "It Must Give Pleasure" at work: the perceived world elicits the feminine character-istics of self, the "soft-footed phantom." Self and world begin to interchange, marry, and from the marriage comes the supreme fiction: the fiction that results from feeling.

This is no momentous new discovery in the poem; Stevens has made it before, several times, in "It Must Be Abstract" and in "It Must Change." At the root of the self and the self's perceptions, the poet perceives rightly, reasons well; attending this is a dissolving of structure, a loosening of what had been too "gauntly" reasoned. In "It Must Be Abstract," for example, when the "balances that happen" happen, there is a mist of the new reality:

> Perhaps there are moments of awakening,
> Extreme, fortuitous, personal in which
>
> We more than awaken, sit on the edge of sleep,
> As on an elevation, and behold
> The academies like structures in a mist.
>
> (I, VII)

The same effect occurs in "It Must Give Pleasure," and in both we hear the rhythm of subdued excitement and pleasure:

> They will get it straight one day at the Sorbonne.
> We shall return at twilight from the lecture
> Pleased that the irrational is rational,
>
> Until flicked by feeling, in a gildered street,
> I call you by name, my green, my fluent mundo.
>
> (III, x)

In both cantos, we are deep in the roots of self-hood, the momentary, irrational, barely conscious and therefore partly unconscious apprehension of reality, that which Stevens had said in *Parts of a World* must remain without description. "We more than awaken," we are at the edge of a new knowledge, but on the edge of sleep: a new knowledge of reality is a new knowledge of the self. Such knowledge mists the world, fogs it up, loosens its structure, permits the speaker—the fantasizing Cinderella (CP 405), the painter in his house (CP 385)—to get out for a moment from under the roof of reason, the structure of reality. When the "roof" of the strict self is blown off in this extreme and personal moment, then the self participates in the world. Only at such a moment can the world be rightly named; it must not be named as an ordering device, not named out of the conceptualizing, reasoning self. Only when "flicked by feeling," convinced that the irrational experience of the moment is the truly rational, only then can Stevens do what he has desperately tried before to do: "call you by name." The act of naming suggests the marriage between Logos and Nameless Dame; the result: "You will have stopped revolving except in crystal." Which is as good as saying that the fluent world, the globe, keeps revolving, nothing has changed. Yet all has changed, for the naming has stopped the world long enough to place the crystal of name around it. While it apparently revolves as usual, it revolves in "crystal." The name that the speaker gives, then, is a crystal name—allows him to "check your evasions" but also "to hold you to yourself." Transparent, the crystal name does not stand between the perceiver and the perceived, as so many conceptualizations do; fragile and precious, the crystal name suggests that this perception is extreme, fortuitous, momentary.

This is the culmination to the poem's long quest for that "pure idea," become here, for the first time in the poem, named. How fragile it is is suggested, perhaps, by the coda, where Stevens seems to take a giant step backward: "Soldier, there is a war between the mind / And sky, between thought and day and night. It is / For that the poet is always in the sun." It is disappointing, after the pleasures of the fluent "mundo," to be back at the battleground, and anticlimactic to have Stevens say, "How gladly with proper words the soldier dies, / If he must, or lives on the bread of faithful speech." But perhaps this coda helps us recognize what R. P. Blackmur has called the "expense of greatness." [2] Stevens' struggle with the "proper words," those sounds for the real soldier from the "fictive hero," sounds that might "Stick / . . . in the blood," should be recognized as a real war for him. The ease with which he swings into the conclusion of "It Must

Give Pleasure," the swelling of that pleasure in the last triad —perhaps we know the heights he has reached by the contrast of the coda. We are reminded, too, that Stevens continues to search for "the bread of faithful speech," his image of communion with reality through words. Not that imagined, but that imagined well and *spoken*, will provide our heaven here.

CHAPTER 6

The World of Words

> "To construct oneself, to know oneself—
> are these two distinct acts or not?"
> —Paul Valéry[1]

In the thirteen remaining years of his life after the 1942 publication of "Notes Toward a Supreme Fiction," Stevens was extraordinarily active. Besides *Transport to Summer* (1947), *Auroras of Autumn* (1950), and the last poems included in *Collected Poems* as *The Rock*, Stevens also wrote all but one of the essays that comprise *The Necessary Angel*, as well as several published in *Opus Posthumous*. No account of Stevens' productivity is complete without mentioning that he never retired from the insurance business, or that he refused the Charles Eliot Norton Chair at Harvard in 1955 precisely because he did not want to retire.

Stevens' correspondence during these last years provides not only a fascinating account of the variety of Stevens' interests and friendships, but a helpful glimpse into the way they interacted with his poetry. In the 1940s, for example, Stevens developed a consuming interest in his genealogy. Although he avoided his hometown, Reading, Pennsylvania, for most of his adult life, in his late middle age Stevens became preoccupied with the people and the places of his family's past. His later work is full of the poetry of place names: the Schuylkill and Swatara Rivers, Oley, Mount Penn, Tinicum, Cohansey. From letters to his relatives and to his genealogist, we discern Stevens' eagerness to establish a sense of continuity with his own past and his Pennsylvania Dutch traditions. Stevens can write of the passage of time as a physical sensation—swimming in "sun-filled water" in "A Lot of People Bathing in a Stream"—and occasionally, he experiments with this feeling from an "ancestral" point of view, as in the second version of "Two Versions of the Same Poem." In "Dutch Graves in Bucks County" Stevens contrasts the "angry men and furious machines" of the faraway battles of the second World War with the equally inaudible dead of his ancestry: "You, my semblables, in sooty residence / Tap skeleton drums inaudibly." One stanza asserts that "the past is not part of the present," but the entire poem is a meditation on that ambiguous relationship.

Stevens' fascination with his family history, an excursion into time, somewhat resembles his vicarious excursions to other places. All his life Stevens cultivated correspondents in faraway places; his experience of a culture was derived not only from paintings, books, and sculptures, but from the even more physical sensations of its tea or fruit or candies. In this long and lovely comment to Barbara Church, who divided her time between New York and Europe, Stevens describes his pleasure:

> It interests me immensely to have you speak of so many places that have been merely names for me. Yet really they have always been a good deal more than names. I practically lived in France when old Mr. Vidal [a Parisian bookseller] was alive because if I had asked him to procure from an obscure fromagerie in the country some of the cheese with raisins in it of which I read one time, he would have done it and that is almost what living in France or anywhere else amounts to. In what sense do I live in America if I walk to and fro

from the office day after day. I wrote the other day to a friend in
Oregon and asked him to try to find Kieffer pears for me this autumn and in that sense I live in America. . . . There are other en-
largements.

(L 610)

It is just such an exquisite life of the senses that makes Stevens
say, "The greatest poverty is not to live / In a physical world" (CP
325). But this letter also shows how intimately related are the life
of the mind and the life of the senses. Stevens' pleasure at eating
a Kieffer pear is more than gourmandizing; he is, in one sense,
consuming Oregon.

Details from some of his correspondence appear in his poetry
in fascinating ways. His young Cuban friend, José Rodríguez-
Feo, for example, wrote to Stevens about giving up a job in Paris:

I gave up the job at the Unesco at Paris because mother was afraid I
would freeze in the Parisian hotels. She happened to listen in on a
conversation wherein a friend of mine described in gruesome details
the fate of an Argentine writer. At night he would go to bed, cover
himself with blankets—protruding from the pile of wool a hand, in a
black glove, holds a novel by Camus.

(L 617n)

Stevens uses this anecdote in "The Novel," around it weaving a
contrasting series of associations: José, "vividest Varadero" (a
coastal Cuban town), a sun like a Spaniard, and summer, in contrast to the transplanted Argentine, red fire, encroaching night,
and winter. In the summer at Varadero, reality spoke in one's
mouth; in the midwinter evening in the North, "tranquillity is
what one thinks." "A novel by Camus," along with the imagery of
disintegration ("day's arches are crumbling"), suggests a mental
passage to symbolic winter: existential anxiety. Art (the novel)
becomes a mirror of reality, a "retrato" (Spanish for resemblance

or likeness) that supplants the real. The Argentine reading in wintry Paris is Stevens' vehicle for describing the metaphysical sensations derived from growing darkness and cold: "It is odd, too, how that Argentine is oneself, / Feeling the fear." The ingredients of this poem are typically Stevens': seasonal, diurnal, and geographical symbols coalescing around a predictable argument; yet the poem differs from comparable poems in *Harmonium.* The anecdote (José's Argentine) is no longer central, but occasional; it is part of the meditation, but not a synecdoche for it (as in, say, "Anecdote of the Jar").

Stevens' letters, full of explications and paraphrases of his poems, are invaluable for charting his changing attitudes; as his definitions of reality and imagination changed, so did his explanations of earlier poems. His comments to Renato Poggioli in 1953 about "The Man With the Blue Guitar," for example, differ from those made to Hi Simons in 1940. To Simons, Stevens explained canto XIX—"Being the lion in the lute / Before the lion locked in stone"—this way:

> The monster is what one faces: the lion locked in stone (life) which one wishes to match in intelligence and force, speaking (as a poet) with a voice matching its own. One thing about life is that the mind of one man, if strong enough, can become the master of all the life in the world.
>
> (L 360)

His explanation to Poggioli begins on the same note, but concludes quite differently:

> Monster = nature, which I desire to reduce: master, subjugate, acquire complete control over and use freely for my own purpose, as poet. I want, as poet, to be that in nature, which constitutes nature's very self. I want to be nature in the form of a man, with all the resources of nature.
>
> (L 790)

Stevens moves from an adversary relationship to a union which blurs the distinctions between his life-long terms, reality and imagination. His continuing efforts to reconcile external reality with imagining mind have been changed by the lessons he learned in "Notes Toward a Supreme Fiction." After he discovered that the poem was itself a process of a never-ending exchange between inner and outer realities, that what he saw outside was what was inside, he was to perform variations on his discovery over and over again. This simultaneously Romantic and Jungian conviction changes both the kind of poetry he wrote and the way he explained his earlier poetry.

Perhaps his attitude toward and definitions of reality and imagination were also affected by his exposure to Continental philosophy with its modern phenomenological attempts to overcome Cartesian dualism. His friendship with Henry Church and Jean Wahl introduced him to the heady world of the Entretiens de Pontigny, a gathering instituted by European philosophers in exile from Europe for the duration of World War II; there Stevens read "The Figure of the Youth as Virile Poet." One important premise of phenomenology is the notion of "intentionality." While the idealist places the world inside his head and the empiricist places it outside his head, the phenomenologist suggests that consciousness is an activity between the subject and the object of which he is conscious. Jean Wahl's article, "Vers le Concret," echoes the battle-cry of phenomenology's founder, Edmund Husserl, who insisted, "Back to the things themselves." The phenomenologists explore the relation between mind and world, committing themselves to the "lebenswelt," the lived world, the experience of the mind perceiving. Stevens' late work similarly integrates subject and object by defining reality as "not that which is but that which is apprehended" (CP 468).[2]

Stevens' abiding interest in the common ground between philosophy and poetry culminated in "A Collect of Philosophy," which he delivered as a lecture in 1951. Looking for "ideas that are inherently poetic" (OP 183), Stevens immediately wrote to Jean Wahl, whose advice was "that no ideas are inherently poetic, that the poetic nature of any idea depends on the mind through which it passes" (OP 183). If we read Stevens' essay looking for philosophical complexity or significant conclusions, we will be as disappointed as he himself was: "When I go back to it, it seems slight; and my chief deduction: that poetry is supreme over philosophy because we owe the idea of God to poetry and not to philosophy doesn't seem particularly to matter" (L 729). The deduction doesn't matter; indeed, one might have gotten there on less tortuous paths. What matters is "the mind through which it passes"—the mind attempting the deduction, needing to make it, and, as Stevens put it, probing for an integration.

Like his essays, Stevens' poetry is impelled by ideas; "Credences of Summer," for example, was generated by his "feeling for the necessity of a final accord with reality" (L 719). But the idea and the poetry of the idea are not identical. *Transport to Summer*, with its central "Credences of Summer," affirms the mind in the same gesture that it affirms reality. Transport, credences—the emphasis is on the mind travelling toward, believing in reality. In "Credences of Summer," Stevens struggles to create a state of mind appropriate to the external reality, a halted moment when the mind neither anticipates nor remembers. "This is the barrenness / Of the fertile thing that can attain no more," he proclaims. Exquisitely evoking a reality at the peak of ripeness, trembling on the brink of decay, Stevens unavoidably elicits the mind's knowledge of the imminent decay. "Look at it," "fix it," "exile desire," he quietly rants, but by the end of the poem, he must acknowledge the mind:

> . . . Soft, civil bird,
> The decay that you regard: of the arranged

And of the spirit of the arranged, *douceurs,*
Tristesses.

Stevens' métier is not the affirmation of reality so much as the meditation that makes possible the momentary marriage of mind and reality. Marriage may be too polite a word for the kind of savage union that Stevens describes in this, his favorite, section of "Credences of Summer":

> Three times the concentred self takes hold, three
> times
> The thrice concentred self, having possessed
>
> The object, grips it in savage scrutiny,
> Once to make captive, once to subjugate
> Or yield to subjugation, once to proclaim
> The meaning of the capture, this hard prize,
> Fully made, fully apparent, fully found.

Stevens is no longer content with the relatively peaceful confrontation between the "lion in the lute" and the "lion locked in stone"; now the two animals grapple in sexual battle. That Stevens translated aesthetic scrutiny into a kind of voyeurism, or sexual "knowing," is suggested by two comments he made to the Irish poet, Thomas McGreevy:

> To wander about among a hundred or more masterpieces (to be magnificent about it) made me feel like a young Sultan just married to his first hundred girls: there wasn't much one could do.

and

> What a secret rowdiness must have been alive in all of you. What an adventure to take such a trip and to know that in spite of your memories of this town and that mountain you were gathering Roma and Venezia and a lot more, just like so many tall black-haired girls. . .
>
> (L 680)

Although the union sought is aesthetic knowledge, the encounter itself is savage and animal-like.

"The Motive for Metaphor" is a helpful poem for understanding how difficult a "credence" in summer might be. Stevens contrasts the half-dead world of autumn and the half-alive world of spring not with summer, but with noon:

> The A B C of being,
>
> The ruddy temper, the hammer
> Of red and blue, the hard sound—
> Steel against intimation—the sharp flash,
> The vital, arrogant, fatal, dominant X.

Stevens jangles every sensory nerve here; we shrink with awed respect from this primary reality. And it is just this shrinking that he criticizes in "Credences of Summer":

> Far in the woods they sang their unreal songs,
> Secure. It was difficult to sing in face
> Of the object. The singers had to avert themselves
> Or else avert the object. Deep in the woods
> They sang of summer in the common fields.

These secure singers who turn from the reality of which they sing come in for recurrent criticism in *Transport to Summer,* for they seek and sing of a reality "there," when, Stevens knows, it turns out to be "here" all along (CP 305).

In his hymns to reality, Stevens affirms "this," "here," and "now" in what becomes a stylistic tic:

> . . . This is the centre that I seek.

and

> . . . This is the barrenness
> Of the fertile thing that can attain no more.

And again:

> This is the refuge that the end creates.

Demonstrative constructions depend on a context to determine their referents; Stevens develops an indeterminacy of reference that can be maddening, amusing, or enriching—depending on one's temperament and mood.

In "Auroras of Autumn," from the book of that title, Stevens returns to the half-dead and metaphorically stimulating world of autumn and compounds the indeterminacy:

> This is where the serpent lives, the bodiless.
> His head is air. Beneath his tip at night
> Eyes open and fix on us in every sky.
>
> Or is this another wriggling out of the egg,
> Another image at the end of the cave,
> Another bodiless for the body's slough?
>
> This is where the serpent lives. This is his nest,
> These fields, these hills, these tinted distances,
> And the pines above and along and beside the sea.
>
> This is form gulping after formlessness,
> Skin flashing to wished-for disappearances
> And the serpent body flashing without the skin.
>
> This is the height emerging and its base.
>   .   .   .   .
> This is his poison: that we should disbelieve.

The "serpent" probably refers to the constellation Serpens, which would be low on the horizon in autumn. "Bodiless," with a head of air, "form gulping after formlessness," the serpent is an imagined structure for a bunch of stars that might take any shape.

Thus the imagined serpent's imagined body flashes "without the skin."

Stevens' speaker is an active perceiver, and it is on his mental process that the poem is fixed; each "this" refers to a different moment in this meditation on perception. "This is where the serpent lives," he says, perhaps looking at the horizon, perhaps stretching out his arms to include all the night sky. Then he asks himself a very Platonic question: "Or is this . . . / Another image at the end of the cave," another delusion about reality? "This" this time refers to his thoughts in the preceding stanza. Moving out again, "This is his nest" has him looking at the earth beneath the constellation; then up: "This is form gulping after formlessness." And finally: an imagined reality, almost a "negative" of ours, where another serpent is "relentlessly in possession of happiness." This comment introduces the speaker's state of mind, and prepares us for the conclusion in canto x about an "unhappy people in a happy world."

I am not convinced that all this sliding around on the same demonstrative construction is entirely successful. Stevens has always exploited the relations between identity and metaphor in the verb *to be*. Yet "Thirteen Ways of Looking at a Blackbird" is taxing to the imagination, while some of Stevens' later poetry is taxing to the patience. What, for example, are we to make of this series from "Credences of Summer," in which "it" refers—I think—to summer (reality):

> It is the natural tower of all the world,
> The point of survey, green's green apogee,
> But a tower more precious than the view beyond.
>   .   .   .   .
> It is the mountain on which the tower stands,
> It is the final mountain. . . .
>   .   .   .   .
> It is the old man standing on the tower,
> Who reads no book. . . .

Stevens' five-line stanzas should be helpful; he has created an appearance of separation and progression: tower, mountain, old man. But is Stevens referring to a literal tower on a literal mountain, say Mount Penn, where a literal old man looks over the ripening fields of Oley, Pennsylvania? If so, what effect is Stevens looking for when he puts himself, the mountain, and the tower in the same construction? Can *all*, including the self, be summer? Or does Stevens mean to suggest a progression from literal statement (the tower as point of survey) to metaphor (the old man in his "ruddy ancientness" might stand for the sun)?

Perhaps this confusion is Stevens' point: a reconciliation with summer means reconciling one's scrutiny and one's metaphors to reality; it means including oneself in a definition of reality.[3] But it is tortuously done, and makes me sympathize with Randall Jarrell's complaint:

> Stevens is never more philosophical, abstract, rational, than when telling us to put our faith in nothing but immediate sensations, perceptions, aesthetic particulars. . . . When Stevens makes a myth to hold together aesthetic particulars . . . [it] spring[s] not from the soil but from the clouds, the arranged, scrubbed, reasoning clouds in someone's head.[4]

To which Stevens would reply, I imagine, "From the head; but of course!" Precisely this self-inclusive reference accounts for Stevens' syntax: "this is" and "it is" include the perceiver in the construction; the demonstrative syntax obstructs our immediate view of the external world by emphasizing the perceiving act itself. Stevens is not particularly interested in the ripening fields of Oley (though he tries to be), but in a view which includes his perception of them, his "this is it!" feeling at seeing them.

Jarrell's distinction between mythic soil and mythic clouds gives us another insight into Stevens, for it explains why "Auroras of Autumn" is a more satisfying poem than "Credences of Sum-

mer." Both are baffling in their indeterminacy, but "Auroras"
yields itself to Stevens' particular forte: myths that spring from
sky-ey clouds, rather than earthy soil. These clouds *are* in Stevens' head, but they are also intensely out there. When Stevens
writes not of ripening summer, but of shape-shifting lights in the
autumnal sky, he has hit on the—for him—perfect symbol:

> He observes how the north is always enlarging the change,
>
> With its frigid brilliances, its blue-red sweeps
> And gusts of great enkindlings, its polar green,
> The color of ice and fire and solitude.

Recall Stevens' fondness for the candle of imagination in "Valley
Candle" in *Harmonium;* in "Auroras," the polar lights include
both the strickening wind and the "enkindlings": "gusts of enkindlings."

These images of fire, wind, and ice recur as symbols of the reality that dissolves myth, leaving the perceiver starkly isolated.
The domestic warmth of canto III, for example, gives way to fire
and wind: "The house will crumble and the books will burn" and
"The wind will command them with invincible sound." In canto
IV, the mythy father—"O master seated by the fire"—cannot survive the question: "What company, / In masks, can choir it with
the naked wind?" The speaker's solitude is the emotional crux of
all the cantos, as he bids "Farewell to an idea" three times over;
each "farewell" witnesses the destruction of some "idea" that
makes the universe a comfortable place to live in.

The first farewell establishes the speaker's isolation. An aging
man walks in his season—late autumn—and in his time of day—
late afternoon. The darkness and cold gather night and winter
around the stanza until the mind can only become a blank: trying
to remember what the white recalls (summer), and trying not to
think what the white anticipates (winter and death). The deserted

cabin of this canto heightens the sense of exclusion in the next canto, removing the domestic scene to some point in the past. The speaker creates the scene as if he were watching from the outside: "The soft hands are a motion not a touch" and "The windows will be lighted, not the rooms." But the scene is hardly meant literally; that mother who is a "shelter of the mind" and "the purpose of the poem" is the comforting archetype to which Stevens bids "farewell."

The father of canto IV resembles Stevens' masculine angel of "Notes," a "master seated by the fire / And yet in space and motionless and yet / Of motion the ever-brightening origin." As in "Notes," Stevens recognizes this mythy father as a projection of his own imagination, yet the portrait is studded with ambivalence: "The father sits / In space, wherever he sits, of bleak regard." This archetypal father is producer and stage manager, but of what? Of nothing, Stevens asserts in canto V, simultaneously denying both pageant and producer:

> These musicians dubbing at a tragedy,
>
> A-dub, a-dub, which is made up of this:
> That there are no lines to speak? There is no play.
> Or, the persons act one merely by being here.

On that note, Stevens turns to the theatrical effect of the brilliant night sky, which has, after all, prompted these associations. Its ceaseless change is meaningless: transformations to "no end, / Except the lavishing of itself in change."

This aimless, meaningless changing is the basis for Stevens' claim in canto VIII that the aurora borealis is "innocent"; like his earlier word "ignorance," "innocence" suggests unwilled, unmentalized reality. In canto VI, it is "nothing," in contrast to the "single man"—the "scholar"-mind—who feels it impinge on "everything he is." Solitude, "arctic effulgence," and flaring fire are correlatives for the death that process inevitably brings; the mind's anticipation of death is the groundbass of this meditation on the "auroras of autumn"—the beginning of a late season in life.

The imagination has always tried to cope with its impending extinction. In the midst of summer, it imagines winter (VII). But "Auroras" is not a long version of "Life Is Motion," where the jovial characters dance around a stump. In the midst of winter, Stevens no longer resurrects summer; instead he wonders:

> . . . When the leaves are dead,
> Does it take its place in the north and enfold itself,
> Goat-leaper, crystalled and luminous, sitting
>
> In highest night? And do these heavens adorn
> And proclaim it?

We are back with the serpent, blinking through the fabulous aurora—now an emblem of the imagination itself. Yet even this enthroned king must abdicate, must "find / What must unmake it." The stars' glittering belts flash, paradoxically, "like a great shadow's last embellishment." The lights of the aurora borealis have become a symbol of being caught up in process, of life blazing its last assertion before disaster. The imagination that meditates on death endorses not "hushful paradise"—an imagined future based on a recollected summer—but "these lights / Like a blaze of summer straw, in winter's nick."

If "Auroras of Autumn" is a hymn to a gorgeous reality, "An Ordinary Evening in New Haven" is Stevens' meandering hymn to a plain reality; it begins where Stevens has begun many times before:

> Of what is this house composed if not of the sun,
>
> These houses, these difficult objects, dilapidate

Appearances of what appearances,
Words, lines, not meanings, not communications.

The poem is the process which allows him to affirm both the reality and the poem of reality:

> . . . We seek
> Nothing beyond reality. Within it,
>
> Everything, the spirit's alchemicana
> Included.

Stevens' comment in "Three Academic Pieces" provides his most significant prose gloss: "What our eyes behold may well be the text of life but one's meditations on the text and the disclosures of these meditations are no less a part of the structure of reality" (NA 76). That "text" of reality has been Stevens' subject since *Harmonium*, of course; what is new is the assertion that his "meditations" are also a part of the structure of reality. Remember that Crispin, of "The Comedian as the Letter C," preferred "text to gloss," yet ended up profitlessly "glozing his life with after-shining flicks" because his creator was convinced that text and gloss, perceived and the meditation on the perceived, eye and tongue, were essentially incompatible. Stevens' later poems are the occasion and process for making these dichotomies dissolve.

His solvents are syntax and metaphor. In addition to the constructions I have noted in "Auroras of Autumn" and "Credences of Summer," Stevens uses a syntactical formula: not x, not y, but (x and y). The images within this construction will vary, but the implication is always "not the perceived" and "not the imagined," but "the perceived becoming the apprehended." Or, as Stevens put it: "Nothing beyond reality. Within it, / Everything." This is making reality the base, of course; Stevens' syntactical genius is to reverse his premise:

> It is not in the premise that reality
> Is a solid. It may be a shade that traverses
> A dust, a force that traverses a shade.
>
> (CP 489)

He accomplishes the same logical sleight-of-hand in poems based on metaphor—that is, meditations on metaphoric activity. A whimsical example is "Someone Puts a Pineapple Together," in which Stevens plays the pedant:

> O juventes, O filii, he contemplates
> A wholly artificial nature, in which
> The profusion of metaphor has increased.

"Someone Puts a Pineapple Together" is the second piece of "Three Academic Pieces," Stevens' essay on metaphor; the poem exists as an example of that meditation which is "a part of the structure of reality."

Playing off reality and imagination as agents in "constructing" the pineapple, Stevens uses geometrical images: tangent, sign, apposites, edge, plane, ellipses, and cone. In this universe, imagination takes its place among the planets:

> It is as if there were three planets: the sun,
> The moon and the imagination, or, say,
>
> Day, night and man and his endless effigies.

Once the "light" from the third planet is admitted, the pineapple blooms with "casual exfoliations." It looks like a hut standing "by itself beneath the palms," a humped owl with "a hundred eyes," or even "yesterday's volcano." Stevens calls these resemblances merely "sprigs," or, returning to the central metaphor, "apposites . . . of the whole." From these self-consciously rendered metaphors for the pineapple, Stevens turns to the pineapple as a metaphor: "An object the sum of its complications, seen / And unseen. This is everybody's world." The conclusion, in which Stevens "proves" that the "total artifice reveals itself / As the total reality," is a tour-de-force:

> . . . It is that which is distilled
> In the prolific ellipses that we know,
>
> In the planes that tilt hard revelations on
> The eye, a geometric glitter, tiltings
> As of sections collecting toward the greenest cone.

Man, who sees everything in a "tangent of himself," participates in the creation of this reality. "Ellipses" are the plane sections of a pineapple-shaped solid; the "prolific ellipses" of man's imagination create a cone which, according to Stevens' metaphysical geometry, is the "sum of its complications."

All of Stevens' late metaphors have this same complex existence: not this, not that, but the other thing that is both "this and that" together. Even when Stevens speaks of stepping "barefoot into reality" in "Large Red Man Reading," it is difficult to determine whether the "text" is reality or the imagination's meditations on it. The "man" reads "from out of the purple tabulae"—a significant mixture of reality's red and imagination's blue—"the outlines of being" which insist: "Poesis, poesis." Stevens has come to see "reality" as the life lived in it; discussions about imagination and reality are conducted, he says, "not for the purposes of life but for the purposes of arts and letters" (NA 147). His purpose is clearly the "integrations which are the reason for living" (NA 155). In the essay "Imagination as Value," Stevens struggles to transcend the position (similar to the one expressed in "The Man With the Blue Guitar") that "the imagination is the power of the mind over the possibilities of things" (NA 136); that is no longer enough for Stevens, who takes on the logical positivists and Freud in his argument that imagination is "the only clue to reality" (NA 137). In "A Primitive Like an Orb," he speaks of a "central poem" which is only "seen and known in lesser poems." Perhaps Stevens is remembering his quotation of Ernst Cassirer: " 'The true poem is not the work of the individual artist; it is the universe itself, the one work of art which is forever perfecting itself' " (NA 136). For Stevens, this possible "central poem" becomes much more than a mirror of external reality:

> . . . It is
> As if the central poem became the world,
>
> And the world the central poem, each one the mate
> Of the other.

This conviction that reality and imagination are facing pages of the same text accompanies a chilling awareness of imminent personal death. In "An Old Man Asleep," for example, Stevens depicts the cessation of existence by suggesting that when the self sleeps, so does the earth: "The two worlds are asleep." When he speaks of "your whole peculiar plot," with its puns on events and burial, and of "the drowsy motion of the river R," Stevens seems intensely aware of an almost threshhold existence. Even more chilling is "Madame La Fleurie," the archetypal mother turned betrayer:

> His grief is that his mother should feed on him, himself and what he
>   saw,
> In that distant chamber, a bearded queen, wicked in her dead light.

Interior imagination, the anima, has grown old and masculine; the comforting mother of earth is now a burial chamber instead of a womb.

Stevens must sympathize with the "drowsy, infant old men" of "Questions are Remarks"; their questions—"why" and "Mother, my mother, who are you"—are remarks about the needs of old men to turn reality into a cradling mother. But only the grandson's "voyant" question—"What is that"—is appropriate to the pageant of "nothingness" before him. An old man's "adult enfantillages" are a failure of nerve and of vision. Yet Stevens several times refers to the "child" asleep in the lives of old men. In his essay on the child archetype, Jung says that "psychologically speaking, . . . the 'child' symbolizes the pre-conscious and the post-conscious nature of man. His pre-conscious nature is the unconscious state of early childhood; his post-conscious nature is an anticipation by analogy of life after death." [5] But this mythic figure of Stevens' old age occurs to a poet relentless in his denials of transcendence. The mind, Stevens says in "The Owl in the Sarcophagus," is a "child that sings itself to sleep." Facing death, Stevens insisted that his "singing" imagination, like an orphan in an indifferent universe, must be a self-sufficient consolation with no endurance beyond its embodied existence.

If the "child" stands for the wholeness of the mind—both its "prepersonae" and its longed-for posthumous beginnings—then Ulysses stands for the mind meditating on its knowledge. In "The Sail of Ulysses," Stevens calls him "Symbol of the seeker" (OP 99); he might be the "ephebe" grown old seeking reality. To Ulysses Stevens gives the speech that sums up the generating impulse behind all his later poetry:

> If knowledge and the thing known are one
>
> .   .   .   .
>
> Then knowledge is the only life,
> The only sun of the only day,
> The only access to true ease,
> The deep comfort of the world and fate.

Stevens' Ulysses is in the tradition of Tennyson's, that old man who cannot rest from travel because experience endlessly beckons:

> Yet all experience is an arch wherethro'
> Gleams that untravell'd world whose margin fades
> For ever and for ever when I move.

So too Stevens' Ulysses:

> Yet always there is another life,
> A life beyond this present knowing,
> A life lighter than this present splendor,
> Brighter, perfected and distant away,
> Not to be reached but to be known.

Stevens' transformation of this tradition occurs in his conviction that the only knowledge we ever gain is self-knowledge. Crossing a "giant sea," Ulysses reads "his own mind"; he learns:

> It is the sibyl of the self,
> The self as sibyl, whose diamond,
> Whose chiefest embracing of all wealth
> Is poverty.

It ought to follow that "The World as Meditation" would be Ulysses' poem, but it is Penelope's—patient Penelope waiting for her "interminable adventurer":

> Is it Ulysses that approaches from the east,
> The interminable adventurer? The trees are mended.
> That winter is washed away. Someone is moving.

Thinking about the physical contentment she will feel when Ulysses returns ("His arms would be her necklace / And her belt"), she feels present contentment because of her confusion of Ulysses and the sun: "It was only day." The sun brings the warmth of Ulysses, so thought and sensation commingle: "The thought kept beating in her like her heart. / The two kept beating together." The poem is reminiscent of the intensity felt in "Notes Toward a Supreme Fiction":

> . . . the strong exhilaration
> Of what we feel from what we think, of thought
> Beating in the heart, as if blood newly came.

The poem's tense shifts complicate the deceptive simplicity, moving from the fragile present tense—"Is it?"—to a narrative past tense—"she has composed" and "the trees had been mended." We are hardly aware when the poem becomes Penelope's meditation rather than her sensory experience: "It *was* only day." Concluding in the conditional and gerundive—"She would" and "never forgetting"—the poem effectively transforms Penelope's meditation into a timeless meditation by the impersonal speaker.

The presence of this impersonal speaker introduces the possibility that the mythic couple symbolizes the external world made interior in the process of personification. Ulysses-sun "awakens the world in which she dwells"; as the feminine symbol of earth, Penelope wears "cretonnes," a fabric usually imprinted with a large floral design. Perhaps the poem is both seasonal and diurnal, bringing spring as well as dawn. As figures of mind, Ulysses suggests solar consciousness and Penelope suggests the feminine figure of imagination; these two figures can never come together, but their "coming constantly so near" is the stuff of poetry.

Like so many of the last poems, "The World as Meditation" is retrospective, begging comparison not just with its companion poems, but with earlier poems in Stevens' canon. Considered with "Sunday Morning," "The World as Meditation" shows the continuity and the change in Stevens' work. Both have the same components: an impersonal narrator, a meditative woman coping with her expectations, and the sun as a central symbol. With its half-mythic, half-domestic Penelope and its complex tense shifts, "The World as Meditation" even achieves the same sweeps backward and forward in time. "Sunday Morning" has the bravura of a condensed *Golden Bough:*

> Jove in the clouds had his inhuman birth.
> No mother suckled him, no sweet land gave
> Large-mannered motions to his mythy mind.
> He moved among us, as a muttering king,
> Magnificent, would move among his hinds,
> Until our blood, commingling, virginal,
> With heaven, brought such requital to desire
> The very hinds discerned it, in a star.

In "Sunday Morning," Stevens strained to affirm a participation in a reality that is primitively physical:

> Supple and turbulent, a ring of men
> Shall chant in orgy on a summer morn
> Their boisterous devotion to the sun,
> Not as a god, but as a god might be,
> Naked among them, like a savage source.

A lifetime's consideration brought the conviction of "The World as Meditation," that the ground of being was neither the sun nor the body's life in the sun, but the thought of the sun, the reality contained in the mind: "It was Ulysses and it was not."

Other retrospective poems from Stevens' last years suggest that the affirmation won in "The World as Meditation" was not an easy triumph. In "As You Leave the Room" (OP 116), Stevens responds to some implied criticism by referring to earlier poems (in order, to "Someone Puts a Pineapple Together," "The Well

Dressed Man With a Beard," "Asides on the Oboe" and "Credences of Summer"):

> That poem about the pineapple, the one
> About the mind as never satisfied,
>
> The one about the credible hero, the one
> About summer, are not what skeletons think about.

But then:

> I wonder, have I lived a skeleton's life,
> As a disbeliever in reality?

An earlier version of this poem, "First Warmth," puts it this way: "Have I lived a skeleton's life, / As a questioner about reality?" The revision from "questioner" to "disbeliever" suggests that Stevens might be wondering whether his incessant questioning did not finally add up to a disbelief in reality—in the possibility of the mind knowing it. The "you" against whom he defends himself could be himself or his critics. Robert Lowell complained, for example, that Stevens' "places are places visited on a vacation, his people are essences, and his passions are impressions"—in sum, that his metaphysics was spoiling his physics. [6]

Stevens' answer—to his critics or his own doubts?—represents a significant departure from "First Warmth," where it was "the warmth I had forgotten becomes / Part of the major reality." Instead, it is "Now, here, the snow I had forgotten becomes / Part of a major reality." In a retrospective poem, the "snow I had forgotten" must refer to "The Snow Man" of *Harmonium*. Stevens goes from his 1940s definition of reality as "ABC," "X," and "summer," all the way back to something like his earlier definition of reality as nothing. This nothing is "part of a major reality"—not *the* reality, but *a* reality, and then only part of it. Even that, Stevens says, is an "appreciation"—enlargement, gain in value, and respect—"of a reality." His diction blurs the distinction between his attitude toward the snow and the snow itself. The poem's conclusion—"as if nothing had been changed at all"—recalls "The Snow Man" who, "nothing himself, beholds / Nothing that is not there and the nothing that is."

Other moments of doubt and affirmation occur in poems the titles of which imply the problem: "The Planet on the Table" and "The Poem that Took the Place of a Mountain." The question brought up by these poems is whether this ongoing "poem" of Stevens' had permitted a life in reality or taken its place:

> There it was, word for word,
> The poem that took the place of a mountain.
>
> He breathed its oxygen,
> Even when the book lay turned in the dust of his table.

In search of an "outlook that would be right," Stevens painstakingly climbed a mountain of his own making. The heart-wrenching power of the poem depends on the conclusion; the rearranger of reality, looking for the view toward which all "his inexactnesses" had led him, finds the very thing which defies rearrangement: the sea. As much with exhaustion as with completion, he reaches the pinnacle:

> Where he could lie and, gazing down at the sea,
> Recognize his unique and solitary home.

It is useless to ask why Stevens' experience of reality is so hard won; the whole premise of his poetry—a premise embraced again and again with fierce courage—is as much temperamentally imposed as philosophically adopted. He could never write an "ars poetica" like William Carlos Williams' "A Sort of a Song," which concludes: "Saxifrage is my flower that splits / the rocks." Stevens simply did not believe that poems, "in the poverty of their words," could participate in the rock-reality, much less "split" it. "We live in a constellation / Of patches and pitches," Stevens says in "July Mountain" (OP 114), contrasting that with the "single world" found on a page of poetry.

At best, he can engage in a kind of metaphysical arithmetic: prologues to . . . , notes toward . . . , parts of . . . , and ideas of. . . . Marshalling the fragments together, scrutinizing the "edgings and inchings of final form" (CP 488), Stevens arrives at something like a whole, a "Planet on the Table." "Ariel was glad he had written his poems," Stevens can say with conviction, knowing that the "planet" on the table represents a special kind of world:

> His self and the sun were one
> And his poems, although makings of his self,
> Were no less makings of the sun.

"Makings"—constructions, compositions. The epigraph to "The World as Meditation" quotes Georges Enesco's "l'exercice essentiel du compositeur—la méditation," to suggest the crucial relationship between the composer and the world he composes. Exploring "reality," we are exploring our thoughts and images of reality, and, therefore, ourselves; the "constructed" reveals only the "constructor."

Stevens is like the man in "Prologues to What Is Possible," pushing against the barrier of meaning:

> As he traveled alone, like a man lured on by a syllable without any
>   meaning,
> A syllable of which he felt, with an appointed sureness,
> That it contained the meaning into which he wanted to enter.

The boat he travels on in "Prologues to What Is Possible" is a metaphor for metaphor; if he discovered and entered the "meaning" he seeks, the "meaning" would "shatter the boat and leave the oarsmen quiet." Even if a man could survive that swim, poetry, with its noisy "oarsmen," could not; the man must remain in "the enclosures of hypotheses"—boats, shores, metaphors. Like Ulysses in "The Sail of Ulysses," the speaker gains only knowledge of that "smallest lamp, which added its puissant flick." But according to Stevens' arithmetic, this addition "creates a fresh universe out of nothingness."

Celebrating the mind's capacity to create a "fresh universe out of nothingness by adding itself," Stevens writes "The Rock." The title recalls a host of images from Stevens' earlier poems. In "Credences of Summer," the rock is an irreducible reality:

> The rock cannot be broken. It is the truth.
> It rises from land and sea and covers them.
> It is a mountain half way green and then,
> The other immeasurable half, such rock
> As placid air becomes.

In "The Man With the Blue Guitar," canto XI struggles to depict the process—becoming—by which parts interact with wholes: "ivy on the stones / Becomes the stones" and "men in waves become the sea." But the sea also "returns upon the men." The concluding image uses "the rock" to suggest not just reality, but "being," "existence": "Deeper within the belly's dark / Of time, time grows upon the rock." So too in "The Rock," where the image suggests neither material reality nor the process of reality, but our life in time and place; the rock is "the gray particular of man's life" and "the stern particular of the air."

Stevens begins "The Rock" by reminding us that memory is mental and therefore fictive:

It is an illusion that we were ever alive,
Lived in the houses of mothers, arranged ourselves
By our own motions in a freedom of air.

Regard the freedom of seventy years ago.
It is no longer air.

"Seventy Years Later" is full of "mind" words: illusion, consciousness, believed, invention, theorem. Far from denying meaning to
these "queer assertion[s] of humanity," Stevens is affirming them
as an "incessant being alive," all we have in the impermanence
that is the permanence of existence:

As if nothingness contained a métier,
A vital assumption, an impermanence
In its permanent cold, an illusion so desired

That the green leaves came and covered the high rock,
That the lilacs came and bloomed.

The "leaves" covering the rock provide Stevens with the poem's
central pun: the leaves are both reality's leaves and poetry's
leaves—pages. It is an elaborate pun that continually dissolves
distinctions between real and mind-made, permitting Stevens to
write a poem that is at once a celebration of poetry (using his definition of "poetry" as an activity of the imagination) and a hymn to
that barren rock which impels man's poetry.

"The Poem as Icon" moves from assertion to assertion: "It is
not enough to cover the rock with leaves," to "They are more
than leaves that cover the barren rock," to the conclusive "The
poem makes meanings of the rock." If the "predicate"—the logical or the grammatical predicate?—is "that there is nothing else,"
then the leaves are everything, as long as we recall the integrity
of Stevens' logic, which moves from an "as if" to an *is*. Making

meanings of the rock creates us; the leaves turn the "whitest eye" to the fertile creative I. Perhaps reevaluating his harsh assessment in "Seventy Years Later" of the "embrace between one desperate clod / And another," Stevens now sees the "leaves" participating in man's seasons:

> They bloom as a man loves, as he lives in love.
> They bear their fruit so that the year is known,
>
> As if its understanding was brown skin,
> The honey in its pulp, the final found,
> The plenty of the year and of the world.

Each season of life brings a knowledge appropriate to it, each one generating the development of the fictive leaves. The knowledge of time comes from the fictive fruit, and at the center of time's fruit is the "final found." William Butler Yeats, in "The Coming of Wisdom With Time," makes a similar equation between leaves and youth, the dead tree of winter and wisdom:

> Though leaves are many, the root is one;
> Through all the lying days of my youth
> I swayed my leaves and flowers in the sun;
> Now I may wither into the truth.[7]

The difference in Stevens' vision is that his youthful leaves are not "lying"—fictive yes, but nevertheless affirming a "particular of being" appropriate to that season of life—and the "final found" itself is a fiction.

The "curative" potential of such a "poetic" process is Stevens' theme. As he says in "Adagia," "Poetry is a cure of the mind" (OP 176). "We must be cured of" the rock, Stevens asserts, implying both "healed" and "preserved." The title of this section, "The Poem as Icon," suggests another meaning for "cure," implying poetry as a kind of "curate" with the spiritual "care" of man's needs in its keeping. Still playing with religious connotations ("The figuration of blessedness"), Stevens puns on the meanings of icon. "Icon" signifies a representation or resemblance (rhetorically, in metaphor and simile; pictorially, in statues and paintings). Thus the poem "as icon" *represents* reality in its words. But an icon is also an object of religious devotion; "the fiction of the leaves is the icon / Of the poem" suggests man's spiritual devotion to his fictions. "Icon" is also a term in semiotics for a sign that signifies by virtue of sharing a property with what it represents. Thus a photograph is an icon, but the word "photograph" is a symbol. In that sense "the icon is the man" because man and his leaves are "icons" of each other: "They bloom as a man loves." Punning on "icon" and "cure," Stevens shows the complex relationships between the barren, meaningless ground of being; man, the meaning-maker; and the "thousand things" that man can make of the rock—and of himself.

As Ralph J. Mills has suggested in "Wallace Stevens: The Image of the Rock," Stevens has borrowed Christian connotations of the "rock" (the Church), the icon, and the cure only to formulate his own peculiarly humanistic notion of redemption through the imagination.[8] Perhaps in this way Stevens is carrying on a private argument with T. S. Eliot, whose prose and poetry insist on the inadequacies of humanism. In "Second Thoughts on Humanism," for example, Eliot argues:

> Man is man because he can recognize supernatural realities, not because he can invent them. Either everything in man can be traced as a development from below, or something must come from above. There is no avoiding that dilemma: you must be either a naturalist or a supernaturalist.[9]

Neither a naturalist nor a supernaturalist, Stevens avoids the dilemma by denying Eliot's premise: man does invent the supernatural realities, and it is precisely because he does that they "exist." Man, the inventor of those realities, is therefore necessarily the "iconic" center of Stevens' poem. T. S. Eliot's "Four Quartets" is a religious meditation on the difficulty of apprehending the Divine Logos with the logos of man; Stevens' "The Rock" is a humanistic meditation on the necessity of apprehending the barren rock to which man's words give meaning.

The poem's insistent and tender mention of spring, summer, and autumn makes the omission of winter conspicuous; the speaker—"seventy years later"—is about to "wither into the truth," as Yeats put it, of winter. But this late-life hymn has all the tranquillity of religious conviction:

> It is the rock where tranquil must adduce
> Its tranquil self, the main of things, the mind,
>
> The starting point of the human and the end,
> That in which space itself is contained, the gate
> To the enclosure.

"Adduce" implies the steps in a logical sequence, the presentation of examples that "lead to" a hypothesis. For Stevens, the hypothesis can be nothing more than man himself, the perceiver of reality and, because he gives reality the only meanings it ever has, the "container" of it.

Among the multitude of Stevens' attitudes toward reality, not one allows him the consolations that give Eliot's "Four Quartets" its religious grandeur. But for many readers, it is Stevens' courage in the face of the abyss that keeps his poetry alive. Perhaps the most courageous act of *The Collected Poems* is the last: by putting "Not Ideas about the Thing but the Thing Itself" as the final poem in the book, Stevens gives the last word to reality.

"A scrawny cry from outside / Seemed like a sound in his mind," the way a bird's song always signifies some awakening of consciousness in Stevens' poetry. But this cry is "not from the vast ventriloquism / Of sleep's faded papier-mâché," Stevens concludes, thereby calling into question the tranquillity "adduced" in "Forms of the Rock in a Night-Hymn." No, this chorister is "part of the colossal sun," an immense reality beyond the mind's sway. Stevens uses his favorite sounds:

> That scrawny cry—it was
> A chorister whose c preceded the choir.
> It was part of the colossal sun.

The bird's "c" pre-c's the choir's, as the c-sounds echo and build to the thundering "colossal sun," then diminish and contract again: "surrounded by its choral rings, / Still far away." The single chorister will also "cede" his song to the larger sound of the whole choir, and thus "precedes" the choir in the sense that the choir too yields to the sun. It is perhaps Stevens' finest poetry, but it is all metaphor: only *"like* / A new knowledge of reality" for the old man in his bed at dawn.

Though I would prefer to conclude by saying that what Stevens gives us when he is at his best and we at ours is a "new knowledge of a reality," in fact he gives us something more rare: the courage to accept the possibility that our every definition of reality is a regulative and saving fiction—an "as if," a "like."

Notes

CHAPTER 1: INTRODUCTION

1. Suzanne Langer, "The Prince of Creation," *Fortune*, January 1944; collected in *The Borzoi Reader*, ed. Charles Muscatine and Marlene Griffith (New York: Alfred A. Knopf, 1971), p. 67.

2. I. A. Richards, "The Interaction of Words," *The Language of Poetry*, ed. Allen Tate (Princeton University Press, 1942; rpt. New York: Russell and Russell, 1960), p. 70.

CHAPTER 2: THE GAIETY OF LANGUAGE

1. T. S. Eliot. "The Love Song of J. Alfred Prufrock," *Collected Poems 1909–1962* (New York: Harcourt Brace Jovanovich, Inc., 1963), p. 4.

2. Henri Bergson, *Creative Evolution*, trans. Arthur Mitchell (New York: Henry Holt and Co., 1911), p. 2.

3. René Taupin, *L'Influence du Symbolisme Français sur la Poésie Américaine* (Paris: H. Champion, 1929), p. 276; the quotation appears in the more readily available *Wallace Stevens: A Critical Anthology*, ed. Irvin Ehrenpreis (Penguin Books, 1972), p. 55.

4. Ezra Pound, "A Few Don'ts by an Imagiste," *Poetry* 1 (March, 1913), 203; collected in *Prose Keys to Modern Poetry*, ed. Karl Shapiro (New York: Harper and Row, 1962), p. 104.

5. Harvey Gross, *Sound and Form in Modern Poetry* (Ann Arbor: University of Michigan Press, 1964), Chapter 1.

6. Joseph N. Riddel, *The Clairvoyant Eye* (Baton Rouge: Louisiana State University Press, 1965), p. 87.

7. The reaction of Stevens' contemporaries can be partially assessed from Part II of the Ehrenpreis anthology.

8. R. P. Blackmur, "Examples of Wallace Stevens," *Form and Value in Modern Poetry* (New York: Doubleday Anchor Books, 1952); reprinted in Ehrenpreis, pp. 61–62.

9. See Frank Doggett, *Stevens' Poetry of Thought* (Baltimore: Johns Hopkins Press, 1966), p. 24.

10. Carl Gustav Jung and C. Kerenyi, *Essays on a Science of Mythology*, trans. R. F. C. Hull (New York: Harper and Row, 1963), p. 173.

11. Erich Neumann, *The Great Mother: An Analysis of the Archetype*, trans. Ralph Manheim, Bollingen Series XLVII (Princeton: Princeton University Press, 1963), p. 65.

CHAPTER 3: INTROSPECTIVE EXILES

1. See Richard Ellmann, "Wallace Stevens' Ice-Cream," *Kenyon Review* 19 (Winter 1957), 89.

2. "Wife" may, of course, be too specific an explanation of this female figure. Many of the passages I refer to in the following discussion, as well as the passage that opens the poem, could refer to that modern muse, the interior "woman" of imagination. I have ignored this dimension of the poem for the sake of brevity, but at the cost of oversimplifying its complexity.

CHAPTER 4: HERO-HYMNS

1. Paul Valéry, "The Persian Letters" in *Collected Works*, Vol. 10: *History and Politics*, trans. Denise Folliott and Jackson Mathews, Bollingen Series XLV (New York: Pantheon Books, 1962), p. 215.

2. Jung, "Psychology and Literature," *Modern Man in Search Of a Soul*, trans. W. S. Dell and Cary F. Baynes (New York: Harcourt, Brace & World, 1933), p. 169.

3. Richards, "The Interaction of Words," p. 70.

4. See, e.g., *The Portable Nietzsche*, ed. Walter Kaufmann (New York: Viking Press, 1968), pp. 448–50.

5. Philip Wheelwright, "Poetry, Myth and Reality," *The Language of Poetry*, p. 33.

6. See Merle E. Brown, *Wallace Stevens: The Poem as Act* (Detroit: Wayne State University Press, 1970), p. 92, for a discussion of the poem as one in which the poet is shaping and defining poetry.

7. Jung, *Collected Works*, Vol. 11: *Psychology and Religion: West and East*, trans. R. F. C. Hull, Bollingen Series XX (New York: Pantheon Books, 1956), p. 12.

8. See Helen Vendler, "The False and True Sublime," *Southern Review* (Summer 1971), reprinted in Ehrenpreis, p. 295.

9. Jung, *Psychology and Religion*, p. 12.

10. William James, *Essays in Radical Empiricism and A Pluralistic Universe,* ed. Ralph Barton Perry (New York: Longmans, Green and Co., 1943), p. 219.

11. See, e.g., William James, "The Function of Cognition," to cite one of many essays, in *The Meaning of Truth* (University of Michigan Press, Ann Arbor Paperbacks, 1970); William Marshall Urban, *Language and Reality* (London: George Allen and Unwin, 1939).

12. Valéry, *History and Politics*, p. 93.

13. William Carlos Williams, *Collected Earlier Poems* (New York: New Directions, 1951), p. 277.

14. James Baird, *The Dome and the Rock* (Baltimore: Johns Hopkins Press, 1968), p. xix, is the source of this etymology.

CHAPTER 5: "NOTES TOWARD A SUPREME FICTION"

1. Helen Vendler, *On Extended Wings: Wallace Stevens' Longer Poems* (Cambridge: Harvard University Press, 1969), p. 196, also notes the pun on existence in "bee": "the new-come bee is the new become and the new-come being."

2. R. P. Blackmur, "The Expense of Greatness," in *The Lion and the Honeycomb* (New York: Harcourt, Brace & World, Inc., 1955), p. 95: "As it is a condition of life to die, it is a condition of thought, in the end, to fail. Death is the expense of life and failure is the expense of greatness."

CHAPTER 6: THE WORLD OF WORDS

1. Paul Valéry, *Collected Works*, Vol. 4: *Dialogues*, ed. Jackson Mathews, trans. William McCausland Stewart, with "Two Prefaces" by Wallace Stevens, Bollingen Series XLV (New York: Pantheon Books, 1956), p. 81.

2. The premises, methods, and history of phenomenology are studied in Herbert Spiegelberg, *The Phenomenological Movement: A Historical Introduction,* 2 vols. (The Hague: Martinus Nijhoff, 1969). Among the host of names that Spiegelberg mentions in reference to the history of phenomenology in France are several closely connected with Henry Church and Jean Wahl. Wahl, moreover, took part in the birth of *Recherches Philosophiques*, a French version of the Husserlian yearbook. Meeting Church and Wahl, Stevens was meeting important changes in European philosophy. Perhaps more important than actual "influence" on Stevens, however, is the common ground between the phenomenologists and those philosophers with whom Stevens was certainly familiar: William James and Henri Bergson.

3. See Isabel MacCaffrey, "The Other Side of Silence: 'Credences of Summer' as an Example," *Modern Language Quarterly* 30 (September 1969), 417–38.

4. Randall Jarrell, *Poetry and the Age*, excerpted in Ehrenpreis, p. 207.

5. Jung, *Psyche and Symbol*, ed. Violet S. de Laszlo (Doubleday Anchor Books, 1958), p. 144.

6. Robert Lowell, "Imagination and Reality," in *Nation* 164 (April 5, 1947), excerpted in Ehrenpreis, p. 155.

7. William Butler Yeats, *The Collected Poems* (New York: The Macmillan Co., 1956), p. 92.

8. Ralph J. Mills, "Wallace Stevens: The Image of the Rock," in *Wallace Stevens: A Collection of Critical Essays*, ed. Marie Borroff (Englewood Cliffs: Prentice-Hall, Inc., 1963), 106–8.

9. T. S. Eliot, *Selected Essays*, new ed. (New York: Harcourt, Brace and World, 1960), p. 433.

Selected Bibliography

Publication information concerning the principal works by Wallace Stevens can be found in the Table of Dates.

I. BIBLIOGRAPHIES

Edelstein, J. M. *Wallace Stevens: A Descriptive Bibliography.* University of Pittsburgh Press, 1973.

Morse, Samuel French, Jackson R. Bryer, and Joseph N. Riddel. *Wallace Stevens Checklist and Bibliography of Stevens Criticism.* Denver: Alan Swallow, 1963.

II. COLLECTIONS OF ESSAYS

Borroff, Marie, ed. *Wallace Stevens: A Collection of Critical Essays.* Englewood Cliffs: Prentice-Hall, Inc., 1963. (Eleven essays on Stevens, including Louis Martz's important "Wallace Stevens: The World as Meditation.")

Brown, Ashley, and Robert S. Haller, eds. *The Achievement of Wallace Stevens.* Philadelphia: J. B. Lippincott, 1962. (Contains important Stevens criticism of the 1920s and 1930s, along with Hi Simons' pioneering essay, " 'The Comedian as the Letter C': Its Sense and Its Significance.")

Ehrenpreis, Irvin, ed. *Wallace Stevens: A Critical Anthology.* Penguin Books, 1972. (A chronologically arranged anthology containing excerpts from Stevens' letters and essays along with reprints or excerpts of essays on Stevens from early contemporary reactions through the developing critical debate of the 1970s.)

Pearce, Roy Harvey, and J. Hillis Miller, eds. *The Act of the Mind.* Baltimore: Johns Hopkins Press, 1963. (A collection of twelve essays which explore the origin, development, and implication of Stevens' poetry of ideas, including a helpful bibliographical essay by Joseph N. Riddel and Roy Harvey Pearce's article on Stevens' late work, "The Last Lesson of the Master.")

III. BOOKS ON STEVENS

(This list incudes only those full-length studies
I have found especially helpful and interesting.)

Benamou, Michel. *Wallace Stevens and the Symbolist Imagination.* Princeton: Princeton University Press, 1972.

Doggett, Frank. *Wallace Stevens' Poetry of Thought.* Baltimore: Johns Hopkins Press, 1966.

Litz, A. Walton. *Introspective Voyager: The Poetic Development of Wallace Stevens.* New York: Oxford University Press, 1972.

Riddel, Joseph N. *The Clairvoyant Eye.* Baton Rouge: Louisiana State University Press, 1965.

Vendler, Helen. *On Extended Wings: Wallace Stevens' Longer Poems.* Cambridge: Harvard University Press, 1969.

Index